Sailing For Home

Sailing For Home

A Voyage from Antigua to Kinsale

THEO DORGAN

PENGUIN
IRELAND

PENGUIN IRELAND

Published by the Penguin Group
Penguin Ireland Ltd, 25 St Stephen's Green, Dublin 2, Ireland
Penguin Books Ltd, 80 Strand, London WC2R ORL, England
Penguin Group (USA), Inc., 375 Hudson Street, New York, New York 10014, USA
Penguin Books Australia Ltd, 250 Camberwell Road, Camberwell, Victoria 3124, Australia
Penguin Books Canada Ltd, 10 Alcorn Avenue, Toronto, Ontario, Canada M4V 3B2
Penguin Books India (P) Ltd, 11 Community Centre, Panchsheel Park, New Delhi – 110 017, India
Penguin Group (NZ), cnr Airborne and Rosedale Roads, Albany, Auckland 1310, New Zealand
Penguin Books (South Africa) (Pty) Ltd, 24 Sturdee Avenue, Rosebank 2196, South Africa

Penguin Books Ltd, Registered Offices: 80 Strand, London WC2R ORL, England

www.penguin.com

First published 2004
I

Copyright © Theo Dorgan, 2004

The moral right of the author has been asserted

The lines from *Poems of Arab Andalusia*,
translated by Cola Franzen, are reprinted by
kind permission of City Lights Books.
Copyright 1989 by Cola Franzen.
The lines from *The Inferno of Dante Alighieri*,
translated by Ciaran Carson, are quoted by
kind permission of Granta Books.

Set in 12/14.75 pt PostScript Monotype Bembo
Typeset by Rowland Phototypesetting Ltd, Bury St Edmunds, Suffolk
Printed in Great Britain by Clays Ltd, St Ives plc

A CIP catalogue record for this book is available from the British Library

ISBN 1–844–88048–6

To Zafer Guray and Oliver Hart

Heaven's net is vast —
though its meshes are wide,
it lets nothing slip through.

– Tao Te Ching

For nothing is harder than to distinguish
the real things of sense from those
doubtful versions of them
that the mind readily supplies.

– Lucretius

Contents

Acknowledgements

I sailed with Oliver Hart, Zafer Guray, Charlotte Hooijdonk, Simon Sweeney, Al Hart and Anne Boyd on voyages that made this book and helped remake my sense of wonder. I am indebted to them for their friendship and for all they taught me, as I am thankful to Sinéad Hurley and Kate Hart of the Oysterhaven Centre.

I am grateful to David Gray, who, my first time aboard the boat, handed me the wheel on *Spirit of Oysterhaven* – then went below to sleep. Those night hours off the coast of Cork, in the company of Harold Fish, made me a sailor.

My friends in Howth Sailing and Boating Club kept me sailing while I was writing this book, kept me from getting landsick.

I owe a debt I cannot repay to the late Giles Gordon. Giles loved good writing, and he loved life – I am not sure he distinguished one from the other. His steadfast belief in this book brought it to a good home.

Euan Thorneycroft, my agent, inherited me. That was a fortunate day for me.

Brendan Barrington is a prince among editors, meticulous, imaginative, patient and sure. I hope he will let that sentence stand.

An extract from the first draft of this work appeared in *The Stony Thursday Book*, edited by Kevin Byrne.

Paula Meehan is my North Star, the home for which I was always sailing.

Bay of Biscay, September 2001

The question uppermost in my mind is, Are boats really meant to do this? We're heeled right over to port; the long swell keeps coming and coming from ahead of us and to starboard, twelve-foot waves knocking us back as the tall sails pull us forward through the driving rain. There's a banshee wail in the standing rigging and water literally everywhere: great white gouts of it coming over the bow, rushing back over the wide decks and seething off either side of the cockpit coamings; sheets of it whipping in our faces, so hard we can barely see ahead; water pouring down our faces, sluicing inside the neck of my oilskins – Simon's, too, no doubt; rain and sea water sweeping down off the heavily reefed mainsail, off the staysail far forward. It's Simon's turn to crouch at the inner end of the cockpit, hunched into himself, back to the deck-house, the waves, the rain. He's trying vainly to shield a cup of tea against the bucking and rearing, the yawing and swerving of a big boat in a big sea, twenty minutes into our watch, not long after midnight, the best part of four hours to go. My feet are braced in the corners of the cockpit; the wheel is heavy, unbelievably heavy, as I lean this way and that against the roll of the boat, shoulders strained almost to bursting, eyes smarting from the half-hail, half-spray that gusts and gusts and gusts in my face.

It has been like this for days now, almost as dark by day as it is by night, or so it seems to my fatigued brain.

Somewhere close by, I sense, is a pit of misery. I can almost feel the sides of it, out there around us in the heaving dark.

What I'm occupied with, beyond and behind a conviction that being right here, right now, is the stupidest thing I have ever done, is a small glow that threatens to rip through my nervous system, a kind of mindflash, some raw exultancy.

I'm watching that more carefully than I'm watching the compass, watching the sails, watching the horrible corkscrew motion as the bow rears and twists, then hangs there an instant before crashing down again into a dark green trough. I am struggling to hold back an animal roar of raw, pure well-being.

I feel absolutely alive, right out to the crackling green aura millimetres beyond the frontiers of my skin. I want to sing, bawl, howl, dance. I want to come off watch and check the plot to find we have held a rock-steady course. The skipper is up next for his solo watch, and I want him to nod, just so, as he checks the log, just once. One sailor to another. Not surprised we've been doing it right, neither pleased nor displeased, satisfied that things are as they should be. All this is going around in my head, not coherently, more like fits and starts of thought, like whitecaps glimpsed from the top or bottom of this roller-coaster we're riding.

There are other strains, too, like snatches of song. My admiration for Simon, not yet twenty, his grasp of what's going on here, the tact with which he balances his superior knowledge of the sea and sailing against the weight of the twenty-seven years I have on him. I'm an ould fella to him, he's ridiculously young to my eyes, but in three or four days and nights of sharing a watch in this filthy weather we have made ourselves into a small but clear-headed team, watching out for each other as much as we watch out for the boat, bending ourselves to a common purpose, alert to signs of fatigue in each other, taking everything in turns, keeping the small flame of morale alight through no matter what weather.

And it has been all about weather these past four days and nights. It's a straightforward trip in some ways, more or less a direct line south from Kinsale in County Cork to Nazaré on Portugal's west coast, about 900 miles. This boat has been down there before; I've been down there before – and it took us a shade under five days. But that was late spring, and this is September. It's a bit late in the year to be crossing Biscay, and even though we made some westing the first thirty-six hours out, planning to ride south with the wind on the beam, or at least comfortably off our bow, we've been hit by a succession of south-westerlies on the nose. We are five on this seventy-foot steel schooner, a small enough crew given the seas we've had and the inevitable toll to be paid in sheer tiredness by watches that leave insufficient time for sleep and recuperation. The others are experienced sailors; all I have going for me is a quickness on the uptake and a willingness to keep coming forward no matter how often you hit me on the head.

So here we are, in the middle of the night, halfway between Kinsale and Cabo de Finisterre, struggling to keep from being driven into the middle of the bay with its treacherous shelf and the mountainous seas that by now will be piling up along its length. Three of us are trying to sleep in what amounts to a large, steel washing-machine drum; two of us are keeping her head as close to the wind as possible, her speed up, our eyes peeled for rogue trawlers or anything else that might emerge suddenly out of the weltering dark. I don't know about Simon because I haven't asked him yet, but I am wrestling to keep the twin demons of fear and exhilaration in some kind of balance – and the thought comes to me: OK,

3

this is tough, it's almost overwhelming, but we have a grip on it, and it's not really going to get any worse than this.

As soon as the thought shapes itself I know immediately that I'm wrong.

PART ONE
Antigua

29 April 2002

English Harbour is full of yachts, 500 feet beneath us. You can see, from God's or an admiral's point of view, what drew Nelson to this place: a narrow entrance to a hurricane-proof harbour, easily defended by a battery here on Shirley Heights. There is a wide bay on the outer side, the bay directly beneath me here, then a second anchorage in there to my right behind the narrow peninsula on which that most English of adventurers built a perfect Georgian dockyard.

It's nearly sunset, still warm, short-sleeve weather. The band on stage is thundering out a reggae-calypso medley. The jostling crowds are borderline casual-scruffy, a mix of locals and yacht crews, wreathed in barbecue smoke, everybody clutching a beer, bobbing to the beat. Sixteen hours ago I was in Dublin, kissing Paula goodbye, scrabbling in pockets and backpack as usual for pen, passport, boarding card and books, my head in a whirl. Now it's dry dust under my feet; tall, slender palms; thick, green undergrowth; a former gun emplacement become a lucrative bar with cooking under flimsy shelters. We are maybe a couple of hundred people: a mix of locals who make their living from seafarers and the sea, and visitors who have made their way here, mostly by sea, mostly from Europe. The rich people, here for Antigua Week in their multimillion-dollar superyachts, are elsewhere, in places where the more a drink costs, the more they feel at home.

I pick up my beer and walk to the low wall at the cliff's edge, look down on the mosaic of mostly white-hulled boats dotted across the green-blue expanse of the rapidly darkening bay. I am looking for our boat, *Spirit of Oysterhaven*, and it takes me a minute or so to pick her out. Normally, which is to say any other time I've looked for her, it has taken no time at all. Seventy-foot schooners are rare in Irish waters, and anywhere we've been with her she has generally been the biggest boat riding at anchor or tied to the jetty. Here she is one among many, and I am, for a moment, obscurely offended by this. That's the second time today I've caught myself feeling proprietorial towards a boat I have sailed on no more than six times, and each time as a lowly member of the crew. It's the kind of evening when, jet-lagged and beer-drowsy in the unaccustomed warmth, I can entertain myself happily for ten minutes or so thinking about this.

On the plane from Gatwick I found myself seated among Poles, heading to St Lucia for a fortnight's charter. As far as I could make out from Julo, the thirty-something skipper seated beside me, they had sailed extensively together in the Baltic and the North seas, never in warm waters. He wanted to know about chartering in Ireland, itineraries, harbours, anchorages. It passed the time away, scribbling possible passage plans first on napkins, then in his notebook. It was only when I found myself drawing a pilotage plan for entering Baltimore, pointing out the deep-water channel, the obstacles to watch out for, that I realized I hadn't had a cigarette for four hours and we were only halfway to Antigua.

The thought comes back to me here on Shirley Heights, as I grind out a butt beneath my heel: the day we leave here, bound for home, is the day I smoke my last cigarette. There,

I think, *that's* why I'm feeling anxious, and I walk back to rejoin my crewmates.

We are four, and we are 4,000 miles from home. The boat was brought out from Kinsale by Oliver, the owner, some months ago. Oliver has gone home to attend to his business; now we are to bring the boat back for her summer season in Ireland. Zafer, our skipper for the trip, is the same wiry bundle of energy I remember from other voyages. Born in Turkey, a sailor since the age of nine, he lives and breathes the sea. Charlotte, the mate, is bronzed and fit, at ease here after spending the Caribbean season on *Spirit*, checking out the chartering possibilities, hosting Oliver's friends. Simon, more red than brown, has filled out a bit since the Biscay trip, but he is still thin and growing, young bones, young restlessness, a ready grin. We sit there, looking around us, getting a sense of each other, four people with not very much in common except this enterprise which will bind us to each other for five weeks or so. For my crewmates, contracted by Oliver, this is work; for me, it is more in the nature of an adventure.

The last time I saw *Spirit* was from a bus pulling away from the dockside in the Galician port of Muros, into which we had run for shelter on the Biscay trip. Coming up the *ria* that night, still wracked with tension, I remember wondering if I'd ever set foot on this boat again. Now here I am, tropical stars bracking the sky over the anchorage, 4,000 miles from home, heading out past darkened hulls, climbing aboard for the second time today, the calypso still echoing from Shirley Heights overhead, settling in the new-varnished cockpit for a last beer, a few words with Simon before turning in. 'Long time,' I say, as we clink bottles. He looks at me for a second, grins, and says, 'Yah, mon.' All I need – the boy thinks he's a dread. Time for sleep.

Forward cabin, starboard side. I heave my gear on to the top bunk, spread a sheet on the lower bunk, and strip. I lie there in the heat and the dark, wish Paula a silent goodnight in my head and fall over the edge into a dreamless dark.

Something taps against the hull. I feel the slight sway of the boat under me, hear a slap of water, another, then recollect where I am. Charlotte hands me a cup of coffee as I stumble out of the cabin; Zaf is bringing toast on deck, and I follow him up the companion steps. Sprawled on the afterdeck, drawing a varnish brush along towards himself, a Rasta introduced as Hector is finishing off the portside deck locker. There's the sweet smell of ganja from somewhere, the higher note of varnish and thinners, the ground bass of thick, black coffee and, as I bite into a slice of toast, the all-pervasive smell of the sea. Some local boys in a dinghy are hanging off the rail, chatting to Hector, one of them lazily holding an extinguished spliff. Hector catches my eye, grins a long, lazy grin: 'Long way from home, mon.' I hand him a coffee, fish a lighter out of my pocket and toss it to the boatman. He lights up, takes a deep, luxurious hit, offers the spliff to me. I wave it away. He offers it to Hector – 'No, mon, I told you, not on the boat.' Hector looks at me for a second, holding the look, a broader grin this time as I catch the returning lighter one-handed. 'Maybe not, mon,' he says. 'Maybe not so far from home, hey?'

A fleet of racing boats is going by, heading out for the day, all bustle on deck as the crews work the sails out of their bags, run up the Kevlar mainsails, bounce once, twice in the standing waves just outside the harbour mouth, then peel away south and west one by one. Inshore, too, it is all bustle – water taxis charging here and there, dinghies coming and going to moored boats. Farther in, knots of people mill purposively on the dock that runs across the face of the two-storey brick and timber buildings. Around the steep-sided horseshoe bay, a lush green vegetation; royal palms rising up out of the undergrowth, towering towards a pale blue sky dotted with puffy clouds. Here and there a splash of vermilion or purple, the white walls and manicured lawns of enviable houses.

There is a great deal to be done, and we are caught between brisk and lazy. I want to balm out in this heat, burn a winter's damp out of my bones. And I want to get down to it, the work that will make us ready for sea. I want to stay here, and I want to be off.

Zaf calls a conference in the saloon. Lists are prepared; tasks assigned. The varnishing is almost done, the finished brightwork gleaming against the seasoned grey teak of the wide decks. There are tools everywhere – around the saloon, outside the engine room, in the cockpit, here and there on deck. Work to be done – on the engine, the gearbox, the generator, the running and standing rigging. Then there's the packing, the digging out of life jackets, stowage of wet weather gear, escape gear – flares, knife, water, compass and so on, all of which will go in a sealed yellow barrel with our passports, ship's papers and money – and finally the big jobs, watering, fuelling, provisioning.

A ship at sea needs to be entirely self-sufficient. This may seem obvious, but to someone like me, still learning the ropes, it's a vast subject for contemplation. Consider the vessel first. The hull must be sound, all seacocks, inlets and outlets checked. The standing rigging, the wire or stainless-steel rods that hold up the masts, must be checked. The forces in play when sails are up are awesome ones, especially on this big schooner. We are wire-rigged, so the integrity of the rig depends not just on the structural strength of masts, booms and related fittings, but also on the absence of fatigue in the stays that hold the assemblage together. You check for signs of rust or abrasion where the wires are bonded to the hull through deck fittings – water can collect in the collars called 'swages' where the wire finishes on a turn. One wire parting under pressure can bring the whole rig down, and in the middle of the ocean that could mean losing a mast, perhaps both masts; in dirty weather, with mast or spar banging into the sides in heavy seas, this could mean breaching the watertight integrity of the hull itself. The hatches must be checked for watertightness, as must the ports along both sides of the hull and in the two deckhouses. The washboards have to be fitted at the top of the companionway; these will keep water out if waves are breaking into the cockpit. So, test them for fit, then store them somewhere instantly accessible. Water making its way in, tons of it in a matter of seconds, especially through a hatch in heavy seas or if she rolls over when broached, can sink a boat in minutes.

The sails have to be inspected for chafe, tears, holes, missing stitches. The headboard – the aluminium plate at the top of the sail where the halyard is attached that will pull the sail up – must be checked. The roller drum on the furling genoa must be checked, perhaps hosed out with fresh water. The running rigging must be gone over; the ropes ('sheets' in shipboard parlance) that run back from the sails to the cockpit winches must be checked carefully for signs of wear, replaced if necessary. The winches themselves must be checked, the drums spun to ensure they are running freely. The life raft must be examined. The gas bottles in their stainless-steel cage on deck at the foot of the foremast must have the regulators checked.

Check the electricals, the instruments – log, speed, depth,

GPS, radar — and the instrument panel itself. The compass was swung before she left Ireland last autumn, that is to say examined for deviation, so that doesn't have to be done, but we'll do it anyway.

Check the gas pipe run to the cooker, the through-hull fittings, the internal lights, the nav lights and steaming lights, the deck lights, especially where wiring runs emerge through the deck. Check the water tanks and diesel tanks, the toilets, basins and showers in the heads forward and aft, the medical kit, the pots and pans, the crockery and the cutlery.

If anything is missing once we're at sea we must improvise from what we do have, or do without. If anything breaks, we must fix it. If anything falls overboard, we cannot replace it unless we are carrying spares. So the spares must be checked — but you can't carry a spare for everything.

As usual in human affairs, there is the imponderable gap between what would be ideal and what we're going to decide we'll probably get away with. Ultimately it's the skipper's call.

Is there enough gas, or will we need a new bottle? There is some chafe on the foresail — does it warrant bringing in a sailmaker? (No.) There's a lot of water in the engine primary filters. Should we change them? (Of course we should, no question.) Should we carry more spares than usual? (Yes, because there is some doubt about the quality of diesel here, justified or unjustified.) The fresh water from the tanks tastes awful — can we trust it over three weeks? (No. We'll buy drinking water in five-litre containers.) Is that a lot of weight? (Yes, but not so much as will affect the trim of the vessel.) Is the medical kit adequate? (Mostly.) On the outward trip from the Canaries there was a surgeon aboard, so we're equipped to carry out minor surgery — there are needles, sutures, disinfectants, painkillers, scalpels, dressings in abundance — but for the usual minor cuts, abrasions and bruises we need a few bits and bobs. We need more sunscreen. We need a lot of batteries, for radios, Walkmans, torches. We need more cutlery, mugs and plates. More tea towels, a few plastic basins – apart from the usual uses, ideal for bringing mugs of tea up above in a heavy sea.

We have shaded, checklist by checklist, from concern for the boat into concern for the well-being of the crew. Here is a tricky area. Is the boat for the crew, a means of bringing the four of us from the Caribbean to Ireland, or are we here to bring the boat over? Both of the above; neither of the above. Bit by bit, as we direct our attention to the *über*-question of what is to be done, we are blurring the boundaries between the boat and ourselves. Perhaps it's from here it starts, the unexaminable sailor's conviction that a boat is, somehow, a live thing, with personality and will and a character of her own. We do the work so that the boat's integrity as a system of systems is optimized; we do the work so that we can make the crossing under the best possible conditions that it lies in our power to provide for ourselves. If we run into trouble, serious trouble, we'll do everything we can to preserve the boat, as a means of preserving ourselves, and as an end in itself . . . but at the end, if there is to be an end, we're not stupid: no matter how deep our affection for the boat runs, she is not alive in the same way we are, and our first and last thoughts will be for the preservation of our human lives. This sense of a boat's being alive in some way is found far more often in sailing boats than in motor boats. We speak of a boat being carried along at the mercy of the wind, every nerve and muscle and sinew strained and thrumming, and we accept the fact of it and the metaphor of it with an abandonment that is close to an acknowledgement of kinship.

Salad and bread rolls and water and juice and yet more coffee tempt us on deck again after a few hours, then it is time to go shopping. Zaf makes for the engine room, where Simon will join him after he runs Charlotte and me ashore in the dinghy to do the provisioning. I've drawn the ace here, I reckon: an outlet for my habitual bossiness and rage for organizing things, plus a bus trip across the island to St John's to satisfy my curiosity about Antigua.

The overloaded Hiace bus might be crossing Connemara or Kerry twenty or thirty years ago. Everyone knows everyone else. We pick up and drop people off at seeming random, as we climb up into the hills. Halfway we change buses, surrounded by hundreds of schoolkids in their various immaculate uniforms, their Nike and Adidas sneakers, their nylon backpacks the same as you'd find on their counterparts in Ireland or anywhere in the world these days. St John's, as we pass through, is beat-up Japanese cars and pick-ups, plantains, mangoes, hairbrushes, cheap cotton clothes piled in the shop windows, buckets and brushes, barber shops and hairdressing salons, two-storey buildings of peeling paint or illuminated plastic-box signs, dogs, oleanders and bougainvillea, policemen in shorts, corrugated red roofs, dust, low cloud, noise, fast-food joints, scarcely a white face to be seen, the young dudes favouring nylon-stocking hats rolled over razored hair, American style, rather than the Jamaican dreadlocks of the guys my age.

The supermarket's in a small, American-owned mall. An unsmiling security guard, a heavyset woman who looks as if she really enjoys both her uniform and her job, checks each trolley as it is wheeled away from the checkouts towards the parking lot. I watch to see what's going on. The shopper hands over the till receipt; the guard goes suspiciously through the trolley, checking its contents against the receipt, then waves the customer on, grudgingly. I am secretly pleased at the thought that when we make our appearance she'll have a hell of a lot of trolleys to go through. Eight, as it turns out, and practically an entire pallet of water. Seventy 5-litre containers, to be precise, rattling behind us as we emerge into the rapidly falling night.

Charlotte, old Antigua hand, has a taxi booked, a friend of Hector's. Danny the Rasta taximan, spliff in hand, surveys the load. 'Whoa! I don' know, mon. Hell, yeah, load it in. No problem.' We're on the axles, the green Hiace full to bursting point, winding our way downhill through one hairpin bend after another in the dark when Danny asks, 'So, where you goin'?' Ireland. 'Ireland? Oh, oh, not me, mon, not me. That's a vaaaast ocean.' He chuckles, shakes his head with exaggerated slowness. 'Not me, mon. Vaast ocean there.' Every trip has its mantra; Danny has just given us the words. We take turns trying it out, Charlotte and I.

But we're not really thinking about the vast ocean, not yet. This is a lot of stuff, and a lot of it is in cardboard boxes, which means it has to come out before we take the food on board. Rule number one for provisioning in tropical ports: no cardboard. Cockroaches nest in cardboard, lay their eggs in it, and are murderously difficult to get rid of once they're established on a boat. Rule number two: all fruit and vegetables to be washed, preferably in a very mild bleach solution, or at least in fresh water. The nearest jetty to the boat is the fuel dock, and we pass a tedious hour stripping packaging, washing fruit and vegetables; then we hail a water taxi and get everything out to the boat. There's an underfloor fridge, as well as an ordinary fridge, so all the perishables go into these. Much of the rest is just piled up in the saloon because we're starved – as are Zaf and Simon after a day spent for the most part in the dark, hot, oily recesses of the engine room. Shower, change, all ashore to HQ, the restaurant on the second floor of the main dockyard building.

The dockyard complex, all ruby brick and white-painted timber, houses the customs office, Internet cafés, a small supermarket and off-licence, galleries, souvenir shops, a bar, a sailmaker's workshop, a small luxury hotel, post office, clothing stalls and much else besides. It was a Corkman by the name of Nicholson who developed the whole complex, starting in the 1960s; the restaurant is run now by a Dubliner, and the maîtresse d' is a thin, nervous, smiling Fermanagh woman. We eat out on the wide wooden veranda, a small and motley crew surrounded by moneyed types, bantering with the staff, at home and abroad at once. There's a table of ten or so sour-faced Northern Irish behind us, the look of lawyers and medical professionals about them, snipping at the staff, glowering superciliously at us. In an effort to help them feel more at home Simon and I are speaking in Irish. The owner stops by at our table on his rounds, florid, expansive and guarded. Much flashing of Rolexes and flexing of designer-yachtie sweatshirts at the table behind us: affluent Ulster is feeling left out. Beside us, a table of four is watching this little comedy. They raise their glasses to us with wicked grins. Delivery crew, led by a tall, white-haired, handsome Welshman, the kind of fellow my mother would have described as a fine figure of a man. John Pearce ('Call me Taff') introduces Gordon the Scot, Rab who is English and a fourth man whose name I never did get, an Irishman. 'We like to think of ourselves as a floating joke,' says Taff, which earns him a venomous glance from the consultant anaesthetist or assistant chief constable at the head of the other table. The talk flows back and forth between our two tables, talk of weather and routes, sail plans and passage making. Now Ulster has two tables to scowl at, but before the excitement gets too much for them the eight of us head for the bar.

Later, sitting on deck while the others sleep, rocked gently by the occasional dinghy burbling past, I have a sudden memory of a morning on Iounissos, the small island off Chios in the Aegean where many of the Greek shipowners have their summer homes. We were chatting quietly over coffee to the owner of the taverna near the landing stage, idly glancing from time to time at a long table of obviously very wealthy men under a vine arbour. One of them half-turned in his seat, deliberately scraping his chair on the concrete to attract attention. He raised a hand in the air, flicked his wrist in a peremptory, insolent gesture.

I can see those men still, and wonder still what it must be like to found your whole character and sense of yourself in arrogance, in a delusion of superiority. I imagine those Ulstermen at sea, when the winds come up and the sky darkens and something pierces that polished armour, whispers in their ears that they, too, are mortal. I wonder, as dispassionately as I can, who will stand and who will crumble. I remember the lines from 'The Ballad of Sir Patrick Spens' suddenly, from school:

> Oh laith, laith were the gude Scots lords
> To wet their cork-heel'd shoon!
> But lang or a'l the play was play'd
> They wat their hats aboon.

I empathize still with that class hostility, even as logic and experience tells me a snob is not necessarily a coward or, when it comes to survival, a fool. I have always had trouble following orders, have spent most of my working life avoiding having to take orders. One consequence of this is that I have mostly worked in jobs where I have been in charge. I would like to think I treated people with respect, built consensus where I could, but I can't be sure of that. One of the things I like about sailing is that I can, as a lowly crew member, acknowledge the authority of the skipper. It must, I think, take a lot of patience to deal with me.

PART TWO

To the Azores

Day 1

The entry in my notebook for 2 May reads: '15.00, cleared Nelson's Harbour, Antigua.'

The day before passed in a whirl of checks and stowage. Most of the tinned, packaged and dry food is gone in under the seats in the saloon. Every tin has its contents written on top in indelible marker – so you can see what's in a can without having to lift it, and also as a precaution against water lifting the labels off. Not much fun in a seaway to be trying to guess whether a tin has beans, jam or chicken breasts in it. Devising a shorthand for this relieves the monotony of the job, as does working out where to stow what, so that all of us can learn quickly which seat to lift for tinned fruit, which for pasta, and so on. It doesn't sound like a terribly serious problem, but it's surprising, on a long journey, how infuriating it can be to find yourself rummaging under seat after seat for a tin or a packet. Temperament on a boat is a delicate issue: we are four comparative strangers, confined in a small space, and petty frustrations can build up with remarkable speed. Already an attitude of willing politeness is setting in: we bump into each other and apologize; when one of us wants a coffee we automatically ask the others if they want one, too; the batteries on Simon's Walkman are running low, so Charlotte digs him out replacements from her stash. These are the mundane foundations for an attitude which could so quickly become a matter of life or death: looking out for each other, being constantly alert to how everyone else is doing.

The lower pilot bunk on the starboard side, opposite the engine-room door, now houses the seventy containers of drinking water. Jammed in behind the canvas leecloth, the mass has a vaguely alien look to it, so it's christened the 'embryo bank'. We're calculating 100 litres per person, which gives us three litres a day each if all goes to plan. That's a lot, but it's prudent to allow a considerable margin in case of breakdown, becalming or other unforeseen delay. I try to imagine what it must have been like in the old sailing days, shipping water from springs by the barrel, having to ration it out on shipboard from sealed casks. Dimly remembered stories – of water parties ambushed when going ashore, of men going crazy from thirst in the doldrums, kept from the water supply at gunpoint by harried officers – flash through my mind, the agreeable stirrings of history somewhat offset by the rumble of a heavy diesel engine as a large boat goes by above, or by the squawk of the radio as somebody raises the customs officer, clearing in after a crossing.

The plan had been to fuel up in the early morning, be gone before noon. As is so often the case with departures, there were snags.

First we discovered that the anchor chains were crossed. We'd been lying to two anchors off the bow, and the chains got crossed because we'd been turning in the wind in the course of the past week. It took a while, and some skilful manoeuvring by Zaf on the wheel, to get this sorted out. Then we raised the port anchor, brought it inboard, unshackled it and stowed it below in the cleared forepeak. The foredeck seemed a mess of warps, lines, fenders and sail bags, though there was method in the madness. When we were ready to run in to the fuelling dock, the second anchor was stowed below, the inflatable dinghy hoisted aboard, the outboard engine also sent down into the forepeak. The dinghy must be lashed securely to the forward coachroof, the engine and anchors lashed to bulkheads below to stop them moving about as the bow rises and falls; then the warps, lines, fenders and sails are fitted in. Heavy enough work in this heat, and Simon and I took turns at being contortionists. Charlotte, meanwhile, was busy stowing sheets, life jackets and spare lines in the deck lockers that don't have fruit and vegetables in them. Zaf made ready the grab bags – little sealed yellow barrels that we will take with us if we have to abandon ship. Both of them have been going through the ship from stem to stern, checking shackles, tackles, fittings, the engine room, the emergency steering gear in the lazarette under the cockpit floor, the cockpit lockers . . .

Now, at last, Zaf fires up the engine, turns her head in towards the fuel dock. We glide up into the harbour, carefully, weaving slowly past a couple of dozen boats at anchor, and tie up by the diesel pump. While the fuelling is going on, Simon and I nip ashore for a few last-minute purchases. The phone isn't working, so I can't call Paula, which leaves me in a state of suppressed rage. Stupid, really, to expect technology to be always and everywhere and at all times available; all the more stupid when it dawns on me I can send her an e-mail from the Internet café. Which I do while Charlotte is getting exit stamps in our passports.

All back on board, we line up along the starboard rail while the cranky young fucker at the fuel dock takes a few photographs for us. Are we off to sea, then? The great adventure, across the Atlantic? Well, not quite; we spend the next hour riding on the engine, more or less back where we rode at anchor, with Zaf displaying superior handling skills in a tight space, while we have lunch and the final briefing. Then, at 15.00, with little fuss, Zaf turns her head to the sea at last, and we cross the bar.

Spirit starts bucking and plunging almost immediately: those standing waves at the harbour entrance mark a line where a surprisingly deep swell runs up against a rock shelf. It looks a lot smoother from inside. We go head to wind, run up the heavy mainsail, first quickly, then more slowly as Simon and I haul on the halyard, a metre or so at a time. The last two metres have to be winched up, and my arms and shoulders are suddenly reminded of how heavy the work can be. Charlotte winds out the genoa, and Zaf brings us round on a course for Guadeloupe. He plans to go south-east for eight hours or so, then turn north; this would bring us well clear of Antigua, on a course, more or less, for Bermuda. It's also a good course if we have to turn back for any reason. The wind's from the east, twenty knots or so, and soon we are heeled on a port tack (meaning the wind is from the port side), then steadying up, the bow wave beginning to course past. We all gather in the cockpit for a ceremonial beer, Zaf and I pouring a libation for Poseidon over the taff rail. For good measure I toss a coin over, too, the glint of it as it spins in the bright air catching my eye.

I have a lucky stone from Paula in my breast pocket and I finger that, then Zaf hands over the wheel to Charlotte, grins, and says, 'It's time?' We walk forward to smoke a last cigarette. We hunch over to shield the flame, inhale simultaneously and straighten up. To port, the commanding bulk of Shirley Heights, silent now; to starboard, far off, a small fleet of racing yachts, their bright spinnakers ballooning; behind us, receding at a surprising speed, the palms and thick greenery of the bay, the pencil masts of the yachts at anchor, the rusty blur of the dockyard buildings with their white accents.

I toss the almost-full packet of cigarettes over the side, feeling a stab of guilt at this minor pollution, a deeper pang of anxiety at the thought of trying to give the blasted things up. The butt, sucked down to the last ember, goes over the leeward rail and – that's it. Jesus, Mary and Joseph, I think, let me not kill anyone. Let the patches work.

We sprawl in the cockpit, one hand on the wheel enough for Charlotte to hold her course; Zaf brings up James Clarke's *Atlantic Pilot Atlas* and the chart – Admiralty 4012, as I dutifully note in my brand-new notebook. The plan is to clear up the east coast of Antigua after we turn north sometime near midnight, then to hold a heading of 010° to 020°, depending on the wind, for as long as it takes us to pick up westerlies south-east of Bermuda. Estimated passage time to Horta in the Azores is twenty-one days. Most boats head out more or less on the diagonal, aiming straight for Horta from the start, motorsailing all the way. Zaf is a sailing man to his fingertips and intends to follow the traditional course for sailing ships bound for Europe, a course laid down as far back as the seventeenth century.

Out there before us are Spanish treasure ships, Portuguese, Spanish, English and French men o' war, Chinese junks, traders and privateers, clippers and merchantmen, all in thrall to the given, the prevailing pattern of winds in this part of the world. It isn't nostalgia that shapes Zaf's decision. Modern boats with (theoretically) reliable engines, in the hands of professional delivery crews, usually motor straight through the doldrums. We are slightly leery of our engine, however, on the general principle, perhaps, that if it can break down it probably will, and the skipper thinks it's the more seamanlike option to allow for the possibility we may have to make the entire journey on the wind.

Nobody says so, but the spell of the journey is beginning

27

to take hold; we have a lively sense of all those who have gone before us in these trackless wastes and wouldn't, I suspect, be too put out if we have to make the whole journey under sail alone.

The safety briefing follows, a brisk detailing of what we will do and how we will do it if we have a fire aboard (everyone quizzed on where the extinguishers are, which ones to use on which kind of fire, safety precautions in the galley); if someone goes overboard (throw anything overboard that will float, especially the danbuoy with its high orange flag, call all hands on deck, punch the MOB button on the GPS, one of us to fix on the casualty and keep pointing to him or her at all times); if we start taking in water; and so on. In all cases, the first thing to do is call the skipper immediately if he's not already on deck.

It is borne in on all of us, not least on Zaf, that the ultimate responsibility in all situations rests on his shoulders. The safety briefing, even on coastal passages, always compels attention. It is a kind of collecting of attention, a reminder that the very sea that bears us up is also, potentially, a hostile environment. Despite the idyllic conditions, we have a long crossing on open water before us, and we are more than usually thoughtful. The rigging creaks, the water gurgles past, a lone frigate bird hovers behind and above us, the red sun is sinking over the still-visible island, and Guadeloupe is a smudge on the horizon ahead of us – but in twenty-four hours' time we will be heading north into emptiness, with none to rely on but ourselves. I haven't been on this boat, haven't been at sea, since that trip down Biscay late last September, and for just a moment a shadow darkens my mind, my stomach contracts; I blink and look around me, reach for the genoa sheet and winch it in a little until the sail stops its unquiet flapping. I look at my hands, doing this as if of their own accord, and

I am calm again. Like that. You get through by doing the work, I remember, and Biscay is once again a long distance away.

For the first day or two, until we have worked ourselves into the run of things, Zaf decides we should do double watches. Charlotte and I take the first formal watch, 20.00 to 24.00. There isn't all that much to do. It's been a long time since I took the wheel on *Spirit*. I plant my feet solidly against the slight roll, settle the rim of the wheel into the cup of my curved hands, let the fingertips absorb the feedback from the rudder and – it's as if there's a click inside my head – I sense the aliveness of the boat. It takes me about an hour to get the hang of it again, to remember how to perceive all the different forces at work, some pushing us left, some right, the dip and absence as the bow falls in and hesitates, the braking effect as she shoulders on through the water, the sudden lightness as a slight gust lifts us and there is a small loss of traction. What I'm putting back together is that indefinable something called 'feel', as much to do with anticipation as with processing incoming information. Bringing the wheel over a point or two before we're pushed sideways, counterpunching before the punch lands. I'm not very good at this; I tend to over-compensate, expend too much energy wrestling with the wheel. On this trip I want to master the art; I also want to learn sail trimming, and I hope to do the lion's share of the navigation. Everything I've learned about sailing I've learned on this boat. By the time I get home I intend to have learned a great deal more.

There's a brief kerfuffle soon after dark when the low clouds on the horizon part and suddenly there is a lighthouse, much closer than it should be. We call Zaf, and he switches on the radar, turns to the chart, flips to the relevant page in the *Atlantic Pilot*. The light on the northern tip of Guadeloupe should be thirty miles off or so, but it looks a damn sight closer. While the radar is warming up, Zaf and Simon join us on deck. We're puzzled, getting anxious, when suddenly we realize what the light is. We are not the first, I later discover, and I'm sure we won't be the last, to mistake a low moon for a lighthouse or for the steaming lights of a large ship coming up out of nowhere. We plough on at a steady five knots or so, jogging towards the island, and Zaf leaves the radar on: there are boats out there, and the night is thickening somewhat. He's being overcautious, deliberately so, and we rise to the lesson, ratcheting our attention up a notch or two. There's an old saying, 'Harbours rot ships and men', and we are all of us conscious of the need to sharpen our sea senses, to keep, in the lovely phrase, our wits about us.

At 21.00 there's a blast of foul-smelling smoke from the engine room amidships. We stop the engine. How not, at this moment, to remember the day in Biscay when much the same thing happened?

There are a lot of sailing boats out there without engines. The near-legendary Don Street famously got so fed up with his that he heaved it overboard off *Iolaire* one day, and never looked back. We are not so purist, much as we like to sail. An engine sits there as a resource to get you out of trouble. Becalmed? Fire up the iron headsail and motor on. Off a lee shore with the wind getting up and the crew exhausted? Fire 'er up and get offside; stand out to sea until it blows over. The wind is free, but it blows when and how it likes – we want our engine, even though we hope to use it as little as possible. So much for romance. Zaf and Simon vanish into the engine room; Charlotte and I keep going, speed falling off a bit as you'd expect, but the wind holding. Diagnosis: it's not the engine; it's the hydraulic gearbox. The clutch plates are slipping, which means we cannot engage gear. Can it be fixed?

We don't know. Colourful cursing ensues, much of it directed at whoever last serviced the bloody thing.

And now the satellite phone makes its first appearance. This is an instrument of torture, forged in the smithies of Tantalus. In theory, you switch it on, dial in your number and a ring of geo-stationary satellites does the rest, routing your call to its destination. The satphone offers the comforting prospect of instant contact with your loved ones, or, as in this case, with Oliver, *Spirit*'s owner. For the next day and a half we'll be in intermittent contact with Oliver, in thirty- to sixty-second bursts. Simon, alarmingly cynical for one so young, has a dark suspicion that the service provider has designed the phone to fail repeatedly, on the grounds that they make more money from the call connection fee than they do from the duration of an average call.

The options in regard to the gearbox are these, we agree over a late dinner:

It can be fixed – we carry on.
It can't be fixed – we carry on.
It can't be fixed – we turn back to Antigua, or we head for Bermuda.

Zaf's analysis – and we are persuaded even though we'll abide by his decision anyway – is this: if we turn back we have to go out again once it's been fixed; if we go on, either we fix it ourselves as we head towards Bermuda or we head into Bermuda, which has far better facilities than Antigua, and get it fixed there; or, and we have a few days to mull this one over, we decide to head on anyway, and make the crossing to Horta under sail alone. Meantime, we go on.

At 24.00 the watch changes. Simon takes the wheel, wearing his life jacket, clipping his harness to a D-ring in the cockpit well. Ship's rules: life jackets are worn when on watch at night; helmsman is clipped on; anyone going forward on deck after sundown clips on to the webbing jackstays which run from stem to stern along the deck. The sea is relatively calm tonight, the breeze is gentle enough, the ship's motion slow and easy – but this is a necessary discipline and is rigorously enforced. Practically the first thing you say to someone as you hand over the watch is 'clip on'. Everyone knows to do it; nobody ever minds being reminded.

Charlotte gets seasick – I'd forgotten that. She works ashore in her own business during the winter, sails for the rest of the year, and has been doing this for a long time. It seems cruel that she should suffer in this manner, that the first four or five days of a trip should be such torture, but she has learned to accept it. She rises and does her watch, stoically; on the handover, she takes her tablet and gets back into her bunk, falls unconscious until the next time. Automatically, we work around this. Hers is the after cabin on the port side: when we are in the cockpit and she is sleeping, we keep our voices down. Tonight, first night at sea, the three of us settle in the cockpit, making desultory conversation, getting used to each other's company, talking of small things, companionable and at ease. Eventually I go below, check our position, speed and course on the GPS, make my first entry in the ship's log. Tea for the watch, then I slide into my bunk with a cup of tea myself. Propped on one elbow, a Maglite angled to light the page, I make the first entry in my personal log. I keep it short, conserving the torch battery. (We don't use ship's lights when the generator's not running, to save power in the big batteries.) There's a pocket in the back cover of my notebook where I keep a photo of Paula. I take out the photo, gaze at it for a while, put it back, turn over to sleep. A thought strikes me: I climb out of bed, look up at an angle through the clear hatch overhead. Yep, we did remember to switch on the running lights. The little things, I think, falling asleep, you have to remember the little things. And never assume you did something; always check, if there is any doubt at all.

Day 2

Friday, 3 May
Pos. at midnight   N   16° 40'
                    W   61° 24'

Sometime during the night we came about and began to head more or less due north. While Simon boils a kettle in the gallery, I am at the nav station, examining the log entry: 'Speed, 5.5 knots; course, 006°; distance travelled, 57 miles; wind, still easterly, 20–25 knots.' The GPS will give us our position on the planet's surface accurate to plus or minus three metres. Satellites in low-earth geosynchronous orbit send information to the GPS receiver on our speed through the water, which can be displayed as SOG, speed over ground; the same satellites give our COG, course over ground. From one small screen, maybe six inches by six inches, we extract this wealth of data. Such luxury! The position fix is pencilled in on the paper chart, usually at 00.00 and 12.00, but, because I'm working on my navigation, I intend to mark the position at the end of every watch. Zaf is indulgent of this, though it makes for a large series of tiny incremental lines, and has the effect of making it seem we are moving very slowly.

Checking the log and the nav information before going on watch becomes an element in the waking-up process, a way station between bunk and deck. It prepares you for the information the offgoing watch will want to pass on – heading, weather patterns, handling and so on. This is all the more important when, as will happen today or at the latest

34

tomorrow, we change over to single watches. With two up, one can always go below to scan the previous situation and retrieve useful information about, for instance, a rising or falling curve of barometric pressure. On a lone watch, you may need to hold all this in your head for four hours. There is a further, psychological aspect to all this. The body experiences the ocean as trackless: there are no landmarks to orient yourself by (if you discount the stars, which are in any case experienced as unfixed); everything outside the boat is unstable, in flux, disorienting. We have a profound need to situate ourselves, a need unconsciously satisfied on the small scale by the sailor's habit of constantly reaching to touch things. On the larger scale, the vectors of heading and speed, our position relative to the nearest landmass, our plotted position on the gridded globe – all these, when computed and shown as an 'x' on the chart, bring peace of mind. At the back of your head, always, is the simple question: If anything goes wrong, how will they know where to send help? The mundane questions also need answering: Where the hell are we? Where are we going? How are we doing?

We are doing very well, considering. Charlotte is murmuring with Zaf as Simon and I join them for tea on deck in the tropical night. The land smells are long gone; there is the fresh-washed cleanliness of salt in the backdraft from the sails, a sense of expansiveness in the starry night. We can see quite well, all the way out to a clear horizon all around. The moon astern is high now, and there is a broad path of silver on the sea behind us. For a long time after the others have gone below, Charlotte and I are companionably silent. From time to time we discuss small changes to the sail trim – we bring in the main a little, let the genoa out full as the wind falls back a knot or two. The aim is to sail her with maximum efficiency always, to keep the slot between the two sails as clear as possible so that the wind coming off the genoa flows cleanly over the taut belly of the main. In this wind we could run up the foresail as well, but we decide to leave it until the next watch change.

Charlotte is really quite ill – it takes a lot out of her to be on deck at all. But she takes her turn at the wheel, never complains, rarely adverts to how she's feeling. It's a curious thing, but I've never yet been seasick, no matter how rough the conditions. This is all the more odd because, like most of my brothers (but not my sisters), I suffer from a nervous stomach, am a finicky eater with an uncertain appetite. It's not unusual for even the most hardened sailors to suffer from *mal de mer*; I am always touched by the tact with which the unafflicted deal with sufferers. I had thought there would be a certain amount of covert scorn for such signs of weakness – of the kind, say, that hardened drinkers display for the capacity-impaired – but unobtrusive, sympathetic concern has been the style always, at least on this boat. Seasickness can be dangerous: the sufferer can become disoriented, weak and inattentive, a situation that may be compounded by the side effects of some of the prescription or over-the-counter medicines commonly used to combat the condition. Anytime I've felt slightly queasy, I've used a pebble held by an elastic band to the inside of the wrist, about two fingers back from the fold line, and this seems to work. Can't remember now where I heard of this, a remedy probably derived from acupressure.

Taking turns to relieve each other at the wheel, each of us more or less lost in thought, we make on through the night as so many have done before us, watching the compass, watching the stars, drifting in and out of awareness of where we are. And so the night passes.

★

It is broad daylight when I come on deck again. Simon grins, and gestures around him: 'Vaaaast ocean, mon.' And it is. A long, low swell, cobalt blue, a thin, transparent lacing of bubbles on each crest; a hard glare off the water, little sound except for the swish of the bow wave running alongside, the occasional creak of the mainsheet running from the boom overhead to the track behind the wheel. The wind's in the east, as is the mid-morning sun, so there's no shade on deck and it is hot. We are careful always of the sun, even in northern waters. It's surprising how quickly you can get burned, even on an overcast day off the Irish coast. Lip protector, sunscreen of at least factor 15, a hat, preferably wide-brimmed, long sleeves and long, light trousers are the order of the day. Secretly, of course, we all covet that crinkle-eyed hardy sailor look, so these tropical days involve a negotiation between vanity and prudence. Apropos, the question of beards: Zaf is already bearded, the sandy scrub on Simon's jawline would pass for a beard in a black-and-white photo, and I haven't shaved for two days. We discuss the pros and cons. Zaf, the old sea dog, decides to go for it; Simon, with some mis-givings, decides to go for it; I decide to give it a few days, but know already I'm going home clean-shaven. I have it in my head that a beard will get in the way of the sun, and when I'd eventually shave it off I'd have a two-tone face. Wouldn't like that. This conversation occupies a surprising amount of time.

The satphone conversation Zaf has with Oliver doesn't. The clutch-plate explanation is abandoned for the moment. The new theory is that it might be the water-cooler; every-thing else was recently serviced. It takes a few tries on the satphone to piece the discussion together, which adds to the general sense of frustration. We talk it out again and again, going over and over the various possibilities as they occur to us, but in the end it comes down to another purgatorial stint in the engine room for Zaf and Simon, while Charlotte sleeps and I mind the helm.

Gloomily, sitting there with one bare foot hooked in the wheel, I consider the vagaries of things mechanical. Things go wrong on boats, naturally they do – things go wrong all the time, with everything – but I am obscurely offended that things should go wrong out here. Perhaps this is a backwash of anxiety from the last trip; perhaps also it is simply irritation that people don't do straightforward jobs in a straightforward manner. I make a list in my head of things that are wrong:

- The life raft in its canister at the foot of the foremast should have been serviced in February; it wasn't.
- One of the two battery banks is out of service. Kaput.
- The water in the freshwater tank is unfit for consumption. (So what? I remind myself, we have plenty of bottled.)
- The freezer under the galley floor doesn't work properly, never has. (Ah, look, it takes about six hours a day of the generator running to keep the bloody thing cool.)
- The cruising chute that blew out on the passage over from the Canaries has been repaired, but probably won't hold; it should have been replaced. (Right, but you don't know it won't hold. It hasn't been up yet. Take it easy.)

I hear myself disagreeing with myself and am dimly aware that I'm maybe just edgy because of nicotine withdrawal.

I give myself over to the pull of the wind on this big, beautiful boat, to her white hull slicing through deep blue water, to the high sun and the small, puffy clouds dotted along the horizon, to the smell of salt on bare teak, the feel of the wind along my bared forearms, on my upturned face. I surrender myself to the forces in play and am borne up and along, a bubble of well-being flexing in my chest. I scratch absentmindedly at the nicotine patch on my arm, strangle the sudden craving for a cigarette, direct my mind into the now and the flow of things.

The boys are back. No luck in the engine room. Zaf scratches his rapidly bronzing bald head. He's irritated and restless. He tweaks the sails (she gets lighter on the helm), tweaks them some more, calls for a slight course adjustment. We all have a good grumble, then Charlotte appears with a magnificent salad and four cans of beer.

I have a sudden flash of what we might look like, seen from a passing cargo ship. The idle rich in their big bloody yacht, lolling along in the sunshine without a care in the world, while the rest of us have to work. Never mind that we couldn't afford a dinghy between us if we were to pool our resources: it seems suddenly disrespectful of our good fortune in the scheme of things to be grousing as we have been.

And another thing, somebody says out of the contented silence, what about the bloody chain for the self-steering gear, eh? What about that?

In theory, with a steady wind and the sails well set, a long-keeled boat like this should be able to steer herself. It doesn't work, for some reason, and nobody can quite figure out why. Zaf goes rummaging in a cockpit locker, emerges with a long length of elastic shock cord and busies himself at the wheel. Ten minutes later, presto! The wheel is lashed in a cat's cradle of line, our new self-steering gear. When she pulls to the left now, in a gust, say, the line going across to the starboard side stretches, then contracts. This pulls the wheel back over again, and settles her on her original course. We applaud our skipper's ingenuity, and christen this new crew member 'Magellan'. The advent of Magellan is noted in the ship's log at 15.27, as is the fact that we are now 139 miles out of Antigua. By midnight it's nearly 200 miles, we're on a bearing of 020° and it is, according to the skipper's entry, 'a beautiful starry night'.

Day 3

Saturday, 4 May
Pos. at midnight   N   19° 24′
                       W   61° 26′

Still on double watches; we go over to singles later today.

For all that we're out here in the comparative silence of the empty ocean, there is claustrophobia to be reckoned with: being confined with three comparative strangers, however amiable, and confined also with oneself. It might seem a paradox, but I feel less constricted when I'm on watch by myself. On a solo watch, while all below sleep, you can mutter to yourself, sing a little, do things with the boat, with no inhibiting sense of audience. I thought about this before coming out: what will it be like, to spend five weeks or so with people I get on with well enough, but with whom, apart from a liking for this boat and for sailing, I have little in common? Nobody on board, for instance, reads the way I do. When I can I'll read one, sometimes two books a day; when I'm not idling or being domestic or neighbourly or working, I spend most of my time with people who read books, discuss ideas, are variously passionate about poetry, fiction, philosophy, painting, politics, the state of our poor Republic. Those are, poetry above all, my most urgent preoccupations. So, what am I doing out here? Perhaps learning again that there are other ways to live a life which are equally valid, may even be more valid than my own. Certainly I don't go sailing for the exercise, or for the social cachet, though I enjoy the strenuousness of working a boat, I enjoy feeling myself rein-habit my body. But now I realize there is something else at work here, too. I enjoy slowing down, stepping outside the confines of a life that has become fixed in the habitual.

It's interesting to be with people who are no more than mildly interested in things that are central to my view of the world. It's good to take a given situation – being together on this boat – factor in the work that has to be done, figure out how we are to do it together, then just get on with it. These responsibilities displace, perhaps even replace, habitual responsibilities. I don't have to feel that being with myself, stuck with myself as it were, is an absolute given. I can stop the nervy self-scrutinizing chatter, for instance. Just stop it. Castaneda has Don Juan talk about 'shutting off the internal dialogue'. I spend some time contemplating this phrase before it dawns on me that, while I am sitting here in the saloon, scribbling these thoughts, Charlotte is stretched out miserable in her bunk; Zaf and Simon might appreciate a coffee. Ouch. Sometimes I love the way my mind works, the way it plays with me. Right now, the thought comes unbidden, I would kill for a cigarette. I get up off my arse and make some coffee, squeeze some lemon into a glass of water for Charlotte.

This morning, at 04.00, the moon waning, some cloud passed rapidly overhead, coming from north-east. An hour later the wind veered south-south-east, came back to east after fifteen minutes or so. The barometer has been fluctuating all day. Our speed has climbed considerably to a consistent seven knots, with a high of 7.6 knots at one stage. Bowling along, course magnetic 020° to 040°, cutting back and forth as the wind swings. We subtract fifteen degrees or so from magnetic course to get our true heading, are still more or less in a straight line for Bermuda. At 15.00 we are 312 miles out from Antigua, about 2,500 miles from the Azores if we stick to our present plan.

Since yesterday morning we've been trolling a lure, a small glass fish with a nasty barbed surprise in its tail. Simon and Zaf are much exercised by their failure to catch anything. They decide to change the lure. OK by me, if they catch something edible, fine. Fishing never appealed to me. I like catching them; I hate taking the hooks out of their mouths, whether or not the poor bastards get put back. If these boys catch anything, it'll probably be a tuna. I shall look forward to seeing them get that hook out.

Clear skies all afternoon. About 14.00 we see a sail to port, about five miles off. Tall sloop rig, Simon thinks a catamaran making for Newport, Rhode Island. Making perhaps two knots on us, perhaps more. Passes ahead, west of north. I try to figure out where Simon got Newport from, then go below, open out the chart, estimate their course and, sure enough, arrow straight for Rhode Island. For the rest of the voyage, any time we see a vessel, I'll practise working out its course, then guess at a likely port of origin and destination for her.

On watch in the late afternoon, I'm perched up on the coaming, the others below, when I wonder, am I doing this trip for the sake of doing it, or so that when it's over I'll have done it? That one has me puzzled for a while, but not half as puzzled as the near-hallucinatory thoughts that were running through my mind before I got up for the afternoon watch: all I've to do is hang on until the Azores, then jump ship, fly home. Or, I could dive overboard. Or, I could just embrace catatonia, lie in my bunk, refuse to get up, wait for someone to make everything better. Thoughts like this make me nervous, as I don't know who's having them. I drag myself out of the bunk in a moment of desperate inspiration, rummage around in my washbag, find the Dioralite in the zipped compartment, stumble out to the galley, tip the sachet into a pint jug of water, drain the lot in two or three swallows.

Eureka! Now I remember where this weirdness comes from: dehydration.

I go check: there are fifty-seven containers of water left. We shipped seventy. Drinking four per day would give us fourteen days, three would give us nineteen. Plenty. I go around, checking that everyone's keeping their fluid intake up.

Around 21.00 we overtake a large, slow-moving cargo ship, leaving her ten miles to port. Zaf points out an apparently anomalous fact: it can be easier to see a vessel in the dark than it is by day. This one is below the horizon, but we see her green starboard light. We check the distance on radar, to give us a reference frame for estimating distance with the mark-one eyeball, the sailor's best friend. It's devilishly difficult to estimate distance over the sea; it takes a great deal of practice. Simon, son of a lighthouse keeper, is the best at this.

On the watch to midnight we have heavy showers – resent having to put on rain gear this far south. It's cool after the showers, the wind gone around to the north. We have to bear away, down to a true bearing of 350° or so. Although this is a considerable way off our desired course, it doesn't matter all that much, taking into consideration the long distance we have to cover. It's hard to conceive of the scale of this journey: from Antigua to Kinsale is about 4,000 miles, the equivalent of, say, Beijing to Moscow, or Casablanca to Johannesburg.

Today has been the kind of day that does your head in. I'm glad to turn in – tired enough for sleep; too tired, I hope, to dream.

Day 4

Sunday, 5 May
Pos. at midnight   N   22° 04′
                          W   61° 12′

On watch this early morning, cold but not too cold, watching
the spreading light burn off the last of the night, I might have
been a different person, on a different voyage entirely. We've
unlashed Magellan – the windshifts and the shortened swell
didn't suit it – and we've been steering by hand. Charlotte's
below making tea and toast; I'm at the wheel, clamped in
the Discman headphones, listening to the fiddle player Gerry
Harrington and the great box player Charlie Piggott. Charlie's
the only man I've ever heard who can play a reel in reel time,
but in such a way that you hear it as if it's a slow air. He did
that one Sunday morning in O'Hanlon's pub in Mullaghbawn,
South Armagh, and I'm still trying to figure out if it was something he actually did, or was my head astray? No matter, I'm
standing there at the wheel, feeling the rise and fall of her through
the soles of my feet, fingertips curled around the leatherbound
rim, my breath ballooning inside me as if the wind is breathing
me – and that music falls away. Now I hear a song in my head,
in Spanish, words and tune, a woman's voice – 'Lament for
Fedérico de Navarro', composed and sung by his mother.

    I should be more startled than I am (where the hell is this
coming from?), but I'm mostly just intrigued. I hear it the way
I sometimes hear the beginning of a poem, that small verbal
nucleus the rest will grow from, and my first impulse is to go

grab a notebook and pen, scribble this down before I forget it. I can't yell for Charlotte to take the wheel, I don't want to wake Zaf, his cabin just inside the hatchway to starboard, and there is some other, less obvious, reluctance, too. I will try to remember this, I think, knowing right away that I won't be able to.

What I remember later, when I do try to write it down, is the song's author and provenance, and something of the story. No more than that. I know, in some unmediated way, that Federico was a young man, only son of a widow, who drowned in these waters, at this time of day, casualty of some naval engagement hundreds of years ago. I think we have sailed through a pocket of air and time, the place where his mother, lifted beyond herself by grief, directed her song. I think that the song, having nothing but the wind and the restless sea to disturb it, has endured here. I say 'I think', but it isn't like thinking, this kind of thing, it has the same impress of 'knowing', that same self-contained presence to conscious-ness, that an image has in an emerging poem when it comes unbidden. A thousand ships could follow the course we are following, and not one of them would pass through the exact intersection of latitude and longitude that we passed through when that song made itself heard in me.

When Charlotte came on deck I'm sure I thanked her for the tea – I hope I did. I have a memory of going forward silently, of sitting there quietly for a long time under the foremast, face to the rising sun, sipping tea, washed by some melancholy for a life not my own. I remember the thought: he drowned, but he did not die. I remember thinking it was strange to have that thought. I said a prayer for him, and a prayer for his mother. An undirected prayer, perhaps no more than an acknowledgement of the *fact* of both of them, the fact of that lament.

But, as Coleridge says, 'these things will by few be understood, by fewer granted.'

I realize, coming back to myself, that we are sailing the Spanish Main. I'd forgotten the phrase until now, one of those lambent and infinitely provocative phrases that seize the imagination in childhood, fill it with towering pictures of galleons and wooden-wall traders, lumbering along, laden with gold (doubloons!), the lookouts aloft anxiously scanning the horizon for the topmasts of some privateer.

The history and fiction of these waters that we know in Ireland is the English version, naturally. It never occurred to me to question this. Now, here, coming to my feet, the warm tropical waters gone blue again, the silver grey of dawn melted away, it strikes me with some considerable force how different the Spanish, Portuguese, French and Dutch versions must be. I feel the thick complexity of these layered and interpenetrating versions darken the air around me, and as suddenly realize I am too tired to engage with this thought.

I am more interested in the brute fact of how we course through the water now, the sails hardened in, the speed picking up a little as the wind freshens. I take my shoes off, go forward to where the night's bow wave has wet the forepeak. I stand there on the wet teak, feeling the cold grain of it through the soles of my feet, and this, for the moment, is enough. This is all I want to feel, all I am capable of feeling. My left hand seeks out the inner forestay for balance; the staysail's aluminium boom bumps softly against my left thigh; a patch of the sun's heat on my right thigh is an adequate fact. The genoa curls and cracks, pulls out into a full-bodied curve again. I look back to where Charlotte stands braced against the wheel. She raises a hand in silent acknowledgement, grins that sunny grin, and I wave back. Sit down again out of the wind; doze.

★

The day passes amiably. We stick to the formal pattern of watches, but people are coming and going, snoozing in the saloon, cooking snacks and meals, tending to the trolling line, chatting, staring off into the distance. Charlotte is back to normal, Zaf is still being driven mad by the engine, Simon is dreaming of surfing, I'm trying to read or make notes – we're all somehow restless and relaxed at the same time. The thing about this kind of passage – stable weather conditions, a steady wind, the boat pulling efficiently – is that there's very little sailing to be done. The wind's down to fifteen knots, but we're still making seven knots or so. The staysail and foremain are out on preventers, the genoa's fully out, as is the main – we're carrying more or less maximum sail, and there's little need for trimming. There is nothing we can do to make her sail faster.

The log entry at 12.00 records our latitude as 23° 26' 17" N. This is, precisely, the Tropic of Cancer. The apprentice navigator feels a right fool when he realizes this only an hour or two later. Another opportunity for improvised ceremonial lost! We have the daily beer when I bring the news, a wistful farewell to the tropics. It all seems to have passed so quickly. Well, tropics or not, we are still a considerable distance due south of Bermuda, and that will do nicely for now.

By the log at 15.00, we've covered 480 miles over water, roughly 420 of which count towards our course. Initially we'd ducked thirty miles towards Guadeloupe, then thirty back north-east, in order to position ourselves for the run north. We are 60 per cent of the way towards 30° N/60° W, the notional point where we hope for westerlies to carry us towards the Azores. If we keep this speed up, we should make Horta in fifteen days overall, the classic average for this passage – but nobody thinks it'll be that straightforward.

In the late-afternoon heat, Zaf and Simon once again sweat

it out in the stuffy dark of the engine room, trying, hoping to discover a problem with the sea-water strainer to the gearbox cooling system. If they find the problem here, then that may solve the overheating.

I'm burrowing for fresh vegetables in the bowels of the lazarette. Charlotte is cheerfully cooking a pork stew and the meat is probably not off. The courgettes, on the other hand, are rotten; ditto half the carrots and peppers; the corn on the cob has an interesting fungus – shades of the *Marie Celeste* – and the tomatoes, perhaps worryingly, are holding out.

Zaf, trying to raise Oliver, keeps getting, then losing, a signal on the satphone.

When he's finished, I try to get through to Paula, with some misgivings. This trip will be the longest time we've been apart in eleven years. Already it is an immense source of frustration to me, our not being able to talk together, to point to things, to pass what happens in the course of the day through both our minds, as we have been accustomed to do. I know that, after the Biscay excitements, she is anxious about my being out here. I know also that, tough-minded woman that she is, she will have evolved a strategy by now for keeping her worries at bay, will have put my absence into suspension in her mind. I worry that breaking in on this protective silence will unsettle us both. For now, though, the question is moot – the satphone sees to that.

My notebook at 18.00 records we are loping north, a long, undulant dip and rise, sun to port, six widths above the horizon, low clouds all around the horizon, small puffies overhead; the light is the kind of bleached purple/fuzzy grey that one gets off the Irish coast at the end of a perfect summer's day.

Off watch, not needed in the galley yet, I spread the chart out on the saloon table. Simon has marked in our latest

49

position, and I am musing over it when I see the notation 'Nares Abyssal Plain'. What? I look more closely. Over there to starboard are depths of 6,340 metres. The vast ocean suddenly acquires a third dimension: down. A long way down. Christ, we are sailing over Switzerland! There are huge mountains down there; we are passing between two of them even now. The hull of *Spirit* is six-millimetre steel. Good steel, sound steel, well cared for, impeccably maintained. But, six millimetres? There's a lightless chasm down there (I look at my feet, at the cabin sole), *down* taking on a tolling, plangent resonance. Down. Down. I bolt up for air, grabbing the *Atlantic Pilot* as I pass the nav station.

There are small traces of cirrus far off to the west, heralding perhaps a change in the weather. It's just about dark as I begin my first solo watch. From now on it will be two hours on, six hours off for everyone. The next watch, Zaf in my case, is the stand-by watch, meaning the first person to call if you think a sail change is needed, if there's a ship about whose behaviour you're not sure . . . It's a good system; it means that everyone gets some guaranteed sleep, a full six hours if nothing untoward crops up. Whatever his place on the roster, the skipper always gets called if the ship is even remotely threatened.

Tonight I'm listening to Furtwängler conducting Brahms and Beethoven, Vienna 1943. I remember the cold, crisp day I bought these CDs, an afternoon in Vienna last November, Paula back in the hotel going over poems for her reading that night. I remember thinking it would be strange listening to this, imagining the audience at the performance where it was recorded, the black uniforms of the SS, the women in furs, the complacency and brute indifference to the human context, the contrast between the darkness of spirit everywhere in the wartime city and the beauty of the music. It never occurred to me I would be listening to this recording in the middle of the ocean. The soundscape is beautiful, but there's a rip of pain in there, too, thinking of those souls who were as moved by this music as I am now, before people sitting in that very audience the night of the recording took a hand in their murder.

The sky is full of stars; there are curious mist wisps racing around the boat, close in, catching the green, red, green, red of the running lights as we rock on.

By now we're more than 500 miles from Antigua. Our official port of refuge (where we run for if we get into trouble) at this point is Hamilton, Bermuda, more or less due north. Just before coming on watch I got through to Paula, gave her our position. Her response was succinct: you stay out of that Bermuda Triangle! Don't want to think about that just now, plenty of food for thought in the depths immediately beneath us. I think of that ship in Heaney's wonderful poem, in the clear air over Clonmacnoise church, dropping anchor in the sanctuary. I think of the Saint on the altar, watching a crewman shinny down to free the hook, remarking that these cannot breathe our air. From nearer to home, there's the story of St Finbarr, patron saint of my native Cork, and his encounter with another monk, Scoithín. Finbarr, rowing across the lake of Gougane Barra, meets Scoithín walking towards him. 'What are you doing, walking on the lake?' 'What are *you* doing, rowing across this meadow?' Finbarr leans over the gunwale, scoops out a redgold salmon, holds it thrashing in the air. Scoithín bends down, plucks the red flower, *scoithín*, from the grasses at his feet. Each regards the other thoughtfully, then, after an exchange of benedictions, Scoithín goes on his way, Finbarr rows on. And that, the annals tell us, is how St Scoithín got his name. Now, out here on the water, my own thinking rearranged, I observe that it was the boatman who named the landsman, and therefore the water is granted the prior or superior reality. Out here on Planet Water that seems perfectly right and natural to me.

We've had clear blue skies all day; now, towards the end of my watch, mist begins to swirl around us. Change in the weather coming, maybe rain again, like last night? At midnight, going back to check the log and have a word with Zaf before turning in, I see our speed has dropped to five knots. The wind's in the east still, but down to eight knots or so, the barometer still high. I wonder about this change in the weather, but have not enough experience to read the signs. Zaf is of the opinion we're going to lose the wind.

Lovely. No engine, and now it looks as if we are to learn first hand that the doldrums is aptly named. The thing is, there's nothing we can do. If we can't fix the engine, we can't fix the engine, and there's certainly nothing we can do about the wind.

We are in the horse latitudes. The Spanish and Portuguese colonial supremacy in their American possessions owed a great deal to the horse, its weight in battle and, above all, the mobility it conferred on their small military forces. Perhaps also to the cognitive challenge it posed to the world view of the indigenous inhabitants – what would you think, having never seen a horse, to see an armoured man on horseback? In any case, many of the ships that plied these routes carried horses on the outward journey, warhorses and packhorses. The trouble with horses, from a sailor's point of view, is that they consume huge quantities of water. So, becalmed in mid ocean, often for weeks at a time, the captains of these sailing vessels were often forced to put the horses overboard if they were to conserve water for crew and complement. It must have looked bizarre, the horses squealing in terror as they were hoisted out over the side, lowered or dropped into the water. I try to imagine them swimming round and round the ship for as long as they were able, then sinking in a flurry of hooves, or falling away behind as a wind came up at last and the potbellied ships began to crawl away. I wonder how long a horse would last out here. Almost I see the rolling, terrified eye, the clumsy head of a charger or mule sweep helplessly by in the fitful moonlight. It must have caused grief and tension on board those ships, putting the horses overboard; the brute necessity so obvious to the seaman, not so obvious, perhaps, to the caballero.

Day 5

Monday, 6 May
Pos. at midnight   N   24° 39′
                   W   60° 59′

Charlotte taps on the cabin door: four o'clock, time to get up. I hear her put the kettle on, sit up, settle a minute or so to get my bearings, feet pressed to the floor. First thing I notice is there's little or no plunging. Up here near the bow, if we have any kind of way on, the bow would be rising and falling, rising and falling. Not happening now. Halyards are slapping overhead, no sound of engine, so we must be still relying on sail, and the wind must have died. Score one for Zaf the meteorologist. Next thing I notice is that the plaster across the index finger of my right hand is far too tight. First thought the boat, second thought the body: that's a good sign. What happened to the finger? Stupidity, that's what. Yesterday morning I was still on deck after not just my watch, but Zaf's, too, when Simon came up and Zaf decided to fly the cruising chute. This is, in our case, a pink and blue balloon-shaped light sail, carried in winds up to twenty knots, the top end of a Force 5, usually flown by us with its inboard end attached to the bowsprit. Setting this sail is a bit tricky, especially if the crew is out of practice, as we are. It takes time for even an experienced crew to get the sequence right so that everyone involved knows without fussing what the others are doing. Anyway, I'm tired, gazing about me on the wheel while they work on the foredeck, and something suddenly goes wrong.

The sheet which has been led aft to one of the starboard winches starts to run out as the unsecured clew of the sail flies up. I have a second to realize what's happening. We don't want it going over the side and possibly getting snarled up in the prop, so I make a grab for it.

Stupid on two counts: first, with one roll still on the winch, the line, under huge power, snaps my hand up against the metal drum; secondly, as my hand of its own volition lets go of the sheet, it sears across my fingers, burning an instant groove into my index finger. The pain is excruciating, one of those pains that instantly freezes the pit of your stomach. The particular trouble with lines on a boat is that they become salt-encrusted and therefore more abrasive – though at the speed that line was travelling it would have cut through the skin anyway. Zaf is as angry as he is concerned, and he's right. I should know better. As it happens, I trapped the tail of the line under my foot just before it whipped out of the cockpit, but that's also a pretty stupid thing to have done: I could have been pulled out of the boat if a coil had wrapped around my leg.

Now I peel the sticking plaster off, examine the wound blearily. It's begun to heal surprisingly quickly, thanks to the tea-tree oil I'd soaked the plaster in. God bless the Anzacs who brought this extraordinary antiseptic to Europe during World War I, and God bless whoever it was, back in the mists of time, who first discovered it.

Anyway, on deck with a fresh plaster, a mug of tea and the Discman. This morning it's Tibetan flute music and Mozart to greet the dawn. The morning comes pale grey, pale pink, without a breath of wind. Our speed in the past four hours has been about three knots, the breeze, what there is of it, gone around south-east. The bar is rock steady; visibility is perfect; an hour after sunrise it is already hot. The genoa's rolled in, too heavy for these conditions; we're wallowing along under main and cruising chute, at least keeping headway. There's a long, slow swell – whatever weather's out there is a long way off.

The internal weather is curious, too. Zaf comes on deck, chuckling, to take his watch. 'Last night, you know, in my dreams, guess what I was doing? Bloody hell, you'll never guess. Have a guess. No? Selling elephants. Could you believe that, eh? Selling elephants!' This morning there's nothing to be done except sit here and watch what happens.

Usually, when Zaf comes on, there is a great stir. First his head comes through the hatch, nose up, sniffing for wind. Then he scrambles up, gripping two mugs of tea ('Jesus, boy, we have to watch it, you know. The Barry's is almost gone!'). Next it's a quick look around, all around, then a slower, more methodical look around. After that it's a careful examination of what sails are set, a tweaking of a sheet here and there, then up on deck, a slow tour, checking everything, missing nothing. By the time he gets back he's wide awake and ready for another mug of tea. So far, every time I've come back up it's to find him ready with a plan: roll out the genoa or roll in the genoa, let the main out further or sheet it in hard, get the cruising chute out of the bag, get the pole up, change mind and get it all down again. The good side to this is, every time he's on deck, I get a masterclass: so much to learn, and no better man than Zaf to teach it. The downside, alas, is that there isn't the remotest chance I'll ever come off this particular watch bang on the button of 06.00 and get straight back to my bunk. But then, I tell myself, I could be sleeping at home, and besides, if truth be told, my own restless curiosity, my need to absorb everything I possibly can about the art of sailing, would keep me up anyway. This morning Zaf is vastly entertained by those elephants. He'll be standing there, the

56

very picture from the antique of the sailing master, pepper and salt of his new beard bristling, and he'll look around, puzzled, and say, 'Elephants. *Elephants.*' He'll look at me, eyes lit with merriment and ask, 'Elephants, you follow me? Elephants. What's that about?'

Beats me. I'm having enough trouble figuring out my own dreams, which I'm remembering with great and, for me, unusual clarity. Last night there were three.

In the first, the late Tiernan MacBride, film-maker, grand-son of Maud Gonne MacBride, appears in a black greatcoat, in high good humour. He wants me to know he hugely approves of this trip, is both surprised and pleased to find me out here. Tiernan, as I know from my friend Kevin Page, was a great swimmer. Indeed, Kevin recalls being on a rescue boat when he was a lifeguard, heading out towards Ireland's Eye off Howth Harbour, and meeting Tiernan a good half-mile from shore, ploughing along like a water bull. I never got on particularly well with Tiernan, but I both like and admire his partner, Pat Murphy, a gifted film-maker herself. Tiernan wants me to know he's very glad I have such a warm and positive regard for Pat. I'm very surprised to find him figuring in my dreams. What leaves the deepest impress in this dream is the strong certainty I have that out here he is in his element.

In the second dream, my good friend Pat Boran is a worried man. He's just discovered that his beloved wife, Raffaela, is a secret firebug! Now what the hell is that about?

The third dream is clearly connected to this journey. I disembark from *Spirit* in Dún Laoghaire, which is on the south side of Dublin Bay, to get on the DART, Dublin's suburban electric train, but the station I'm standing in is actually Sutton on the north side of the bay, and I'm getting the DART in order to join the boat in Dún Laoghaire, meaning to go on watch. I bail out at some station which is and isn't Lansdowne

Road on the south side, only to realize I am only half dressed and only halfway there. Unsurprisingly, I wake from this somewhat bewildered.

What the three dreams have in common is a Technicolor vividness, a sense of the hyper-real which is not usual in my dreams. It's the same for Zaf, though neither Charlotte nor Simon finds this happens to them. What holds my attention here is not so much the contents or narrative lines of the dreams, more the sense they give, in the afterwash, that spheres of consciousness, or at least of attention, are becoming porous to each other, that the contents and structures of one kind of thought are beginning to interpenetrate others. It's also noticeable that the body is beginning to fend for itself without my conscious direction, to orient itself to complex movement of its own volition, to look out for itself almost as if it were an autonomous entity. I am beginning to pay a different kind of attention to being alive, here, now, in this delimited world, at once familiar and unfamiliar.

I put on more sunscreen, drink more water, start thinking about breakfast and the engine. Simon and Zaf reassemble the heat-exchanger, fire up the engine and for ten minutes or so we surge ahead. Then the bloody thing overheats again, and we switch it off. By 14.00 we are going nowhere. Charlotte, laconic as ever, records in the log: no wind, no speed. That about sums it up.

The crew sprawls on deck, working on our tans. We are trying to read, or sleep, to cut down on movement, let frustration slip on by as we carefully refrain from talking about our predicament. I can see how, after a few days of this, we might begin to get on each other's nerves. In some way I had hoped for a few days like this, a chance to write a handful of poems, maybe. It doesn't happen. In fact I have to force myself to write my daily notes. Deeper than the desire to write just now is the overriding impulse to experience this trip as absolutely as I can, with no withdrawals into the habitual places of silence and reflection I have nurtured in myself all my life.

A happy consequence of this plenitude of time is that meals are elaborately planned and executed. Even better, from the cook's point of view, the boat is relatively stable. Cooking on board can be a horror story. The galley is amidships and to port. That's good because midships is the part of the boat that moves least in a seaway. You have to imagine the boat as a kind of see-saw, the bow and stern plunging up and down, up and down, with the fulcrum, the midships, moving far less. This picture is both true and misleading. It's true as far as the longitudinal axis of the boat is concerned, but sometimes, especially in lumpy seas, the whole boat will fall off a wave: imagine your kitchen suddenly dropping three feet through the air on to a hard surface. Then there is the yawing, the rolling, the lurching from side to side, the corkscrewing – it's easier to have the galley where it is, but only relatively so. Zaf doesn't cook, a deficiency he makes up for by enthusiastic help with the preparation and the washing-up – the latter another horror story in its own way, though perhaps more psychological than physical. The rest of us do our best, the degree of ambition brought to the job a direct function of the movement of the boat. Sometimes it can be so bad that all cooking is done in one pot, simply because it's impossible to keep more than one pot on the cooker. Stews are the great stand-by of the seagoing cook, stews and pasta. You can pre-pare a pasta sauce, wrap the pot in a towel, cook the pasta, drain it, pour the sauce in on top of the pasta and, presto, with only minimal burns and scalds, a hot meal for the crew. This, as you might imagine, can grow monotonous, so most cooks make the effort to do a little better than this.

The gas cooker on *Spirit* is mounted athwartships. There are three burners and an oven, although, as with most boat cookers, this latter is better at casseroles than at anything which is sensitive to a cold spot in the middle of the oven. There are 'fiddles' (low rails) around the edges of the cooker, and movable bars of ingenious design which screw on to the fiddles to more or less keep pots in their place.

The ideal seagoing cook would be a masochistic, fireproof contortionist with an aptitude for juggling, an agoraphobic, a hygiene freak, a fast worker, a cordon bleu graduate, an acrobat, a strong-stomached Buddhist saint. Here in the doldrums, the only requirement is that it be your turn to produce a meal.

Charlotte, as a consequence of her Caribbean season just past, is particularly adept at conjuring up the most complex and luxurious of salads, today's being a good example: fusilli al dente, chopped pineapple, green olives, onion, cubed ham, pine nuts and shredded Chinese leaves, drenched in olive oil, lime and lemon, garnished with curls of Parmesan. You must imagine this washed down with ice-cold Carib beer, enjoyed at their leisure by a rapidly bronzing gang of four cut-throats, lounging under a high sun, giving every appearance of not having a care in the world. In reality it must be understood that we are a deeply serious professional delivery crew, engaged in a task that is both perilous and demanding, engineless in the horse latitudes, at the mercy of the unforgiving sea.

That fucking gearbox, as it is affectionately known, occupies a great deal of our attention and our conversation. This afternoon it also occupied a great deal of my time. Fool that I am, I get to feeling it's unfair to Simon that he's been helping Zaf all the time in the engine room; equally foolishly, I think it might be good experience for me to take his place. As a consequence I spend four hours in the heat and oily stink of the engine room, as Zaf takes things apart, cleans them, puts them back together again. My only consolation is that I don't get a fit of the screaming heebie-jeebies.

Over and over we rehearse diagnoses of the gearbox problem that become hour by hour more unlikely. As things stand, we have ten to fifteen minutes of motoring if we should need to drive ourselves out of trouble.

At 19.30 or so the radio sputters, breaking the torpor. Charlotte answers. Sailing yacht *Lightness of Being*, looking for engine oil. Nobody else comes on the air, so it looks as if we are the nearest vessel, ahead of them to the north-west. Zaf says to tell them we'll help them if we can, depending on what quantity they need. They don't make it very clear why they need oil, or how urgently. They sound possibly German, but might be Czech, given the name. We repeat our position, they acknowledge, end of exchange. A quick look around confirms they must be somewhere over the horizon; in any case, we are constantly scanning all around us – a ship making twenty knots can be on top of you in half an hour, from hull-down to far too close. It gives us something to do, getting up now and then to scan the brilliant, far-off haze to the south-east for a sail.

Mist again after dark, the log at midnight records our slowest speed yet, 0.4 knots. That's less than one-sixth of normal walking pace.

Day 6

Tuesday, 7 May
Pos. at midnight   N   25° 20′
                W   60° 17′

Just after dawn, at 07.00, *Lightness of Being* makes contact again. Zaf's instructions are to ask them for a proposed rendezvous point based on both our courses, given that we are unable to motor in their direction. I relay this to them; they say they'll get back to us.

The wind today is all over the place. It starts off in the west, about fifteen knots, then drags around to north-east. At one stage instead of 070° we were making 170°. It would have been bad enough to be going nearly due east instead of north, but to be heading back the way we came, as near as dammit to due south . . . that's the pits. By mid afternoon we have five to six knots on the clock, rain, squalls, confused seas and the wind still in the north-east. I make soup with rice and canned vegetables, and tuna mayonnaise with salt crackers. Washed down with pots of Barry's tea, this cheers us all up. For a while. Zaf and myself are, it must be admitted, fixated on Barry's, a real Cork thing. The Bantry Turk is, if anything, even more devoted than I am to the elixir, and the others rag us unmercifully about the imminent demise of our carefully eked-out supply. 'Christ almighty,' says Zaf, 'it's bad enough being off the fags' – and I wish he hadn't said that as, patches notwithstanding, the only way I can keep the nicotine with-drawal at bay is by resolutely shutting down whenever the pangs make themselves felt. This time the craving is so intense that I only calm down when I promise myself three cigarettes as soon as we reach the Azores. Only three, mind.

There's a sudden rain shower while we're changing sail; young Simon runs for the shampoo. Cheers all round. Robust proposal that his feet should be immersed in tea-tree oil, shampoo and water while he sleeps. I'm sorry myself now I didn't move fast enough to shower alfresco and for free. An unexpected bonus of the fresh water in the tank being undrinkable is that we have plenty for washing, but there's an inclination, admittedly not very rational, to conserve this water. Charlotte, an old 'schooner chick' – her words – claims you should be able to wash thoroughly using no more than a mug of water. Well, yeah, right . . . I'm curious about the term, doesn't she find it a bit dismissive, patronizing? She is puzzled by the question. 'No, that's what all us girls on the schooners used to be called.' By the men? 'Yes, of course, but us chicks call ourselves that, too.'

I'm down below at the nav station, having just calculated we have 620 miles up, when Zaf, trying the satphone without much hope, gets through to Oliver. The engineer back in Ireland has had a thought: would we drain the light gearbox oil, replace it with a heavier engine oil, and see what happens? Would we? We'd sing to the fucker at this stage if we thought it would work. We go to work, Simon and Zaf upended in the engine room, cans and trays and tools being passed back and forth, the drained oil carefully stored in a marked container until we can dispose of it in Horta. The engine oil is poured in. The theory is that, being of a much greater viscosity, the heavier oil will keep the clutch plates engaged.

Zaf stands in the engine-room door while Charlotte fires up the engine. All above and around is overcast. Not a scrap of blue. There's a puff of oily, black smoke astern, then a steady burbling from the exhaust, a spurting of cooling water. We set the revs at 1,200 and settle to see what happens. After fifteen minutes Zaf checks the temperature: it's cool. Thirty minutes, cool. Simon's entry in the logbook at 17.30 expresses our feelings: 'Gearbox still cool!!!' So is the weather. The wind is from the north-east, about ten knots, and we are heading north-north-west, motorsailing now, trying to compensate for making so far to the east earlier today. There is a perceptible sense of satisfaction aboard: we are no longer at the mercy of the wind. We still want to sail as much as possible, even if not to our optimum course, but now we have another option, and that makes a huge difference. We are all so cheered up we're not even really bothered when Charlotte announces that tonight's dinner will use up the last of the fresh meat.

We are all on different time clocks here. Zaf, I suspect, would stay out sailing for ever if he could. Simon has been away from home for, what, four months? He wants to get home, see his family, see his friends, go surfing. Charlotte has done the Caribbean season, is going back to start preparing the boat for summer chartering in Irish waters – it's all much of a muchness to her. As for me – well, what? Part of me is enjoying the trip entirely for its own sake: I like being out here, jumped at the chance to do this run, would be happy to stay out here, as long as we're moving. Part of me wants to be home by the first week in June, before Paula goes off to teach a workshop in Scotland – I'm coping reasonably well with missing her, but I don't want to add another week or ten days to it – and another part of me just wants the trip to go with maximum efficiency, wants to make the Azores as fast as the weather allows. Is this a kind of competitiveness? There were boats of roughly comparable size due to leave Antigua the day after we did, and I would hate them to make Horta before us. I like the idea of sailing the boat to her maximum, of making the best use of what wind there is. I am a bit disquieted to find this leads so effortlessly, albeit until now unconsciously, to wanting to do better than others.

I'm fed up with trying to sleep in that cabin. Last night it took ages to go over: I was simply unable to persuade the body that every time the bow plunged down it would then come back up again. I lay there with my eyes open, trying to persuade myself of this, knowing it was so, but could not stop myself feeling that the sequence was down, pause, down again, pause, down again . . . no logic could supervene. Tonight I lay my sleeping bag out on the seat, port side of the saloon. This is my favourite place on the boat: midships, so it doesn't rock so much; over the deepest part of the keel, so there is nowhere near as much slamming when the bow crashes into a wave. I've slept here through storms when it would have been impossible to sleep in the cabin, not least because the noise forward is so much greater, not to mention the danger of slamming my head off the bottom of the bunk overhead (which I have done). Here in the saloon there is a greater sense of space; better air, too. I have the advantage of being deaf in one ear, and I sleep with my good left ear in the pillow, so the noise of people passing through rarely wakes me.

The wind tonight is north–north–east, so we're on a starboard tack, the heading 325° – all of which means that we're heeled over to port, and there is a natural tilt into the side of the hull. This makes for a very snug berth, and the best sleep I've had on this trip so far.

Day 7

Wednesday, 8 May
Pos. at midnight   N   26° 24'
                   W   60° 30'

From my notebook

In dream go to James Galway (!) concert with an old friend
from days of wine and dope. As we enter there is a Michael
Hartnett lookalike (for a sec I think Michael himself) reciting
Michael's poem 'Grandmother' on stage, backup singers ready
to go in bridal white and veils; then young lads in quartered
tweed caps, open-neck white shirts and open waistcoats go
scampering thro' audience – a kind of *Riverdance* tribute to
MH. We proceed thro' what are now RDS [Royal Dublin
Society] grounds, on further towards the building where our
seats are, and emerge on to a lane which falls away into a sea
of fog in a vertiginous San Francisco curve, a curve so steep I
know it is the curve of the world. I foot-waltz a derelict car
into a garage, out again to let . . . cops, is it? . . . exit; then in
again. I'm off down the hill, a middle-class woman and a
young black girl discuss the Dow index on the sidewalk; in
the middle of a bunch of kids a twelve- or thirteen-year-old
says, in a refined Dublin accent, 'My name is *Gluais*. I'm going
to be an actor.' I think, Ireland! Their teacher smiles wanly,
and says, 'I'm trying to start them with Europe,' and I say, not
sarcastically, 'Try them with *elsewhere* or *out there* first.'

★

When I'm dreaming, I usually know somewhere inside myself that I'm dreaming. This past week, though, dreams have been so vivid that I usually start the day by soaking a cloth in cold water and laying it on my neck. Cool down the reptile brain.

I stop, as usual, at the nav station on my way through. At 01.00 we had 80 per cent cloud, at 02.00 40 per cent, patchy cloud until now and, when I crane my neck around to look up, almost a clear sky at present. It was a warm night according to Simon, our average speed is six and a half knots and, again according to Simon, we had a high of 7.8 knots when the cloud was at its thickest. The wind has been at best north-east, is still more or less from that quarter. Ideally we'd like south-easterlies at this point, to drive us on up to where we can expect the westerlies that we will ultimately need to make Horta. We're close on 700 miles out of Nelson's Harbour, still heading almost directly for Bermuda.

Magellan is back in service, doing an excellent job, so there's little to do in the way of helming. Someone, I don't know who, has made a nest of flat cushions on the bench behind the wheel, so I sprawl out there, collar turned up, and vegetate for most of my watch, getting up stiffly every ten minutes or so for a thorough look around.

The wind is steady, fifteen to twenty knots, there's a long, low swell again, we're holding our course well, so when Zaf comes up to relieve me there is nothing for him to do.

'Right,' he says, 'what would you say is our estimated time to the Azores?'

Down to the saloon, strong, pale dawn light. Get out the *Atlantic Pilot*, the chart, the dividers. Work out an exact distance from our present position along the likeliest course. Walking the dividers along the line, reading off the scale, making the calculations – all of this is strangely satisfying.

When I have a figure for distance to Horta I go back to the GPS, use the cursor to tally a series of chords along the curve which is more or less our course, just to have a figure as a rough counterbalance to the one I've worked out. There's enough of a correspondence to make me trust the original figure.

Say we have 1,795 miles to go. If we can make seven knots – or 168 miles per day – then we will need eleven days to reach Horta. At six knots, we'll need twelve and a half days; at five knots, fourteen days.

The most reasonable estimate, it seems to me, is twelve and a half days: we should be able to make an average of six knots without too much trouble – if the engine holds out. Zaf reckons that's about right, though he would add on a day or two for the unexpected. Despite all the engine vicissitudes, the day spent becalmed, the unsatisfactory wind direction, we are more or less still in the frame he suggested the day we raised anchor.

Lunch today is ravioli with egg pasta, salad of lettuce, apple, dried fruits, croutons, mayo. The water around us is a deep, deep blue. We are scudding along, well balanced, in high good humour, teasing each other about the danger and social disgrace of landing after a transatlantic crossing fatter than when we set out. Not much danger of that, though: these idyllic conditions are hardly going to last, and we all know that testing weather can make you lean and mean overnight. We are a small crew for so large a yacht: if it comes down to days of heavy work on the helm and with the sails, we won't be long shedding a few kilos.

A mooching kind of day, a day for small, self-imposed tasks – tidying of food lockers, washing of floors, airing of cushions. It's like a mood that passes through us, an unspoken thing of instinct and example. We find ourselves coiling lines, relashing the dinghy, tidying the deck lockers, rearranging the stuff in the cockpit lockers, washing down the folding table in the saloon, tidying the bits and pieces of gear that accumulate on the nav-station desk. We hum to ourselves as we go about the boat; when someone makes tea or coffee, they'll be sure to dig out some biscuits as well, some kind of treat.

Somewhere along the line I find myself, pen and notebook in hand, inspired to make lists. It's always a good sign with me when I start making lists, the outward and objective sign of waking up inside, a kind of acceptance of the need for orderly *doing*, as opposed to absent-minded being. These lists are distillations of our conversations over the past few days, and I decide to leave out the more unattainable propositions; Zaf, like all skippers, has big plans for what the owner should be spending – a new suit of sails, for instance, a new generator . . .

Chores in the Azores

Ship

- Run off water, clean and/or replace filters, fill tanks (Buy pump?)
- Diesel – get filters? Top up tanks
- Gearbox seals – have fixed?
- Cruising chute – have stitched?
- Fwd head – repair
- List med chest contents; top up
- Gas bottle/s
- Water jug plus filters
- Heavy gloves for cleaning
- Autopilot chain
- Impeller for generator

- Coffee pot
- Table knives
- Set of allen keys

I sit back and examine the list. The cruising chute that blew on the Canaries–Caribbean leg was repaired on board, and there is some doubt about it lasting. We could strengthen the repair ourselves, but it's probably OK if we wait until Horta, have a sailmaker do a proper job. The forward head, opposite the galley, has become blocked. Zaf, God bless him, then Simon, reluctantly, have tried to unblock it, but whatever's wrong is proving intractable. A harbour job, we decide, and we use the aft head now, across from the nav station. The disadvantage of this is that the aft head is very close to both Zaf's and Charlotte's cabins, and the noise when you flush it is quite loud, a bit tough on sleepers. (Zaf reminds us of an old trick: putting a few drops of cooking oil in the valve cuts down the screeching noise when you pump.) Taken all in all it's not a bad list, one week out; apart from the gearbox, nothing major has cropped up.

Crew

- Laundry
- Provisions, include water in containers if needed
- Excursions
- Souvenirs
- Hotel room?

We're doing very well in the food stakes. If the wind came right and the forecast were in our favour, we could cut and run for Kinsale directly and probably not have to go on short rations – well, not very short anyway. Water might be a problem; I don't know enough to know. We're doing very well, and now that it's getting cooler in the evenings we probably won't have a problem keeping dehydration at bay. We could, at a pinch, boil the water from the tank, but then we mightn't have enough gas . . . these are not pressing considerations, of course, but it's useful always to calculate and recalculate your strengths and weaknesses, evaluate your changing options.

Laundry on board is a constant preoccupation. Because we have to provide for two quite different climates, we have more clothing than you might expect. For the home waters, even in early June, we'll need warm layers, bulky fleeces and sweaters, trousers or jeans, seaboots, thick socks, heavy oilskins. For this first leg we need shorts, light long-sleeved shirts, light trousers and so on. We've all tended to minimize the tropical gear, which means there is constant washing of T-shirts and shorts, underwear and smalls, a constant flap of washing on the guardrail. There are lines crisscrossing the engine room as well, necessary when there's rain, a good idea even when there isn't because the salt picked up by anything hung out aloft means things never get quite dry.

The idea of taking a hotel room arises from a long, desultory conversation in the cockpit regarding personal hygiene on boats. Down here in these latitudes we spend a lot of time on deck; we wear light clothing. It's easy to keep up with the washing. You don't, in short, get very dirty or smelly. The sailor's secret weapon in this regard is a packet of baby wipes, which keep the delicate places fresh and healthy without using water. Forget daily showers: once every three days is comfortable, and people have been known to go for a week, two weeks before eliciting pointed remarks or theatrical sniffs from crewmates. But we fell to musing about long baths to ease aching muscles, repair bruised bodies, float off layers of pore-deep salt. There is a move, then, to take a hotel room in Horta, with a bathroom which we can all use in turn. A small dose of hedonism to dream about.

Not that *Spirit* is particularly austere. Seventy feet is a lot of boat; except for lunch and dinner we don't have to be together all that much if we don't want to be. Each of us has a small cabin, cramped in real terms, but a priceless private space nonetheless. Still, if you think of it in terms of four people sharing a small apartment for five weeks, without ever going outside . . .

When the sea is up and the wind is up we feel far less claustrophobic. Partly this is because we are kept busy trimming sail, keeping the boat balanced and on her heading, but there's something else, too. It's to do with the wind. It is very rare to be on a boat and not feel the wind, however slight the breeze may be. Almost always there is a wind from somewhere, and the wind has an invigorating effect on even the most sluggish spirit. When I'm feeling muzzy-headed, dull with introspection, physically uneasy, it is almost always a sovereign remedy to go on deck, to take the helm for a bit or to go forward, sometimes all the way forward on to the pulpit boards beyond the forestay. Up there you can feel the whole motion of the boat, the whole forward drive of it, the power that the wind has to lift and drive these fifty tons. Something of the same lift comes into your spirit, then, a sense of being borne up and out and on beyond yourself.

Still, though, a long bath in water as hot as you can bear, thick steam redolent of lavender, say, eucalyptus, rosemary . . . then the thick towels, the soft carpet underfoot, the soft land breeze from the tall windows, the wide, white bed, sleep where nothing about you is moving, the floor and the ceiling and the walls shadowed and solid and fixed . . .

All this is, perhaps, a tad premature. Mid afternoon we're 740 miles out of Antigua, and we all feel, for what seems the first time, that this really is going to be a long journey, not just to Horta, but all the way home.

Now there's a new instruction for those going on watch: check the gearbox temperature. This is not a high-tech operation. In the engine-room floor, treaded sheet steel which lifts out in sections, there is a hole directly over the gearbox. You put your hand in the hole, carefully reach down about fifteen inches and feel the top of the gearbox casing. If it is no more than warm, everything's OK. You do this carefully because your exploring fingertips have to ease past a metal coupling rotating at high speed; you also need to be careful in case the gearbox is too hot to touch, so you end up with your fingertips hovering for a second or two in its heat aura before you actually touch it. Everybody practises this while things are calm, to get used to doing it before it has to be done with the boat slamming about or falling off waves. The good news is that one after the other we can report that the engine-oil trick is working. Today, with the winds light and from the north-east, we are able to keep a good bit closer to our preferred track by motorsailing than would be possible under sail alone. Nevertheless, our heading for most of the day is about 340° magnetic, forty to fifty degrees off our ideal heading. Just before sundown we spot a big ship about seven miles off the starboard bow, heading south. She's making, Zaf's estimate, no more than five or six knots, which means she must have engine trouble. We tack to let her pass, tack again to go astern of her.

This is the first big vessel we've seen since Antigua, and I speculate that she's a banana ship. We loved the banana ships when I was a kid: we'd cycle down to the docks to watch them being unloaded, by hand in those days, and would generally score a box of green bananas from a soft-hearted docker if we hung around long enough. There was a protocol to this: you had to wait without asking until someone gave you a box; you had to split the contents up immediately, out of sight, then get lost. Our mothers knew better than to ask where the big green bunch hanging in the kitchen window had come from, and we knew better than to volunteer the information. Banana boats, for some reason I've never worked out, are always the best-painted boats in harbour. The ship off to starboard was white, resplendently so, and it may have been this, as well as a wishful surge of remembered sentiment, that persuaded me she was a banana boat.

Pleased as he is with the born-again gearbox, the skipper decides to rest the engine overnight. This means sailing in a falling wind, so we go back to four-hour double watches: very likely the wind will go around, so we'll need two on deck to handle sail changes. It's cold for some reason, the first night we've thought it cold, and there isn't much talking in the cockpit; you doze or you keep an eye on the wheel, and every now and then one or other of you goes below to make tea and a sandwich, or to raid the snack bag.

We have a new cause for concern: the steering gear keeps making the most alarming noises, a kind of grinding creak one moment, a sharp crack the next. We've been in the lazarette, under the cockpit sole, with torches; we've examined the offset quadrant the steering cables run from, linked by a geared shaft to the wheel column, but there's nothing obviously wrong. In some ways we'd prefer it otherwise: if we could see something wrong, we could try to fix it. As it is, there's nothing we can do. Charlotte is the most philosophical, takes the view that the rudder is answering the wheel and will probably continue to do so; we shouldn't worry until some-thing breaks. Then we attach the backup tiller (a complicated business) and carry on. I never know with Charlotte if she's in denial or is just being sensible. It's also possible, of course, that she *knows* everything is all right, but we don't find out that she knows because it doesn't occur to us to ask her. We others take a gloomy relish in extrapolating from minor worries to catastrophe at the creak of a shaft. I am suddenly reminded of the young Finnish journalist who thought to break the conversational ice, on meeting Samuel Beckett, with 'It is a fine day, yes, Mr Beckett?', receiving for his pains the terse Hibernian answer, 'So far.' (I should record here that many provenances are offered for this story. This is how I heard it first.) Anyway, Magellan is back on duty and, if anything goes wrong, we can always blame the mute and defenceless web of shock cord.

At midnight, under a clear and starry sky, we spot the masthead light of a sailing vessel away off to starboard. This is possibly *Lightness of Being*, not heard from for some time now. We decide against hailing them, figure they can see us if we can see them, and if they still are in need of engine oil they can hail us.

Day 8

Thursday, 9 May
Pos. at midnight   N   28° 04'
                    W   61° 43'

This morning's calculations, my bit of recreation when coming off the dawn watch, give the following: we are 240 miles south-west of Bermuda and 1,770 miles from the Azores. The past two to three days have been a doldrums passage, making the best time and distance we can, but relying on engine rather than sail power. Dispiriting. The wind has gone east-north-east, and our heading has improved to 010° magnetic, but we are much too far west for our liking. The days are getting longer – streaks of dawn light this morning at about 04.30. By 08.00, the wind freshening somewhat, we are back to two-hour solo watches, and Magellan is once again temporarily retired. Last night's ship gave us a weather rundown: there's a big high up at 31° N, where we are bound in hope of north-westerlies or south-easterlies. About twenty-four hours away, by my reckoning. A further calculation suggests we are now twelve to fourteen days from Horta.

Well, I ask myself, perched on the forward coachroof, mid morning, coffee in hand, where are we? In the middle of nowhere is one answer. Clipping the corner of the Sargasso Sea is another. In oceanographic terms, this oval-shaped sea is bounded by latitudes 20° to 35° N, longitudes 30° to 70° W. It is the only sea without land boundaries and has intrigued mariners since at least the time of Columbus – who tried to find the bottom here, but failed. Not surprising, perhaps, as it's 6,000 metres down on average. The Portuguese named this part of the Atlantic for the large quantities of seaweed resembling grapes, *sargaço*, which carpet much of this mysterious region. The Sargasso rarely releases anything that gets caught in it, due to its inward-spiralling currents. Sailors in wooden ships seem to have believed it was the weed itself which trapped vessels here, though they were probably failing to recognize the greater role played by the fluky and light, sometimes entirely absent, winds. The notorious Bermuda Triangle is still to the north of us, and we see in fact very little sargassum. I find myself dwelling pleasurably on the fact that the city of Zaragoza in Aragon derives its name from the same grape that named, as it were, this sea – a city famous for its rioja, a bottle of which we happen to have on board and which we will drink with lunch today.

I have been living as much as possible in a continuous present since we crossed the bar at English Harbour, as if the frame of this journey, in time and space, is an envelope outside which I do not wish to trespass. But it would be unfair to Simon not to set down his theory (or his version of someone else's) about why ships vanish so regularly in the Triangle. What he believes is that great masses of seaweed fall to the ocean floor and rot, producing vast quantities of methane. Every now and then, a volcanic tremor releases a giant bubble of gas which, arriving at the surface, transforms the solid sea into an unstable mix of gas and water. Anything sailing a patch of sea so affected finds the water no longer buoyant enough to hold it up and plunges into the unfathomable deeps. Well, I don't know. There are thermal vents all over the sea floor in this area, but I would have thought sunlight was needed to convert vegetable matter to methane, and these are notoriously sunless deeps. But, I like the image, straight from a sailor's tale, and we are, after all, sailors.

Simon and Zaf are a little cool with each other through the morning. Big row last night. Zaf was on the radio to that ship passing south, getting the weather, calling out what he was getting for Simon to write it down. 'Fifty-one,' said Zaf. 'Are you sure he didn't say sixty-one?' Simon enquired. Zaf exploded. He's sick of this endless questioning, everyone, especially Simon, always doubting him, as if he didn't know his trade. This was quite a spectacular outburst, shocked us all, and Zaf went on muttering about it all night, driving us all quietly daft. I tried to make the peace, with marked lack of success. It gnawed away at me until I figured it out this morning. English is Zaf's second language. He speaks it very well, but he isn't at home in it as he would be in Turkish. Simon is a bright lad, very bright, but has a twenty-year-old's extreme reluctance to explain himself. He thought he was asking questions just to make sure they were both agreed on what they heard; he imagined that the words he used, the inflections in his voice, would convey his intention to be helpful. Zaf thought he should just write down what he's told. Fathers and sons fall out like this, I think, and all around us in time, in this lost quarter of the ocean, skippers and junior officers have been falling into a similar misunderstanding for centuries, are still falling.

Should I try again this morning to make the peace? How best to approach it? I am conscious that I, too, have been pestering Zaf with questions for days: how far along are we? Should we be making more east, cut the corner? How sure are you there will be westerlies at 31° N? And so on. It is quite possible that these naive and direct questions are also being misunderstood as insubordinate. In a less formal situation, I know, I would wade in robustly, think nothing of it, but I am very conscious here of the primary need to maintain the skipper's authority, and of my status as the lowliest form of life on board this particular ship.

I am sitting on the lee rail amidships, feet dangling over the edge, when Zaf comes forward with two coffees, still muttering about Simon. I tell him that I am fascinated by the abyssal plain scudding along beneath our keel. I tell him it makes me nervous, the idea that all that stands between us and the lightless nightmare of it is a six-millimetre hull. I tell him how sailing's so new to me, that I come to it from a lifetime of questioning everything around me, that I have spent nights unable to sleep in my bed, feeling myself to be no more than a gathering of electrons floating on a gathering of electrons.

'Jesus,' he says, 'do you think like that all the time?' A lot of the time, I tell him. He looks at me wonderingly, genuinely perplexed. 'Doesn't that drive you mad?' he asks. Sometimes it does. I tell him that being on a boat is still a bewildering experience for me, a source sometimes of great anxiety. Like in Biscay last year, I tell him, I was scared because I couldn't understand what was going on. I kept thinking the boat was going to go over. He considers this for a while.

'This boat weighs fifty tons,' he says. 'Look up. How much of the weight is above the deck?' I crane my head back, consider the two towering aluminium masts, figure in the weight of the sails. 'Not much,' I say. 'Right,' he says. 'Now, think of the keel as a deep, heavy pendulum. The boat can swing over until water is washing along the sides of the deckhouses, even over the tops of them, and that pendulum will swing her right back over again. You can't imagine,' he says, 'what it would take to knock this boat over. And another thing, if you keep all the hatches shut, and water can't get in, this boat literally can't sink.'

I think he's genuinely astonished that I have not understood this before now, but then, as I tell him, I never asked anyone directly to explain it, and nobody volunteered to either. We consider this for a few minutes in companionable silence. 'Fucking hell, boy,' he says, in a Cork accent more convincing than my own, 'no wonder you'd be nervous if you didn't know that.' He's laughing now, and I tell him, 'Well, that's why I'm always asking you questions. I want to know things, so I ask you questions. Like, why will there be westerlies up at 31°? Why aren't we cutting across slightly, to shorten the run to the Azores?' He starts to explain, stops, look at me shrewdly, and says, 'You're trying to tell me something else?' 'Simon,' I say, 'he asks questions because he wants to get things right, only he's not old like me. He gets stubborn.' I get a grim look at this; the head turns away. There's a short silence before he turns around, grins at me, and says, 'All right, all right, I'll talk to him, but, fucking hell, these young fellas . . .' Then he hears himself, stops, and we both burst out laughing. How to explain to the impassive Charlotte on the wheel that this little inboard storm is nearly over? Maybe I'll just let that go.

Zaf is a born seaman. Like all people born to a trade or an art, he seems a living element in the play of forces that swirl around him in his chosen medium. He has the requisite formal qualifications, but so have hundreds, thousands of others; what gives you confidence in him is, well, that you have confidence in him. You just know that no matter what the sea throws up he'll have a response. I've studied him carefully, am intrigued to see how he works the boat. How he watches the wind, constantly; how he watches the sea, the sails, the tension on sheets, the telltales in the standing rigging. How he listens to the engine; how even when he's sitting there enmeshed in the conversation, his eye will dart off to follow a sudden movement, his head will cock at a new sound. He has also, and I am touched by this, a profound concern for the safety and well-being of the crew. I've met too many gung-ho sailors, hard chargers who think that an uncomprehended order can be clarified if you shout louder, a neophyte put at her ease by a show of swagger. I've seen Zaf send someone below if he thinks he or she needs sleep, or take a double watch to let an exhausted sailor rebuild his strength. There's a dose of common sense in this, of course: a tired crew member is a danger to the ship, liable to make rash judgements. Nevertheless, in Zaf's concern, there is always a measure of considerate human feeling.

For all the complaining we did when the engine was out of order, now we feel cheated when it comes on, as it does to-day at 16.00. This feeling is perverse: apart from helping us to keep up our speed, the engine gives us hot water through the calorifier, and keeps the batteries topped up. At night, if we're in an area where the skipper thinks the radar needs to be on, crossing a recognized shipping route for instance, then we are better off with the engine running – the radar is a heavy drain on the batteries. For all these reasons it makes sense to run the engine, but still there is a particular pleasure in sailing on the wind alone, and we are reluctant to give it up.

I get Paula on the satphone, and the first thing she says is, 'Quick, give me your position.' I read her the latest lat/long from the GPS, and she explains that she has found a great weather website, one that will zero in on a given set of co-ordinates. She's hooked into a satellite that will allow her to zoom in on a particular patch of ocean, and has been trying to work out if the resolution can be made fine enough for her to see us! This annihilation of distance is a new kind of phenomenon, and is very interesting from a psychological point of view. Just how far apart are we? Her voice in my ear, my voice in hers; me reading instruments to find out where on the ocean's surface we are; she using the same data to call up a picture of where we are. Overhead, spinning soundlessly past in their orbits, the shining satellites that fetch and receive the data we are exchanging. We are, in this conversation, an event, a set of digital pulses in a binary universe.

We know, even down at the cellular level, that we are phenomena in a universe of raw energy. What we know of ourselves as creatures with minds and bodies and desires is a different kind of knowledge. The telemetry knows me as a source or absence in the digital, energetic exchange – I am either on or off, there or not there. I know the satellite as an object; I can learn what its components are, what funding package produced it, what political and social uses are envis-aged for it. Whether it's on or off, I know it's there. I know its history and can estimate its likely future. In acceding to its function I acknowledge the validity of its language. It has no interest, however, in mine. I know how my body feels today, how it yearns for the companionable proximity of Paula's body. The satellite is not present to itself, even as physical object. I think the dissonance this split sets up is dangerous: to allow myself to be deceived in regard to Paula's proximity here is to disorient myself in the body space I inhabit.

When I asked Zaf earlier why he doesn't phone Anne and their two daughters at home, he never really answered, just said he'd call from the Azores. I thought at the time this was a bit cold, and it surprised me, given the fondness with which he constantly speaks of them. Today, moping on the foredeck after talking to Paula, I get a glimmer of what he seems to have long ago grasped: these conversations are in some sense without substance; they leave the mind for a time in no place, neither here, where we actually are, nor at home.

For all that, once I've worked things out in my head and am back, absolutely, on the boat, I am warmed by the thought that Paula is at home, murmuring to herself as the hard drive hums, working the keyboard in search of a picture of where in the world I am. Besides, it'll be dead handy if she spots a tropical storm heading our way – though the old sea dog will probably have sniffed it on the wind long before NASA picks it up.

A very clear night, cold and crisp. The moon has finally dwindled down to nothing, but the sea is bright with phosphorescence. Coming off watch I note that a duvet has appeared on the mate's bunk.

Day 9

Friday, 10 May
Pos. at midnight N 30° 01′
                  W 61° 21′

Another clear and beautiful dawn, colder than yesterday, the
transition from milky pearl grey to washed-out blue almost
instantaneous. On with the engine! In the scuppers, port side
forward, a flying fish is jammed between the gunwale and a
pipe. We've had them on deck nearly every morning since
departure, small stiff mullet-like things, the wings hard despite
their gossamer appearance. Simon points out that the tail is
asymmetric – the lower portion is longer than the upper.
Watch, he says later, as a few go speeding by, watch what
happens with the tail. Eventually I get it: the fish launches
itself out of the water, wings hammering, then as the tail dips
into the top of a swell it beats furiously, the sculling or
sweeping effect giving lift and forward impetus. (Long afterwards I came upon a curious book, *Creatures of the Sea* by
Frank T. Bullen, published in 1908 by, of all things, the
Religious Tract Society. On the subject of these curious
creatures, Bullen has this to say: 'In order that the *Exocetus*
may indulge easily in these aerial excursions, it is provided
with a very much enlarged swim-bladder, which, when
inflated, fills the whole cavity of the abdomen. There is also
in the mouth another bladder that is filled with air through
the gills, and both these inflations are performed automatically
at the moment the fish leaves the water. The bladders are kept

full of air while the fish is on the wing, but the moment it touches the water they are deflated, allowing the fish to plunge as rapidly as it wishes to the limit of its depth, which is not very great. These bladders are an excellent substitute for the air cells within the bones of birds, and make of the fish a veritable bird while on the wing.') In the books of my childhood, flying fish always seemed beyond exotic; I thought of them as light, rainbow-hued, transgressive as any shape-changing thing in a story or myth. In the light of morning, they are small, compact, muscular things, dull silver in colour, as gormless-looking as most fish. Plus, they don't fly, as birds seem to do, for the exhilaration of it, for the grace of efficient hunting with minimum expenditure of effort: they fly only to escape predators, which gives their jerky little rushes a mean and panicked air. We use them as bait for the fish we have yet to catch.

Inch by inch, mile by mile, we are clawing our way north, making a very little east. We want 079° for Azores, are making at best 030°. The plan is still north for westerlies; they *should* be there, says Zaf, but this is sailing, no guarantees. And of course if we do get winds it'll probably mean cold and wet, as well as fast. Always a trade-off.

For the past eight hours the winds have been east-north-east, averaging fifteen knots, gusting as high as twenty.

In the days of sail, the men o' war would have had the best of it in these latitudes, I reckon, compared to the merchant ships. So much more to do, when wallowing along in the light winds. On the merchant ships, could there have been as much to do with your time? The point of naval discipline was to build a hive-mind responsive immediately to the word of command, to train the officers to give orders, to train the men to obey them, and to train all to consider themselves always and everywhere unthinking instruments of the captain's will.

So, keep 'em busy. All the accounts we have of merchant ships, on the other hand, suggest the men were worked to the bone when it was needed, allowed to relax when not. Anxious to be doing something myself, here, now, I think I'd have preferred the navy.

Somewhere about the middle of the morning, drifting along in what was a much more hesitant and fragmentary daydream than the above might suggest, I came to with a start. Bollocks, I heard my saner self say. You wouldn't have lasted five days on a navy ship before you'd have found yourself dangling from the crosstrees or knifed for a shilling. And it's true, between the leavings of various aristocracies on the upper deck, bound to infuriate me, and the cut-throat escapees from the hangman's noose on the lower deck, I would have come to a swift end.

I don't know which is worse, the juvenile fantasy or the mordant realism, but I recognize the signs of tiredness, the sulky mind tossing and turning, so I head below for a stretch-out which becomes a deep, fathomless sleep. I wake in mid afternoon, fizzing with energy, thoroughly rested for the first time in a week.

The generator's on, so we have 240 volts. I plug in the electric kettle, take a quick look on deck to see what's happening. Zaf's in shorts and shades behind the wheel, humming away to himself. Simon's deep in a surfing magazine, perched on the coachroof on the shaded port side, his feet immersed in a bucket of sea water. The sun is warm out of the wind, so Charlotte's stretched in her usual place on the starboard deck, topping up the tan.

Another idyllic afternoon of sunshine, trade clouds around the horizon, cirrus in streaks overhead. Bearing 030° to 040°, not so far from Bermuda, motorsailing. The windseeker is flying, poled out from the forward mast. It's like a cruising chute, but cut from a lighter cloth, a good light-winds sail, greyish white, heavily stitched all over for reinforcement. I like it when we fly the chute or this windseeker; something in the full-bellied shape of them, pulling with the wind, that makes you feel the wind is partner to your efforts to go forward.

Everything you do on a boat has an effect on the senses. Just now, looking forward, feeling through my feet that the boat is in the groove, seeing the windseeker and main taut and full against the blue sky, the angle of heel about fifteen degrees, the deck canted against the horizon just as it is, the thrum of the wind almost a music, I feel a muted and sober joy as clean and clear as the white-flashed waves tipping past us, the blue, undulant swell flowing clear to the horizon.

Simon looks up and all around him, back at me; I grin at him, turn to catch Zaf's grin, his head bobbing in affirmation; Charlotte raises herself on an elbow, index finger holding down the page she's reading, marking her place, and smiles at Simon, at me, at Zaf – a moment I can only describe as full communion, all of us caught in a bubble of pure consciousness of the here and now. Simon extricates his feet from the bucket, unfolds himself like a long, improbable jackknife, throws his hands in the air and lets out a long whoop of animal joy. Zaf looks at him merrily over the top of his glasses and says, deadpan, 'Good man, Simon, thank you. A cup of tea would be very nice.'

I sit in the bow cage, bare brown feet dangling to either side, clutching a mug of tea, white water rushing beneath me as we rise and dip, rise and dip. I'm thinking that nobody I know has been this way before when I suddenly remember that last night I dreamed of my grandfather, my father's father. Now I understand what brought him to mind. He came this way as a newborn infant. The family story has our great-grandfather in New Zealand at the turn of the twentieth century, hoping to set up a business shipping grain to Ireland. His wife, Annie Martin, goes out to be with him, but doesn't like it there, decides to return home. She takes passage, pregnant, on the White Star Line ship *Rimutaka*, Captain E. H. Greenstreet. Off Cape Horn she goes into premature labour, gives birth to my grandfather, dies. She is buried at sea, and my grandfather is baptized by the captain, christened Theobald Martin Rimutaka Greenstreet Dorgan (Theobald for his father, the name having come into the family in admiration of the great republican Theobald Wolfe Tone). My grandfather would be brought up in Passage West, County Cork, by two maiden aunts and their brother, formerly a doctor in the United States Navy.

I have wondered before now at my own laziness, my reluctance to undertake even the rudimentary research that would clarify, perhaps undermine, this pretty story. Today, I understand that reluctance. When I was a boy and heard this story, all my daydreams were of escape, of a more ample elsewhere. In the confines of this story, this inheritance, was a latent permission to dream myself into whatever life might please me best, a life where I might even find myself one day at sea in the tropics, crossing the path my grandfather made as a child, going north to a country of which he could know nothing.

In last night's dream he was trying to give me something, and now I remember our last encounter. He had, it turned out, two half-sisters living in New Zealand, daughters of his remarried father, a man he never knew. They had made contact, and planned to visit him that summer of 1972. I was nineteen, had made my own plans, intended to work the summer in New Jersey. That gruff man loved me, I knew that, and I loved him, though I didn't know it at the time.

I just thought I liked him, the way he would draw me out, tell me things. That month of May before I left he drew me aside in his tiny, high-walled garden. 'You know those two from New Zealand? They never married. They've a big farm you know, about 2,000 acres. I'm going to get them to leave it to you.' Did I believe him? Was he serious? No way to tell. All I could think of, beyond the nuisance of exams, was the utter freedom of being alone in the United States. I spent a hard-working, hard-partying couple of months on the New Jersey shore, and I got home to be told by my mother that he had died in the early summer. They'd decided not to tell me, had known how much it would upset me. The aunts had changed their plans, did not come to Ireland, vanished from the story, or from all but the story. I never did get that farm, a matter of little regret to me, but a fertile place to go dreaming in over the following years when the press of immediate reality turned sometimes sour and thin.

The wind is freshening; the last few dips have brought water coursing over my feet. I raise my empty tea mug to the sky: grandfather, *salute*! My turn on the wheel. I scramble back.

At 22.00, coming off watch, I plot our position, log it, note that the night is starry and cool, the wind east-north-east, the engine on, our speed five knots. I note also that Simon is scrubbing out the saloon. My head is full of clear, simple questions: Who wet-nursed the infant all the way home? Did his father ever get in touch with him? How did he feel about the sea, my grandfather? What happened to the farm? And then a thought strikes me, I go rummaging in the bookshelf, dig out a world map. What route would you take from New Zealand, east about or west about, Cape Horn or the Cape of Good Hope? No one to ask, but I fall asleep knowing something has changed in me: this time I want to know; I want to test the story.

Day 10

Saturday, 11 May
Pos. at midnight   N   31° 42′
                    W   60° 22′

Round midnight last night we swung on to a course of 085° compass, 070° true. (We always give compass course for the helmsman or woman, true for the navigator working on the chart.) All being well, we will hold this course to the Azores. At 04.00, coming on watch in the rising light, I saw a sail way off to starboard, making much the same course as us. The mysterious *Lightness of Being*? Or someone else? I grew very tired on watch, so I went below to sleep. My eyes hadn't properly closed over before I was shaken awake: 'Quick, get the video camera. We've caught a fish!'

Grab the camera from the skipper's cabin, stumble up into the cockpit. Zaf and Simon are crouched in the starboard quarter, Simon lunging with a gaff, Zaf on his knees, half out over the gunwale, wrestling with a large fish. There's a huge tangle of line in the cockpit; the yellow winding frame lies snapped in two pieces at the foot of the binnacle. Magellan has a firm grip of the wheel.

They haul a large, blue fish on deck, wrestle it past the winches and over the genoa sheets, and dump it halfway along the starboard side. It's a bluefin tuna. There's a jabber of excitement and dispute, but we finally agree that it must be thirty kilos and that it needs to be dispatched. Charlotte's sent below for a sharp knife, reappears and is shocked when Zaf plunges it deep into the fish's brain. Struggling to record every instant of this unexpected drama with the video camera, I fall back on the traditional cold heart of *cinéma-vérité*. Nothin' to do with me, pal. I'm just the recording apparatus here.

The morning is sultry, a sulphurous light everywhere, the wind has died back. We're slatting about, wallowing even, hove-to now, and there is a lot of blood in the scuppers. This is one powerful-looking fish, pure function in fin and streamlined body, built for speed. Bluefin have been clocked at more than fifty kilometres per hour. I look back. There's nothing to suggest there are any more out there, though once they used to swim in huge schools. That lure has been trolling along behind us for ten days now without a bite. Suddenly we are looking at an awful lot of fresh protein.

Zaf keeps up a running commentary as he butchers merrily away. 'See this?' – he zips a long cut up the belly, rips out a handful of guts – 'Lovely stuff. See how fresh it is?' Splash, over the side. Hacks the head off energetically. 'See this? Best part of the fish.' Splash, over the side. Tail off, brandished aloft. 'Think I'll keep this for a trophy.' Thinks about it. 'Naw.' Splash, over the side. I'm clambering about all over the place, trying to record all this, wondering whether the deck will ever come clean, despite the buckets of sea water which Simon is sluicing over carnage and butcher. Now Zaf has a bread knife, serrated edge, with which he is sawing off big, thick steaks, four of them. The rest of the fish, a big chunk weighing maybe ten kilos, is wrapped in plastic and sent below to the underfloor freezer. Up to his armpits in gore, brandishing a knife in one hand, a steak in the other, the skipper triumphant poses for the camera. For a second he might have been a figure out of the old days, the effect only slightly marred by the peaked All Blacks cap tipped boyishly back on his bronzed head.

Simon, meanwhile, with the optimism of youth, figuring that if there's one there must be more, already has the line rebaited and back in the water. Suddenly there's a roar from the stern, we all rush back and, sure enough, there's something big and powerful on the line. Zaf shoulders past. They haul the line in between them, and inside a minute there's a vicious-looking barracuda-like creature coiling and thrashing about under the quarter. *Spirit*'s stern quarters are cut back quite deeply, curved in under the cockpit, so there is very little side as such against which to hold this fish. It's a long, thin, muscular beast, about five feet long, with very sharp teeth and murder in each rolling eye; though Simon has the gaff well sunk in, nobody wants to see this thing crashing about on deck or in the cockpit, and we're all relieved when Zaf finally wrestles the large hook out of its slavering jaw and the creature returns to the deep. What was it? Zaf says, zargana. I've never heard of it, am in no hurry to see one again. I'm half-expecting to see sharks, given the amount of blood and tuna offal in the water. It's hot, and it crosses my mind we could have hove to many times in the past few days, gone for a swim. That might have yielded some unexpected excitement.

I need a sleep after all this drama, but am no sooner gone over than woken again. Simon has spotted what he thinks may be a life raft in the water up ahead. I grab a boathook, go forward, put the glasses on it. It comes up alongside minutes later, a twelve-foot orange cylinder, stencilled 'Property of Western Monarch, London' in black lettering along its length. Cone-shaped at one end, it's extensively barnacled along its waterline. We pass it slowly, watching for lines trailing in the water, then let it go by. We can't even make a satisfactory guess at what it might be. It doesn't have a military look to it, so it probably isn't one of the extensive array of sonobuoys which the US Navy maintains all over the world's waters;

it doesn't seem survival-related, has no obvious hatches, broken antennae or other indicators of what it might be used for. Just a small, unimportant mystery, we decide, and watch it recede.

I make a third attempt at sleep, but it's no use. I'll never get over now. Marinated tuna steaks for lunch, pan-fried with herbs, plus salad and Chilean merlot. We bask in the cockpit, enjoying the hard life, listening to Zaf and Simon replay their hunters' triumph. And replay it, and replay it. I feel like an indulgent uncle, mellow and fortified.

Then, out of nowhere, cloud. It's turning cool. Could these be the north-westerlies we've been waiting for? No, as it turns out. Consult the *Atlantic Pilot*: at this time of year we'd need to be at 38° N. We motorsail on.

The dominant colour of the sea is a deep cobalt blue. We got used to this surprisingly quickly, considering how accustomed we are to the green-grey-black waters of Ireland. I've spent hours on end, these past ten days, sprawled in the cockpit, perched on the coamings or on deck, my back against the coachroof, just looking at the water. Mind empty, or near empty, perhaps turning a simple thought over and over, but in any case gazing at the water. So much more water than land on this planet. Between the height of water at the Equator and the height at either pole, there is a fall of thirteen miles because the earth is not a perfect sphere. I read that somewhere this past winter. We are sailing downhill for home, then. I remember in Biscay last autumn, going south, the body sense I had that we were sailing uphill; I convinced myself that I thought this because we were butting into south-westerlies, the waves piling up before us so that we seemed to be climbing them as steps on a very long, very gradual slope – but now I'm not so sure I wasn't just sensing what is a literal if barely perceptible truth.

We are being borne along, in part, by the great sweep of the Gulf Stream, that immense current that sweeps right up to and past the Irish coast. Most people never venture on the sea. Many venture into it, at the coastal margins, but never travel on it or through it; millions never lay eyes on the sea in the course of their lives. Yet the sea is the birthplace of our weather, the reservoir for our water and hence, by the magic of convection and rain, our food. It is our dumping ground, our highway to the growth of empires, our place of dreaming and nightmare, our most reached-for metaphor. It is the place whose seeming emptiness we have always regarded as a repository of meaning: 'They that go down to the sea in ships, that do business in great waters; these see the works of the Lord, and his wonders in the deep.' My attention this cool afternoon is fixed not on the wonders of the deep, but the wonders of the surface.

The sea is never at rest. I have seen in Uzbekistan the vast desert of the Kara Kum, flat and undifferentiated, stretching away to the horizon in whatever direction one looked. Even there, I remember, the eye will recoil from emptiness, go actively searching for minute gradations in height, in texture, in colour, the evidence it knows it will find that nothing on earth is featureless, be it natural or man-made.

We call the sea 'empty', 'featureless', and this is a crude and lazy shorthand, a way of saying 'I'm too busy to look, to see this as it is in itself.' The water around and beneath us is full of life, a ceaseless buzz of activity, chemical and biological processes, the coming and going of life forms and other phenomena, of growth prompted by photosynthesis, acts of generation, geothermal and tectonic movements, currents, pressures, winds – a cauldron of becoming, of being and of ceasing-to-be. This the mind knows, my mind knows it looking over the side, and yet if I go below now, after scanning the horizon, and somebody asks, 'Anything out there?' I'll more than likely say, 'No, nothing.' 'Anything out there?' in this context means anything unusual on the weather front, any ships to be seen, any whales or dolphins, anything out of the ordinary?

I could, however, answer the question as if it were literally meant: blue-green water to all sides, a low, long swell from the east, where the wind's from, the tips of the swell laced with short strings of transparent bubbles, the face of each triangular wave glassy and tending towards translucent near the top, the back scored with ripples, thin bands of lines like fingerprint whorls, caused by the wind's action; I could try to say how each wave is different from all the others, that the last one I noticed, which slapped us amidships as I turned to go down the companionway, was maybe a half-metre higher than the run for the past half-hour, had a scarf of white foam trailing off it, that the hull lifted a little more than usual to let it go under, that a scrap of foam flung ahead of the wave tip hit a stanchion, dividing to either side of it, disappearing almost at once in a faint stain on the deck.

I could try to describe the sounds the water makes, the slap of it on the hull, the faint antiphon when it falls away, the run and gurgle of the bow wave, the susurrus when one wave overtakes another and their crests merge in a flurry of foam; then there's the modulation in the sound of the wind, each instant unrepeatable, as it courses over the endlessly vary-ing surface of the water. I could try to describe the keening in the rigging, the taut hum of air rushing over the surface of the sails, the crash of bundled halyards, the creak of the hull, the coming and going roar of the engine, burble of the exhaust, hiss of water from the propeller . . .

I would exhaust my questioner's patience even before my meagre store of words ran out because most of the time, sailing, we very much want to take the sea as a given. 'Empty' means 'nothing to worry about'; it means we are still afloat, still going forward. The sea is never still, and in that sense is profoundly alien to the animal self in us that sees always in movement the possibility of danger. Movement is inherently unstable, and when we are at sea we are moment by moment, in the most obvious and inescapable way, unstable ourselves. If the wind gets up and the seas get up, then the sea state and the wind conditions will move to the forefront of our attention, but still we will think of the sea as featureless. We have what you might call a psychic investment in the belief that the sea is, essentially, empty; we literally cannot see that the ocean is full to the brim, is brimming over, with itself. I have seen people sit for ages, simply staring at the sea, and if I ask them what they're looking at they say the same thing always: nothing in particular.

Down below, Simon looks up from his surfing magazine. 'Anything happening?' he asks. I say, 'Nah, nothing.'

Charlotte calls, 'Come and see.' Jellyfish is what we see, a drift of Portuguese men-of-war, purple and sky-blue tendrils dangling, a little semi-transparent dome-shaped sail on top of each, to catch the wind. We eat chocolate with our coffee, staring out at the sea.

I manage a brief contact with Paula, just enough time to give her our coordinates. I'm getting very little information on how she is getting on; next time I'll try to get in first with the questions. I try to imagine what it would be like if I were at home and she were out here. My head would be full of perils, potential disasters, dangers – I'd never imagine how placid it all is, and if she were to say that's how it is I would imagine she was just sparing me, keeping me from worrying. When I got back from the last trip she teased me unmercifully for doing that to her; I would be there on the phone, reassuring her that everything was fine, while she would be sitting there at her computer watching the very storm I wasn't telling her about, trying not to let me know she knew.

The log entry at 20.00 is laconic: 'Skipper attempting self-immolation.' We are hove-to, the dome barbecue clamped to the after rail, and Zaf is spraying lighter fluid on the stubbornly smouldering charcoal. Great gouts of flame and smoke are billowing up, and eventually the coals catch, settle to a steady red glow, and we slap on the marinated tuna steaks. About forty-five seconds a side is all it takes. It just flakes away in the mouth, the freshest fish I have ever eaten.

At midnight a vessel passes, big ship, maybe eight miles off to port. We try calling her for a weather forecast, but get no reply.

On the edge of sleep, I recall last night's dream. I am crossing Cork city in a howling gale. Sheets of rain are falling, so heavy and thick I can only move forward through the streets in the intervals between each successive one. I have never known such rain, such darkness on the wind, such an obvious assault from the heavens. I am desperate to cross the city, driven by an imperative I cannot establish, am bewildered to find myself on these streets, and all the bridges are down. All of them.

Day 11

Grey, cool and cloudy at dawn. A pomarine skua appears, then another. They sweep around us in wide circles, keeping their distance, not dipping into the wake as gulls would. I know what they are because I scribbled a description, and Simon, marine wildlife expert by appointment, looked it up. From time to time we see a petrel, occasionally a tropic bird, but apart from a daily shearwater there's very little to see in the way of fauna.

Poring over the chart (1,214 miles on the clock now), I am joined by Zaf. 'Good,' he says, 'we can more or less keep to the rhumb line now.' The what? I go to look it up.

The shortest distance between any two points on the surface of a sphere is a 'great circle' joining the two points and having its centre at the centre of the sphere. Therefore, the shortest distance between where we are now and the Azores is a segment of a great circle. The problem for the humble navigator is the Mercator projection which is the basis of our charts. Join any two points on a Mercator-based chart with a straight line and you don't, unfortunately, have a segment of a great circle. A segment of a great circle produced on an ordinary chart would be a curve. There are two ways to mark this curve on a chart: the first, and most usual, is to make an educated guess; the second and only accurate way is to find a chart based on a gnomonic projection and work from that.

A gnomonic projection is essentially a perspective projection in which, according to *The Oxford Companion to Ships and the Sea*, part of the surface of a sphere is 'projected from the centre of the sphere on to a plane surface tangential to the sphere's surface'. On a chart based on this projection, any two points connected together give a straight line which is in fact a segment of a great circle. The trick is to list a series of intermediate points along this line, note their coordinates, then mark these points in their appropriate positions on a standard Mercator-based chart. This appears on your chart as a curve. Now obviously you can't sail a compass course along a curve, so the navigator marks a series of straight lines, chords to the curve, which gives him a succession of courses to sail. These short, straight lines are called 'rhumb lines'.

Well, we don't have a gnomonic chart, we have Zaf, and he makes an educated guess at what the curve should be. He pencils it in, but it's more a contribution to my education than it is a navigation aid, as we are sailing or motorsailing as much as we can, and we go where the wind dictates as long as it's in the right general direction. Great-circle sailing, or rhumb-line sailing, is of great importance to navy and cargo ships, as it gives the most economic course to steer for any given journey. To sailors it's a time bonus if they can sail down the rhumb line, but otherwise of little practical importance. Still, I'm glad to have learned this. *The Oxford Companion* offers me this gem for my notebook:

The gnomonic chart became popular with the publication by Hugh Godfray in 1858 of two polar gnomonic charts, covering the greater part of the world ... Although it was generally believed that Godfray was the original inventor of this method of great-circle sailing, it is interesting to note that a complete explanation of the construction of a polar gnomonic chart, with a detailed explanation of a great-circle route from the Lizard to the Bermudas, appeared in Samuel Sturmey's *Mariner's Mirror*, of 1669.

Samuel Sturmey, by God, what a name for a navigator! And his sample great-circle route isn't that far off our own course at present; if I were to mark a direct route to Kinsale and another to the Azores, then Lizard to the Bermudas would split the arc of difference between them. I grant you this signifies nothing very much, but it's a pleasant diversion on a morning with 50 per cent cloud and a distinct drop in the ambient temperature.

We go east now more than north, ten days from the Azores if we manage to average six knots.

Yesterday's long, languent swells are gone, replaced by small, precise grey waves, bad-tempered, clipped, hostile. The day is out of sorts, the wind batting about all over the clock.

From the log:

01.09	North-east	0–5 knots
02.02	North-north-west	5–7 knots
04.13	North-west	10 knots
06.30	South	10 knots
08.15	West-north-west	10 knots
09.39	West-north-west	10 knots
14.00	West	14 knots
19.00	East-north-east	20 knots
20.22	North-east	17 knots
22.47	North-east	15 knots

Everyone is tired, but nobody's really getting sleep. It starts off cool and cloudy, then becomes still and sultry, then in the afternoon it greys over and we get cold rain. Imperceptibly, the dress code is shifting from shorts and T-shirts to oilskins. Early this afternoon I went rooting in the bottom of my kitbag, checking to see where my socks are.

We're all in a strange mood today, somewhat melancholy, withdrawn and broody. Everyone's inclined to stay below, for the first time since we set out. Generally on the day watches we keep each other company; it's rare to pass an afternoon on your own, as I did today. With everyone below busy at unseen stuff, I got stuck into some sail trimming off my own bat. The engine's been off since 11.00 or so, since the wind went west a bit and gave us a chance to stretch out. With the breeze consistently on the port side for the first time on this passage, the main and foresail are boomed out to starboard, and the boat looks completely different. It's a bit like driving on the wrong side of the road. I go to ease out a few rolls of the genoa and have to stop in the middle of what should be a reflex action by now, think it through. The winches are on the wrong side, as it were, the mainsheet behind my back sloped at a different angle. In a way it's enjoyable, as I have to think out the power geometries minute by minute. In another way it's disconcerting. Just when the hands know instinctively what to do when, say, the wind freshens or we're hit by a sudden gust, I have to stay my reflexive response, take a few seconds more to be sure my response is the right one.

There is an agreeable edge to the melancholy the day and the work engender. It has the feel of a childhood Sunday, a winter's day with soft rain, little light, nothing particular to do. The acid taste of near-boredom. Bit by bit, putting the bow over to balance her against a big wave coming in, easing out or hardening up with the wind shifts, leaning now this way, now that, hauling the wheel over, putting my back into it, I feel myself come slowly into a kind of quietude, a sense of complicity with the boat and the set of the sails and the sea. When it comes to handing over the wheel I am almost reluctant to go below, but minutes later, ensconced in the saloon with a mug of tea and a book, I am glad to be away from it, in out of the weather. I don't want to stir for the rest of the day.

The saloon is the great salvation of this boat. Midships, it takes in the full beam; teak-panelled with a curved white tongue-and-groove headlining, it's about eighteen feet square with ample headroom, well lit by day through oval brass ports, the companionway hatch in the after end giving light and air. At home in Dublin I've seen smaller studio apartments, and taken together with the galley forward of it and the head forward and to starboard it's an immensely liveable space. I come and go here like a gypsy ghost; that dark shape on the settee when you pass through is me deep in a sleeping bag, face turned outward towards the sea only inches away. Mostly, though, this is the social heart of the boat. The polished teak table can seat eight people comfortably, has been known to accommodate a convivial twelve. If you come in here from the cockpit, through the narrow corridor past the engine room, the first impression is of polished teak walls and floor. On your right there's a deep hanging locker, faced with woven cane, where we keep the linen – sheets, towels, tea towels, pillow cases – along with the bag of signal flags, some spare waterproofs, some deck harnesses, a few lengths of useful line. Forward of this and ahead of you there's an L-shaped seat, lockers above the longer length, whiskey, rum and cereals in the lockers. More food in the lockers underneath, tools in the seat against the forward bulkhead. Sometimes you'll find one of us crashed out here, catching a quick nap. The forward head is on the other side of the bulkhead, to the right of the next passage forward. To the left is the galley, with its serving hatch to the saloon. Still in the saloon, the great teak table is on the port side, in the centre of a horseshoe of soft blue upholstered seating. Food storage here under the aft and side seats, a diesel tank for the generator under the seat against the galley bulkhead. The lights are set in the white-painted headlining, low-wattage, one of them red for night vision. You can isolate any light or group of lights, move through the saloon at night using only one light, not waking any sleepers. There are removable wooden companionway steps at the after end, a hatchway above which comes out through the raised coachroof just forward of the mainmast. The hatch is kept secured at sea, though the foot-high doors facing aft are often open for ventilation. The saloon is our great answer to claustrophobia, especially in inclement weather. You can sprawl out here, hold crew briefings, spread charts and pilot books out on the table, write, eat, play cards, sort things, mend things – it's been dining room, sleeping quarters, bar, reading room, workshop, store, doctor's surgery, sick bay, sailmaker's loft, sanctuary and oratory.

Everything here feels sturdy, seamanlike, timeless. It's the wood, of course, the moulded handrails that run around under the coachroof, the solid portlights, the vertical grabrails, the exquisite joinery work. You are reminded that steel and timber together make a powerful specific against disaster. You feel protected, secure, braced against anything that may come. Your hands and your hips have strength to work with, fixtures and surfaces to swing from, bounce off, when you lurch across the open spaces in a heavy sea – I've seen people swing into the saloon as the bow goes down, flop sideways on to a seat as it comes up again, throw themselves forward on the next downroll, all with the matter-of-fact insouciance of an acrobat, entirely unconscious of what they are doing.

Right now there's no need for acrobatics; we're moving

gracefully through the water, maybe ten degrees of heel, a smooth and easy motion. Simon is chopping vegetables in the galley, head bobbing to the insistent beat of whatever it is he's listening to today. Mostly, as far as I can tell from the sound leaking out of his headphones, it's monotonous techno – too much bass, too much tinny hiss from the hi-hat. Well, when I want to annoy him, that's how I describe it. The galley is perhaps too small for a boat this size. The work surfaces, finished in stainless steel, the sinks, the pot store and the cooker make an almost perfect circle, with a small gap to squeeze in through. The cooker's on the forward bulkhead, three gas rings, a gas oven. It might be better on the port side, gimballed to allow for the ship's rolling. As it is, it's a complete bugger to keep pots and their contents secure in a seaway, despite the ingenious pot-clamps that screw on to the fiddle rail along the front of the hob. Facing the cooker, that's to say facing forward, you have the sink on your left, the work surfaces behind you and to your right. The space you have to dance in is about five square feet – and you do dance when you're cooking, you dance and you get bruised. We all have a ring of bruises around our hips, from lurching and crashing against edges and corners when reaching for a pot, washing dishes, coming in and going out.

On rough days, when we can't open the overhead hatch for ventilation without getting soaked, the cook gets a great deal of solicitous sympathy from the rest of the crew, not all of which is aimed at deflecting or defusing his or her bad temper. A great deal of off-watch chat hovers around redesigning the galley or otherwise solving the problem of working in there.

My suggestion of a few days ago – that we should ship a cook so fat he has to be squeezed in and therefore, axiomatically, cannot get bruised – offended Simon's sense of logic:

Yeah, but how would he get at stuff in the lockers? Charlotte, very seriously, explained to him that I wasn't being serious, which only had the effect of further confusing him.

Zaf leads us off on a new tangent by suggesting inflatable, wraparound protective aprons for the cook, and Charlotte brings the whole conversation to a close by saying, 'Well, I'm not really bothered, really.' Which confuses us all.

The forward head is opposite the galley entrance, to starboard. There's a shower, a washbasin and a temperamental toilet. Shaving in here is a real treat on a rough day: you brace your arse against the door behind you, your bent knees against the locker under the washbasin, your elbow on the rim of the basin; then, face lathered, you close your eyes until you're sure you've caught the rhythm, open them at the null point when the boat is all the way down and scrape a quick swathe of foam off before the upswing starts; pause, let her come down, feel the null point in the pit of your stomach, scrape, pause, and so on. Every so often, just to add interest, the helm changes course or we get hammered by a rogue wave. The supreme art is to lift the razor off your face *exactly* at that point.

The best way to start a day at sea is to stagger into the head immediately upon waking, piss copiously, wash all over, shave without cutting yourself, then go up on deck with a mug of fresh coffee and a cigarette. I realize with a start that I haven't really been thinking about cigarettes for the past three or four days. A guilty thought occurs to me. I reach through the galley hatch and tap Simon on the shoulder: 'Simon, have I been in bad temper for the past few days?' He looks at me blankly, then it dawns on him. He gives his best wolfish grin. 'Dyin' for a cigarette are ya? No, we were saying it yesterday, there hasn't been a word out of you. You're a bit tense like, but you're doing fine.' Uh huh. But right now I'd smoke ten, one after the other.

I go have a look around on deck – Zaf on the helm, not much chat, wind fresh, maybe 50 per cent cloud. Cold. I go below again, check the log, the chart, the GPS. Tidy the chart table, go take a mug of tea from Simon, curl up under my sleeping bag and nap.

Tonight's sunset is sulphurous pale yellow, vaguely menacing and northern, rather than benign and tropical. Back to sleep. Wake, eat, go on watch. Wind north-east, cool, sea monotonous. Charlotte's log entry says: 'Good to be sailing again.' Zaf's, later, says, 'Motoring again.' These entries seem to sum up the day we've had. In the embryo bank on the lower pilot bunk, half the water containers are empty. They squeak and squeal as they are squeezed between the full ones.

Day 12

Monday, 13 May
Pos. at midnight   N   33° 02'
                    W   55° 55'

Mozart again to bring the dawn up after a night of motoring. Zaf as usual is up with the lark (and the tea), ready to take a sextant sight, but the sun has disappeared behind cloud. I love these empty mornings on Planet Water. The greys and oranges and blues.

There's a deep, rolling, oily swell. Still high pressure here, though the barometer is down. The swell suggests big winds 350 to 400 miles to the north. There's a big container ship to port, heading east, probably for Gibraltar. It's a grey and lumpy morning, very Irish in some way. Charlotte's log entry at 04.00 praises Magellan, quite rightly. He's still hard at work, stretching this way and that, keeping us on our course all through the morning and into the day.

Today everything is behaving well. The gearbox is staying cool, the boat is tracking straight and true, the wind is staying obligingly steady in the north-east and now it is glorious, burning afternoon. Two more container ships go by, heading east like the first.

Taking over the helm now, Sweeney from Mayo, skinny in shorts, gangly, red-haired, scrubby-bearded, immersed in a surfing mag; wandering off course in some dream of a major wave. I yell back at him, 'Did you know there's an old Irish poem about the wanderings of Mad Sweeney?' He doesn't get it, but Zaf does, goes spluttering below to check the temperature of the gearbox, leaving Simon mystified. I'm on the port side, halfway along, near the preventer on the fore-main, leaning back against the dinghy strapped to the fore coachroof, my feet in a bucket of sea water, belly to the sun. We're on a heading of 085°, hoping to keep south of what is evidently a shipping lane. Zaf is back up, has gone forward of me, working on his tan, gabbing away merrily, ignoring the moving pen as I try to scribble in my notebook. Charlotte's to starboard, working on *her* tan.

I'm reading *Poems of Arab Andalusia*, translated by Cola Franzen. So lucid and exact about this earth. I copy these four lines into my notebook:

> When the wind blows
> I make sure it blows in my face
> the breeze might bring me
> news of you

There's a low swell; we dip and rise very little, so I go forward into the bow, sit there looking back, making myself a mind video for the winter. Behind me, canted forward, stainless-steel open rails make a cage to protect us when we're working right forward. Welded and painted angle iron gives a footing, a kind of truncated bowsprit. Oliver had boards fitted on top of this framework in Antigua, but now I see they are lifting; one is already gone – the guys just screwed upwards through holes drilled in the angle iron, when they should have used bolts. The water slapping up against the boards as the bow plunges will knock the rest of them off before long. The stay on which the genoa is fitted is attached to the bowsprit here, the roller furling drum which winds in the sail at knee level. Immediately in front of me is the anchor windlass with its twin drums, and the pipes down through which the anchor chains are led from the drums to the chainlockers in the forepeak below. Last year we found water had been getting into the forepeak through these narrow pipes, even though they'd been blocked off by having rubber gloves shoved into them – the foredeck must have spent most of that trip underwater. Now Zaf has hammered wooden bungs in.

Access to the forepeak is through a large, transparent Lewmar hatch to my right looking back. Directly in front of me is the inner forestay, a thick wire running to a point seven-eighths of the way up the foremast; to this stay we can fit the high-cut yankee or a storm jib for heavy-weather sailing. Both sails are triangular, as are the foresail and the mainsail. The genoa, set from the forestay, is a full-bellied sail that, fully extended, overlaps the foremast. At the moment we've set main, fore and genoa, so the other sails are bagged below in the forepeak. The staysail is hanked on to the next stay in; this stay has a light aluminium boom attached, and the boom end is fixed to a short track on deck, with a block-and-tackle system to allow us to pin it out to whichever side we choose. There are smaller Lewmar hatches over each of the forecabins and the galley, for light and ventilation – and escape if necessary. Running around the entire deck is a gunwale maybe six inches high, capped with varnished teak. Stainless-steel stanchions, set on the gunwales at regular intervals, provide the support for the twin lifelines that run along each side; there is a more solid arrangement of horizontal bars around the stern.

Between gunwale and faded teak deck are the scuppers, steel channels to shunt away water through letter-box slots in the hull sides. To my right and left, lashed in the scuppers, are the aluminium poles we can use when flying the cruising chute, windseeker or spinnaker. The inboard end clips to a fitting on the foremast; the pole is extended out to the side, controlled by a halyard for uphauling or, reeved through a block, for downhauling; the line used to pull the pole towards the stern is called the 'afterguy'.

Next, going back, is the foremast, maybe sixty feet tall, with a boom permanently attached. We set the foresail (or foremain) here, a heavy sail that never comes off when we're at sea. The foresail, like the main, has a set of plastic sliders fitted at intervals to its luff, the edge of the sail that's vertical and nearest to the mast when hoisted. These sliders fit into a groove on the mast, and the sail is then hoisted by muscle power as far as we can take it, the last few feet brought home on the winch. The halyard that we haul it up by, together with topping lift, spare halyards and other lines that run up and down the mast, is a great source of noise, at sea and in harbour, as are the same lines on the main mast. That characteristic slapping noise you hear from a boat in harbour when the wind is up comes from these lines banging against the mast, and we take great care to minimize this noise by keeping tension on them. Quite apart from irritating your nervous system, this noise is a sign that your lines are being beaten to death. The foremast, like the main, is over-engineered, heavier, thicker in section, than it needs to be. This boat in general is over-engineered, a great comfort in a blow, though it does slow us down a little.

At the foot of the foremast is the life raft in its fibreglass cylinder, its painter securely fastened to the deck. If we have to abandon ship we heave the cylinder overboard, the painter keeps it attached to the vessel, a compressed air charge is fired by pulling the painter right to the end, and the raft inflates. We hope. Next to the life raft, in a cage of stainless-steel bars, are the two gas bottles, their yellow paint blotched with rust. Lashed to the forward coachroof, between the fore and main masts, the dinghy we use as a tender is still inflated – because it's another life raft in case of need.

The two forward cabins are under the foredeck, as are the galley and the forward head; the saloon is under this forward coachroof, and the hatch at its after end comes up under the boom on to the block-and-tackle system with its rail on the deck that allows us to set the boom out to either side, or haul it in as the case may be. Here is the widest part of the boat; we have a beam of about eighteen feet.

Now the mainmast is towering over us, about seventy feet, as tall as the ship is long. The winches are heavier here, as are the halyards and topping lift and other lines. The main, like the foremain, stays permanently on when we're at sea, lying in folds lashed to the boom when not hoisted. The mainsail is the primary driving force on the boat, a heavy beast, of synthetic cloth like all the other sails on board. It's a stiff cloth, too, coarse enough to skin your knuckles on, a recalcitrant thing when it comes to handling it.

Under the after coachroof are the engine room and the pilot berths, the skipper's cabin on the starboard side, the mate's to port, a small head between mate's cabin and engine room. At each corner of the coachroof there is a highly varnished deck box, the lids secured with webbing straps. We keep fruit and vegetables in one, spare life jackets in another, while the other two are crammed with lengths of webbing, lines and ropes, shackles, blocks and other bits and pieces that might be wanted in a hurry. The main boom stretches back over the cockpit, the mainsheet fixed to a wide track at its after end.

The cockpit is protected by high coamings, also teak-capped, and here there are two big heavy winches and one small winch on either side. The larger winches, the primaries, we use to control the genoa, a big sail with a huge load on it when it's full. The others we use when the cruising chute's up, or any of the other headsails.

Back in Antigua, Hector did a fine job of varnishing the teak cockpit, but after only twelve days the varnish is rubbing smooth in patches. Here in this well much of the work on the boat gets done. The wheel's here, fixed to the binnacle with its compass on top, and here, day or night, there is always someone working. We manage the sails from here, steer, keep watch, eat when the weather's fine, keep company with each other in most kinds of weather, day or night. In the lockers under the seats are cans of oil, fenders, buckets, boathooks, some of our many toolboxes, a tray of shackles, trays of nuts and bolts, a kedge anchor, some pumps, mooring warps, the deck awning, containers of waste oil, the petrol tank for the outboard engine, spare diesel cans and the yellow barrels with water, emergency rations, flares, a hand compass, the ship's papers, our passports, some charts, money, a knife, a whistle, torches – all the stuff we'll take with us if we have to abandon ship. The emergency tiller is down underneath us in the lazarette, may we never have to use it.

At sea we don't use the forward hatch, so all traffic up or down goes through the cockpit. The engine controls are at the helmsman's left, the instruments to his right. The life buoy's behind, and the Irish tricolour on its staff is always a living thing, shifting or slatting or billowing in what wind there is. This is where you come when you want to know what's going on aboard or out there on the boundless sea. When I'm ashore and dream myself back on board, it is always here in the cockpit I find myself, sniffing the wind, checking the set of the sails, scanning the horizon, watching the companionway to see if there's any sign of somebody coming up with a cup of tea.

Which ends the reverie with a pang. We've run out of

Barry's, I remember, and walk back to Zaf, still sunning himself, so that we can enjoy a good grumble, regret again that we didn't think to bring a bigger supply.

My turn in the galley tonight. What to cook? Something with tuna. I go rummaging in the saloon, lift the seat, prop it with a cushion. Here are canned, packeted, jarred and boxed riches. Tin of pineapples? Yes. OK, curry – why not? Rice, then, and a jar or two of madras sauce – no, one korma, one madras. Up on deck, root through the deck box with the vegetables in it. Onions, tomatoes, garlic, lots of. Back down to galley. Lift hatch in floor by recessed brass rings, one broken. Stow hatch to one side. Off with lid of freezer, out with shrink-wrapped hunk of tuna. Close fridge, unwrap tuna, stare into space, estimating quantity. Saw off slab of tuna, wrap and replace remainder, hatch back down, scrub hands, cut tuna into chunks. Rice into cold water, stand bowl in sink in case of splashing. Pause for a moment, register motion of boat. Good, on an even keel, speed a steady six knots or so, engine on.

Open hatch above head, not so much breeze: good, it won't blow out the flame on the cooker. Our favourite pot is the pressure cooker because it's very deep. Dig that out, and the heavy frying pan. Chop garlic coarsely, also onions. Wedge pan on cooker with pot clamps, pour in olive oil, light flame. When hot, fry off tuna chunks carefully. Lift from pan when done, tip into pressure cooker. Next, fry off garlic and onion. Tip contents of pan, oil included, in on top of tuna. Remove pan from cooker, put to one side. Stick on a kettle of water.

Take out bowl of rice, stand it on worktop, on folded tea towel to stop it sliding. Rinse and chop tomatoes, into the pot. Open jars of sauce, tip contents into pot. Stir, sniff. Which way is this going? Towards sweetness, I think; drain pineapple juice into glass, tip fruit into pot, drink juice. Next? Chilli sauce. Jar in locker overhead, sniff, two teaspoons. Hell, add a third. Stir, sniff.

Not bad. Bottle of water, add water to one sauce jar, lid on, swish vigorously, tip into second jar, repeat, tip liquid into pot. Stir. Kettle boiled, make pot of tea, pan into sink, washing-up liquid, hot water, wash, dry, replace in cave locker. Rinse out glass, pour tea into mugs – are we all awake? – four mugs then, 'Simon! Tea!' He comes, with biscuits, takes away three mugs. Dig out casserole dish and lid, light oven. Carefully bring sauce to slow boil, stirring gently so as not to break up chunks of tuna. Oven now hot, pour sauce into casserole, swish water from kettle in pot, pour in with sauce, stir gently, lid on casserole, casserole in oven. Wash pot, put drained rice into pot, add three volumes of water, on to stove, boil, turn down, lid on, leave to simmer very slowly. Wash chopping board, knives, spatula and can opener, drop jars into rubbish bin – food residues go over the side, everything else is double-bagged, stored in lazarette – dry and store everything. Now, hot water in washing-up bowl, four plates immersed in hot water to heat. Always amazing, how quickly food goes cold at sea.

All ready to go as soon as the rice is done.

I don't know if it's like this for other people, but I find when I'm cooking at sea that it's done with complete consciousness, moment to moment. Some of this is to do with working in a confined space, some is to do with working in a relatively unfamiliar space, but mostly it arises from the salient fact that a galley at sea is a potential disaster zone. Doing things neatly and well is something you get into, partly because there is a sense of evolving order as the passage goes on, and one attunes oneself to this; there is also the consideration that neat equates with efficient, which further equates with safe. Thus, it is rare to find someone in the cockpit, not helming, who doesn't automatically tidy the rope falls, pick up incidental debris, secure something that's worked loose.

The good mate springs a pleasant surprise when she produces a bottle of champagne at dinner. We are now, at 20.15, halfway between Antigua and landfall in the Azores.

There is a moment after dinner when I am churlishly resentful that, pleasant as the meal was, I wasn't eating it at home. I reach in the pocket at the back of my notebook for the photo of Paula I keep there, sovereign specific for whatever ails me.

The wind is in the west for my trick at the wheel, and I spend a pleasant two hours on the after-dinner watch helming with a following sea. Another sovereign specific: solitude at the helm with enough strength in the wind to make it interesting, and enough weight on the helm to let you feel your own strength as you drive the boat on.

Day 13

Tuesday, 14 May
Pos. at midnight   N   33° 58'
                    W   53° 16'

Westerlies all through the night. They last until about 10.00, when it backs north-west. We are still closer to Bermuda (or Cape Cod for that matter) than to the Azores, but we're on a good heading, averaging 095°, and making good speed.

According to the log – can't figure out whose handwriting it is – Magellan went on strike soon after midnight. Back to helming by hand. Well, at the moment nobody really minds because, with these winds holding at fifteen to twenty knots, the genoa poled out to port and the cruising chute flying high off the bow to starboard, we are bowling along goosewinged. Goosewinging, twin headsails poled out, one to each side, gives a lift to the spirits. It also, in this instance anyway, helps even out what had been a considerable rolling, with big crests running under us from astern.

Simon was napping in the saloon last night, so I slept, or rather didn't sleep, in the forecabin. Surfaced in pre-dawn, as the immortal schoolboy joke has it, feeling grumpy.

Dressing, I realize it's been more than thirty hours since I wore a nicotine patch. I put the last one on. If I thought there were some cigarettes aboard I'd search the ship, inch by inch, stem to stern.

Yesterday, I thought about manoeuvring up close to that

container ship, asking them to put some cigs overboard in some kind of container, then thought, nah, I can last.

Charlotte, coming off watch, catches my mood. I am very touched when she reappears, not long after going down, with a mug of coffee and some toast. I've already had tea, tea she makes unfailingly before calling me on watch each morning, but this unexpected extra kindness is moving, the more so as she does it with the same undemonstrative matter-of-factness with which she does everything. The three of us tease Charlotte all the time that she never, ever tells a joke – we, on the other hand, never seem to stop. God knows where we get them from, or for what dark reason we remember so many between us. When she's gone below, straight to sleep, I fall to wondering at her patience with us. Zaf has been so long in Ireland he's *hibernicis hibernior* by now, but Charlotte seems immune to the Irish disease, that sense of doubleness in language which characterizes our complex and unstable attitude to English. Or perhaps it's just that the Dutch don't tell jokes, or maybe it's just Charlotte?

A cloudy morning, fitful gusts from time to time, the sea unpredictable, moody I'm tempted to say, were it not that the coffee has woken me just enough to let me understand that I'm projecting. So I try to stop doing that.

The best way out of these crossgrain mornings is to quieten the mind and go in after last night's dream. I switch Beethoven off, remove my cap, cool down, concentrate on steering with my fingertips barely touching the wheel, and after a while it comes back to me.

The dream featured a very small boy of eight or nine, very thin, pale, blondish, who needed to be brought to see a psychiatrist friend of mine, a very eminent man. It wasn't 10 a.m. yet; it was only 2 a.m., too early for our appointment, so I said I'd look after the child for a while. Meanwhile, out of I forget where, a fey girl child appears – and now I'm taking both of them very quietly out in a row boat. There's an extraordinary silence in the boat, and I realize after a while what's happening: he is falling in love with her, she has been waiting aeons for him, and I am just the boatman.

Then I am in a post office/Internet café, and they (felt presences) have things mixed up. Mick Hannigan, Director of the Cork Film Festival, is involved somehow; Martin Mahon, former Director of the Dublin Film Festival, ends up with Hannigan's table and papers, a rich find for a fellow film buff – and then there's a world-weary but not unkind Garda sergeant examining the tachometer of a harassed truck driver who seems a decent sort of fellow, and I'm anxious because it's putting-out time on the beach in this seaside town and we've seen the wee girl go off trustingly with some people and the small mute boy is very distressed, as fearful for her as I am . . .

That's as much of it as I can piece together, and it has me baffled. I am still feeling uneasy when Zaf comes buzzing up, sniffing the wind, doing his usual whirlwind tour of the deck. I go below, make coffee, shower and shave, wake myself up. Simon has appeared when I go back up, and I take the wheel while he and Zaf set about hoisting the chute, poling out the genoa.

I'm standing there at the wheel, looking at the sails, when I realize that I am inhabiting two times at once. The last time I noticed myself paying attention was standing here watching the sails go out; then, how and when I don't know, I seem to have fallen into some circular repetition of the morning, ending up here, now, remembering everything since 04.00 at the same time as I'm thinking, 'This is my first experience of being conscious since I went to my bunk at midnight.' Suddenly I hear the wind again, and the voices from the foredeck;

the helm is a live thing in my hands, my right leg has gone to sleep and my coffee, when I reach for it, is lukewarm. Don't be worrying, I tell myself, you're only out in the middle of the ocean. Why this last should have been such a comforting thought, I couldn't tell you.

At times of dislocation, check your location. I head for the nav station when Simon comes back to take the wheel. We're 1,500 miles out of Antigua, about 1,200 to Horta. Since last night, I notice, we've begun to talk not of miles travelled, but of miles to be covered yet.

Somebody always appears over my shoulder when I'm playing with the figures. This time it's Zaf. 'Well, what do you reckon?'

I tell him, ETA port of Horta, Faial: a.m., Wednesday, 22 May.

'What did I say in Antigua, eh? Twenty-one days?'

I nod. We have a pleased skipper. He pops his head around the corner, calls up to the helmsman. 'Simon, boy, you'll be buying us all beer next Wednesday!'

'Yeah? Cool! How do you figure that out?'

Zaf tells him, gives him a breakdown of the figures. Charlotte sleeps with the door of her cabin permanently open. Nothing seems to wake her until it's time for her watch. Now she cracks an eye open, says, 'Wednesday?' Zaf nods, says, 'Yep.' 'Ah,' she says, and goes back to sleep.

Simon is from the smallest Gaeltacht (Irish-speaking district) in Ireland. We've been in the habit of speaking together in Irish since our first trip together. It's a perfect outlet for grousing: we can mutter away mutinously to each other when something or someone is getting on one or the other's nerves. It also forces us outside the language set of the boat.

Irish has become an escape for Simon and me into a wider

world. Simon's is a little rusty from lack of practice; mine is maybe more fluent. His, on the other hand, is the language he spoke from birth, while mine was learned in school, and though I've kept it up assiduously it *is* a second language to me. It's funny to watch his body language change when we speak Irish. He becomes more boisterous, more assertive, more given to reflection, too. He's conscious, I think, of his youth, is inclined to be uncomfortable in some ways with the rest of us, unfamiliar with our frames of reference. I was poring over the chart the other day, set a course for Cuba, for practice, and it wasn't long before Zaf and I were talking about our childhood memories of the Cuban missile crisis. Charlotte was born just about that time, but nevertheless has a sense of Cuba's history since the revolution, her own views on world affairs, on Latin American politics and so on. We were chatting away desultorily about these things until Simon broke in: 'Do you know something? I haven't a clue what ye're talking about.'

When he and I talk in Irish, though, he speaks of his family, of his childhood growing up on the remote and often storm-tossed coast of the north-west, of his father the light-house keeper at Blacksod, his mother the teacher. When he speaks in a general conversation about his sailing experiences, it's always in terms of adventures; he speaks in anecdotes. When he speaks in Irish to me, he talks of what fascinates him about the sea, of his reasons for going to sea, for becoming a yachtmaster; of his wish to captain his own boat, to travel the world and visit the best surfing beaches. We sing snatches of songs we both know; I recite scraps of poetry from the schoolbooks; we make up terms for the weather; we wonder what the hell, in the larger scheme of our lives, we are doing out here. It's as if the alternative language delivers us into a different kind of comradeship. It's also a kind of memory prompt. *Ar mhaith leat cupán tae a bhuachaill?* (Would you like a cup of tea, boy?) is gentler, somehow, than its English equivalent. For him it evokes home; for me it acts as a reminder that I have a life in which I am not the least experienced person aboard a schooner in the middle of the Atlantic. For both of us, speaking in Irish reminds us that we *are* Irish, and around this thought we have built a whole ongoing dialogue about our island nation that somehow doesn't realize it *is* an island nation. I'm not sure I fully realized it myself until I started going to sea.

Simon is nearly as fascinated as I am with my late vocation as a sailor. The sea was the great omnipresence in his life since he was born; it's the most natural thing in the world for him to have become a sailor. I started sailing only four or five years ago, completely by chance, and he's intrigued by this sudden passion. I talk to Zaf about this a little, but his interest is generous and practical: he has appointed himself my teacher, greatly to my benefit. How or why I got into this is of no real concern to him. With Simon the question widens out. He wants to know how it could be that growing up in the port city of Cork, with the world's oldest sailing club just down the harbour, I didn't start sailing sooner. And we both want to know why far more Irish people don't sail, why we have such a poorly supported fishing tradition, compared with Iceland, say. We ask ourselves how any government could have let the Irish Shipping Company sail on to the rocks. We wonder how it is that there are so many songs and poems in the Irish language having to do with the sea, so comparatively few in our English-language song and poetry. We only ever seem to have these conversations in Irish. He might never ask me in English, to take a curious instance, why and how I make my life as a poet; in Irish he keeps coming back to it.

This morning, chattering away on deck, it's driving us both crazy that neither of us can remember the Irish term for 'shearwater'. Every single morning since we set out there's been a shearwater swooping about us; it appears at dawn, just before the sun clears the horizon, always astern, just hanging there. It stays around most of the day, disappears just before sunset. Is it the same one every day? We don't know. I suspect it would tell us if we only knew how to address it in Irish! I have developed a fondness for the shearwater; this is a Cory's, with a slow wingbeat, and a way of flying close to the surface of the water, often vanishing behind swells until its white underbelly coasts into view again on a strong downbeat of its wings. They live out here, going ashore only to breed. Perhaps that's why I like them (it?) – we are in the company of a creature wholly at home in these wastes, which makes us feel slightly more at home ourselves.

We sail the daylight hours today, engine off, the wind swinging between west and north-west. The steering still makes the most alarming noises, a loud mechanical creak followed by a wrenching click any time we move the wheel more than ten degrees to either side. The first time this happened I had my heart in my mouth. Anticipating what might happen builds up a considerable anxiety, and more than once I found myself wishing the bloody thing would just give, and we could fit the sturdy emergency tiller. It wouldn't be much fun steering so heavy a boat on a tiller set low in the cockpit, but it would at least be solid and sure. Zaf, no doubt, would set up some improbable jury-rigged apparatus involving short lines and shock cord which would allow us to use the tiller from the relative comfort of seat or coaming, but it would still be harder on the back than steering by the wheel. Anyway, we've got used to the noise, have more or less come to accept it as an unavoidable eccentricity of the system, rather than a source of potential trouble. Every now and then, though, it makes us uneasy.

The long swell has been building steadily all day, to the point where, near sunset, we estimate the wave height at nine feet or so. Zaf is looking thoughtfully back in the direction of Bermuda, and I know what he's thinking. There must have been a bit of a blow back there, perhaps west or north-west of the island. We're getting steady winds all day, ten to fifteen knots most of the time, and *Spirit* is averaging five to six knots over the ground, a good pace all things considered. We put the engine on when the sun goes down; the green and red running lights up forward become slowly more distinct as darkness comes over us and we forge on into the night. The engine is a kind of heartbeat after dark, as comforting in its own way as the safety umbilical we clip on automatically when we come on deck.

I had the wheel at sunset while Charlotte and Simon went forward to bring in the cruising chute. It's lore if not law (Oliver's remembered phrase) to reduce sail before dark – this limits the likelihood of anyone having to go on deck at night if the wind gets up.

Simon and Charlotte clip on the combined life jacket and lifeline we all wear, snap shackles on to the webbing straps, the jack stays, that run stem to stern along the side-decks. I watch them go forward at a half run, position themselves at the rail, wait without turning around or speaking for me to slack off the cruising-chute sheet where it's cleated off at the winch. There's a short length of line fixed to another cleat beside the wheel; I tie the free end to the wheel rim to hold her steady, move to the winch, press the flat of my left palm to the coils of line on the winch, to hold them, undo the free end of the sheet. Then, keeping the tension on the sheet, I carefully take a few turns off the winch drum until there's only one left, then take the strain, feel the chute pull away from me slightly. Now I let it off, slowly, slowly, the chute pulls away up and forward, then begins to collapse, losing its shape, spilling wind and power until its clew comes fluttering down to where Simon, one elbow hooked in the shrouds, begins to gather in the sail. He undoes the bowline in the clew, ties the sheet around the nearest stanchion with a quick hitch. I pull in a little slack on the winch, for the sake of tidiness, then go back to my station at the wheel. Charlotte, on the halyard at the foremast, gives Simon slack progressively as he gathers the pink and blue cloth to him in armfuls now, then she lets the halyard and the peak of the sail come floating down to the deck. She unshackles the halyard, clips it to the frame around the gas bottles, then both of them bundle the sail in to its sailbag, Charlotte holding the neck open, Simon plunging the material in, making sure that tack, peak and clew are at the top for the next time the bag is opened. Finished, they lash the bag to the bottle frame, trail their lines back to the cockpit, swing in, unclip and settle there for a moment to catch their breath. The whole operation has taken about five minutes, and what I notice when we're done is that nobody needed to talk – we all three of us knew what was to be done, then just did it. This is only as it should be, but silence is more often a feature of work done after dark than it is of work done in broad daylight.

Day 14

Wednesday, 15 May
Pos. at midnight   N   34° 28′
                    W   50° 25′

Exactly at dawn, bang on schedule, the daily shearwater. It's a cloudy morning, visibility only moderate. It's cool after a starless night, and the bird is banking ahead of us, its wingtip catching the light as it turns to drift back down the port side, hesitate, come up astern and hang there in the backdraft from the mainsail. Unlike a gull, it shows little interest in scraps tossed overboard – there's usually the soggy remnants of a biscuit or two left over from the night watch. I've brought my notebook up with me because I had such a vivid dream I want to record it before it fades. I rarely write at this time of day, partly from fatigue, more often because the shift from dark to light is often accompanied by a shift in the wind, and there's little free time at the helm. Today is relatively calm, perhaps because the morning sun brings little warmth, and the wind is steady in the north-west, so I have a little time to write. The shearwater prompts me to make an effort to recollect what birds we have seen so far.

Birds of this Passage

| Frigate birds | environs Antigua |
| Tropic birds | as far as 28° N |

Shearwaters	constant so far
(Cory's)	every morning at dawn, a solitary; occ. couples
Pomarine skua	one sighting
Great skua	numerous singletons, one pair
Petrels	occasional
Swallow	one, 'he have a roundy head'

That last notation bears explaining. The short-story writer and schoolteacher Bryan MacMahon told me a story of having two pupils whose school results began to bear an uncanny resemblance to each other's. One of the boys, clearly, was copying. Bryan had a pretty good idea which one, but natural justice demanded that he determine the matter beyond doubt. He set the two of them a test, keeping them back after school to write an essay, seated on different sides of the classroom of course. The assigned topic was the swallow, and Bryan's report of what ensued, if I might venture to reproduce his speaking style, went something like this:

Well, sure it only took a couple of minutes. I checked the bright lad first; read the opening paragraph of his composition. If it wasn't good, it wasn't bad, and there was substance there at least. But the other fella! He had got as far as his opening two sentences, and was now halfway down the pencil in his anxiety of chewing, seeking inspiration in that immemorial Helicon of the desperate schoolboy. I picked up his page, read: 'The swallow is a migratory bird. He have a roundy head.' And there, for all eternity, the lad was prepared to let the matter rest. There was nothing more to be done or said. I took up their papers, told them to go home.

But what was a swallow doing out here? Last year in Biscay, in the middle of the night, in high winds, Simon and I saw two swallows land on the boat, appearing to vanish under the dinghy lashed to the forward coachroof. They'd circled a number of times in the stern light, the white light atop the flag staff behind the wheel, and we were quite certain from the forked tails what they were.

All night we've been motoring without a scrap of sail across three contending swells from abaft the beam; taken together they make for a confused sea, too much for Magellan to handle. Now the wind shifts from north-west to south-east with perfect timing, just as Zaf comes up for the 06.00 watch. That's a big windshift, 180 degrees, so we put her head into the wind for a few minutes, haul up the main, then set the genoa on the port side.

I'm looking forward to a rest, but Zaf is unhappy with the fishing line. It needs to be brought in and rebaited, so I stay on the helm while he does this. Zaf has a new money-for-drink scheme: we'll go longlining for tuna once we reach the shelf off Faial. He reckons that we could put out four lines, and take maybe eight 30-kg bluefins before we run in to Horta. That close in we wouldn't have to worry about refrigeration to keep them fresh, and we could make US$3,000 to $4,000. I can't decide if he's serious or not, but we have fun speculating about what we might do with the money. Various options are explored, but when Simon comes up with the ten o'clock coffee the frontrunner is: we tie the boat up in the marina and fly home with the ship's papers, present them to Oliver together with a flight ticket to Horta, and head off to drink the balance in Kinsale.

'How far is it, anyway?' Simon asks. 'What, to Horta?' 'No, to Kinsale.' OK, that needs a different chart. I go rummaging in the drawer under the chart table; dig it out. Spread the chart on the saloon table; draw in a faint pencil line from Faial to Kinsale. I make a guess at the great-circle route and draw that in freehand. With the dividers we take turns in measuring the distance, and come up with an agreed 1,140 miles. Simon takes down the *Atlantic Pilot*, with its useful tables of prevailing winds by time of year. We can reasonably count on moderate westerlies for this passage, so we settle on an average of five knots boat speed, basing this on the ratio of wind speed to speed over ground on this present leg of the trip. This leads to an estimated passage time of ten days from Horta to Kinsale. Back up to Zaf in the cockpit with a question. 'How long are you reckoning on spending in Horta?' He mulls this over for a bit. 'I reckon three days.' 'OK, then we make it Wednesday, 4 June in Kinsale.' He thinks about this for a while, says that's about right. In her uncanny way, the mate surfaces instantly from sleep. 'Did you say the 4th?' 'Yeah, more or less.' She looks thoughtful for a while, nods, closes her eyes again. How does she do that?

I go below, shave, wash, strip, slide into my smoothed-out sleeping bag, turn my face away from the light, stretch my legs as far as they will go and feel sleep pour into me as if I were hollow from crown to toe.

I wake from the most vivid flying dream I have ever had.

I am zooming (but I don't know how) towards the Irish International Trading Company premises in Cork, trying to catch up with Charlotte, take over the boat from her, when I realize she is sailing a sail: there is no boat. I am trying to figure out how she can be stopped at the South Terrace traffic lights, then she's gone, and it's me now with the sail pressing me from behind. So I let go and we're off. Sheer exhilaration. Up, around, past bus queues, down through a labyrinthine boys' school built on a hill, down level after level until I'm in some kind of community-action workroom. My friend Mike Youlton asks for some help, I say sure, then, somehow, the sail is being flown out the door at the bottom of the steep hill by myself and Jack Lynch, the actor and storyteller whom Mike and I know from the Anti-Nuclear Movement days.

Jack is an adept flyer; he darts here and there with a flourish. Sometimes I'm flying solo, I see this through his eyes and through mine from a distance; sometimes it's both of us there, and the point of view is common to us both.

He's wearing green and is as blissfully happy to be flying as I am. Then some cartoon baddies (bikers!) steal the sail, but we get it back at a Garda checkpoint. All very jolly, all very bright-coloured.

Should we go up to see the Ticknock Headers? Sure, why not! The Ticknock Headers was a slightly disparaging name given to a hippy/anarchist nucleus in the Anti-Nuclear Movement, several of whom are friends of Jack's. Ticknock, in the Dublin mountains, was a large, sprawling house with a floating population. Like Mike, we belonged to a more politically hard-nosed fraction of the loose-knit movement, and now I notice that Mike is a bit disappointed in Jack and me – at our frivolity?

Off with us anyway, up and up and up, over huge cliffs, stomach-squeezing. Up and up and up – such strange houses, even a two- or three-house Regency terrace! One house is just Potemkin, tiles and concrete and blank windows wrapped around a bare rock. A large, grim, forbidding house, red brick, blue tiles, cement render. 'Is that Art's?' 'It is.' We circle the house, home to a one-time friend of Jack's, a man who walks around me when I run into him now as if I were some kind of dangerous and volatile local Antichrist.

I wake up. My stomach is still going up and up and up, somehow attuned to the rise and plunge of the boat.

My first thought is to stumble back to the GPS, check what's going on. The wind has picked up, gone south-south-west; we're making six and a half knots. Good. I head back to my berth, reluctant to get into conversation with anyone, anxious to keep hold of this disturbingly high-coloured dream.

Like many people in the Western world I have a head crammed full of ill-digested reading. Again like many, I have developed an idiosyncratic way of reading my dreams, a perspective pulled this way by Jung and a plethora of teachings on dream as symbolic enactment or script, that way by various cognitive theories which focus on the physiology of brain activity in the dream state. My own way of understanding dreams is, I suppose, to relate to them as I relate to what is going on when I 'get' a poem, then try to understand how best to rewrite the drafts subsequent to the first so that it ends up both coherent and not untrue to its originary moment. In other words, I treat dreams as if they come from the same place as poetry, are couched in a similar language, require for their being understood to be recast in the half-conscious light trance in which I revisit poems.

The waterborne buoyancy, the salt-laden air, the panelled walls and the shifting lights and glooms of the empty saloon make a sympathetic environment for this work.

The drive of the dream is obvious. This is a story of airborne movement, of physical exhilaration, liberty and skill of movement, joyous, exuberant – and simply mapped on to the body's experience of sailing. The swoops and dips, the ascents and descents, the navigation of the self borne up on air – all these are easily intelligible and acquire, perhaps, a greater persuasiveness from the fact that, as I lay dreaming, my body must have been experiencing similar movements. The locations, too, are interesting. The Irish International Trading Company was a warehouse operation in Cork when I was growing up; I never did find out what it was they traded in, except industrial salt, but the name always hooked my imagination as I cycled by. I was born on the South Terrace, in a nursing home that has now become a seaman's hostel. The school and its many levels, its mix of formal and informal education, mirrors the geography of hilly Cork, as the Dublin mountains locate me in the present moment of my life. The cartoon villains, the cooperative police with their roadblock, are, I suppose, figures for my situation at sea, where I am at one and the same time in constant if theoretical danger and preserved by authority. If I should choose to read a lesson into this vivid dream, it is to do with what being at sea has made me realize about myself.

I have choices in this dream, personified in Mike and Jack. Mike reminds me there is a strain running through my life of assumed responsibility as a politically conscious citizen, operating in the public domain. Jack, an actor and storyteller, a gentle and humorous man, reminds me of another strain, more personal, interior, a sense of myself as a writer with no responsibility to anyone but myself. Say, the commissar and the yogi.

Which has what, I ask myself, to do with the price of fish? I took up sailing suddenly, just before I resigned not only from my job, but also from a raft of committees and boards of various kinds; I moved out from the city centre to a seaside suburb, in order to live quietly and write. I understand the dream to be telling me that I feel guilty about choosing my own interests over service to others, but that I've made my choice, chosen flight over the long march through the institutions, and that this is OK. Did I need to be in the middle of the Atlantic to learn this?

I am ruminating morosely over the reductive things that happen if you think about dreams, when the sun comes through the hatch above me where I'm washing up in the galley and there's a 'pop' somewhere inside me, and I feel the same lift coming up through my feet as I felt when flying in the dream. I go up on deck, where Simon and Zaf are grinning broadly, sharing their happiness at the grace and power of our progress through the water. I think that now would be a perfect moment for a cigarette, let the thought hang there, let it fade; I am seized by a great feeling of well-being, a buoyancy in the heart, an aeration, a sense of possessing the moment and being possessed by it. For one of the very few times in my life, for how long a time I can't tell, I feel as sure and confirmed in being alive as, I sense, it is possible for me to feel. Then that fades, as the dream is beginning to fade, and I bend to tidy a halyard that has shaken loose from its cleat on the mast.

Charlotte has made lunch. It's warm again, if breezy, and we eat in the cockpit, everyone perked up by the speed we're making, the sense that *Spirit* is in the groove. It was a real Irish morning, says the mate, already beginning to anticipate the coming charter season in home waters. We're more regretful than she is, I think, that we're leaving the tropics behind – though Simon's homesickness is getting stronger by the day. We're happy to be sailing well, as happy as children are when a game's going well; like children, we live in body time more than head time when things are going smoothly, we carry ourselves as if we had no care in the world – but naturally we do have cares, and I think this adds an extra savour to what we count as play, the sense each one of us has of the attentive adult inside us who watches over our actions.

I've found a new spot to sprawl in for the afternoon, between the deck boxes on the after coachroof, behind the mainmast. Cushions and sleeping bags are wedged in the shrouds on all sides, to air in the welcome sun; I commandeer one long cushion, a seat from the saloon, to furnish my nest out of the wind's way. Half-sitting, half-lying there, scribbling my daily notes, I feel the pen hesitate, then move on, flying over the page like an aerial or magnet drawing the words down from somewhere else. I know it's the first draft of a poem because I'm watching the words appear on the page at the same time as I am forming them, or they are forming themselves, in my head. I trust the process because it happens, and because anything I've written that has an afterlife as what I call a poem begins like this.

There are major problems with the draft, as I see at once, and I underline some phrases, scribble alternatives in the margins here and there, in an attempt to cage the thing in, to hold it there in suspended animation until some future day when I will be able to summon a clearer head. I know immediately I'll not finish this while I'm on the boat.

At 18.30 we are exactly 1,000 miles from Horta, 1,700 from Antigua. It has been a restorative afternoon; we are all slightly groggy from the sun. We drowse through dinner, each of us in a world of her or his own. At 21.35 the engine comes on, and everyone not on watch heads for the horizontal.

Day 15

Thursday, 16 May
Pos. at midnight   N   35° 08′
                   W   47° 43′

Two entries from my notebook tell today's story in mini-
ature.

Patches all gone now, eked out 7 over 14 days, and I'm hurting.
It's been sometimes very difficult – but I haven't lost my temper
once.

A barrelling day under sail, 179 miles in past 25 hrs (16.30 as I
write), faster under sail than under sail and engine.

As I came on watch, preoccupied with the nicotine question, the wind went around to the south. We have a following
sea, which means a deep, steep swell keeps lifting the starboard
quarter, a great swooping sensation if you're in good form, a
profoundly uncomfortable one if you're not.

I didn't sleep very well. We all wonder how single-handers
manage; we wonder also if their reputation for a slight
dementedness can't be directly traced to long-term sleep
deprivation. Charlotte is the one among us who has the best,
most ruthless attitude to sleep. When she has no duties to
perform, Charlotte is usually in her bunk and sound asleep.
Simon is distractable when the sailing is interesting, on call at
odd hours of the day or night for sail changes and that kind of

thing, so, though he sleeps well, he doesn't sleep half as much as a growing lad needs to.

What keeps me awake is, I suppose, curiosity and the novelty of being out here. I always want to know what's going on, I'm always anticipating things going wrong, and I am, after all, in the grip of nicotine withdrawal. Zaf sleeps least of us because he feels at all times responsible for everything that happens. I daresay he's right; we are a relatively inexperienced crew. He is, for instance, the only one aboard with a good working knowledge of diesel engines. The rest of us, between us, could bring the boat to port under sail if anything should happen to him, but we'd be a worried lot if we hadn't a functioning engine. Zaf must also know how much we would be dependent on his heavy-weather expertise if we should find ourselves in a blow. On top of these considerations there is the simple truth that he worries topics and thoughts the way a dog worries a slipper or a stick. He will riff for hours on end about something or other that's annoying him. He knows these gearboxes – you can't repair them when they go wrong. Only thing is to throw them overboard. If it were his gearbox he'd throw it overboard. Overboard, that's the place for it. You can't repair these fucking gearboxes. Once they go, they're gone. Should be fucked overboard. And so on. And so on.

When we're all in good humour, we tease him mercilessly about this relentless drone. When we're tired or cranky and irritable, it's maddening. When Zaf is in good humour and we tease him, he laughs; when it's his turn to be in bad humour, I'd like to say that we tease him anyway, but we don't. We stay quiet, and get driven crazy.

There are times when we all drive each other crazy. Simon sulks when he's feeling down, gets frustrated, bottles it all up, imagines he's keeping his thoughts to himself – but it takes no art at all to read his mind's construction in his face. When Simon's unhappy about something he drives us all nuts. We all agree that Charlotte must, surely, be irritable like the rest of us, but we can't tell. She never once, in the whole trip, shows a sign of irritation.

I am sure there are times when I drive the others mad, but I don't know how. They don't, or won't, tell me. I can make a guess at the things about me that drive people crazy: God knows people have queued up all my life to tell me my failings, and some of this has sunk in. I'm a pretty good hand at self-accusation, too, but in this case I am at something of a disadvantage: what normally drives friends, coworkers and Paula crazy is not necessarily what gets on the nerves of my fellow crew. I can make a list of probabilities, I suppose: I probably talk too much; I probably ask too many questions; I probably worry too much about things that make me nervous, but which accomplished sailors take in their stride.

Which morose but true reflections need to be balanced with the other signature of this curious day, the magnificent sailing conditions we are enjoying. Internal weather, Mr Keats notwithstanding, does not always mirror external weather, nor vice versa. From 07.30 we are on the wind alone, and making very good speeds. We average 7.5 knots through the day, in mid afternoon we show 8.8 knots for a giddy thirty minutes or so, and Zaf saw 10.2 on the clock at one stage. Simon is dead keen to be on the helm, whooping when he is, never far away when someone else is having fun. This boat loves to sail on a broad reach, the wind at an angle of forty-five degrees from behind. We power along under genoa, fore and mainsails, pretty upright considering the pressure of the wind, throwing a fine fan of spray skywards when we roll and the leeward gunwale scythes through the green water.

Hour by hour we take turns on the heavy wheel, sweating

despite the stiff breeze, opening ourselves out to the weather, the brisk scouring away of ill temper. Charlotte and Zaf embark on a cleaning binge, sweeping and mopping and scrubbing, delving into the recesses of lockers, opening what hatches they can, letting the salt air drive through the boat, drive the demons out. An inspiration to Simon and to my cranky self. For the first time in weeks it is possible to pass by Simon's open cabin door without going weak at the knees. An elaborate theory that something small and furry crawled in there to die has had a long currency among his shipmates: no corpse is uncovered when the Sweeney tornado has finished its work on the cabin, but we find buckets of socks and trainers lashed to the leeward rail, and we fear that tonight's dinner will taste strongly of eau de Cool Young Dude, or whatever it is he has been spraying cabin, bedding and self with. The shearwater seems to hang back further than usual today when our lad is on the wheel.

Towards sundown a big squall threatens from behind. We all climb into wet gear, Zaf in what Charlotte calls 'Glandore Cowboy' style: wet jacket, shorts, high Dubarry boots. Irresistible photo opportunity.

Zaf and Simon bring down the cruising chute. Maybe I should go up and help? Charlotte on helm, confusions, recriminations, shouting for the first time on this trip – I suddenly decide I have no interest in this; I'm staying put. They want to play cranky sailors, let 'em.

Day 16

Friday, 17 May
Pos. at midnight   N   35° 42'
                   W   44° 10'

I check the log on my way up at 04.00. It's been a rough enough night, I'm guessing, from the work point of view. There is a heavy north-westerly swell with many breaking crests, and the wind is swinging between fifteen and twenty-five knots. These conditions can place a ferocious strain on the shoulders – *Spirit* needs nonstop helming in a following sea.

Mozart's Requiem and the rising and widening of the light balance the muscle ache, but I feel every minute of my two-hour stint.

Zaf bounds up on deck. Where does he get the energy? The cruising chute must go up. Wait for Simon? No, he'll do it himself, now. And up it goes, eventually, and the engine comes off. Every single time that engine is switched off I feel a lightening of the heart.

Last evening and night we were making 7.5 to 8.2 knots fairly consistently. It is quite something to see the effect on all of us of a knot or two's increase in the daily average. Our spirits lift as the boat lifts to the swell and the wind. We face into the day under cruising chute, foresail and main, the fore and main boomed out at an angle of maybe thirty degrees. For days now, as a matter of course, we've been rigging preventers, lines from the booms to the deck that will stop us from accidentally gybing.

The accidental gybe, when the wind goes around suddenly and slams the boat on to an opposite tack, is something every sailor tries to avoid. The sudden strain on gear and rigging can be catastrophic, can even lead to dismasting. When you gybe like that the boom can take the head off someone unwary enough to be standing in its path as it crashes across.

The other cause of a sudden, unplanned gybe is a tired helmsman or helmswoman; their attention wanders, they may even nod off for a moment, the boat is pressed round by the wind and then, bang, everything slams over. It's a good read on Zaf's part to provide against both of these possibilities.

By mid afternoon the wind has veered north, may go on into the north-east as the depression above and to the east of us continues to track away ahead. Anything less than sixty degrees off the bow will screw us up, but we are reasonably confident that we'll make Horta next Tuesday.

We continue to worry about the steering. Now there's a looseness, a sense of play in the wheel which means it takes longer to feed her back into the wind; there's a cushiony rather than a crisp feel to it. Zaf immediately extrapolates this into catastrophic gear failure in forty knots of wind with fifteen-foot seas, knockdowns, engine-room flooded – lovely. I never know, when this happens, whether he's just thinking himself out to the edge of possibilities, or if he really thinks this is a likely scenario.

Later we learn that the generator can't be used because, it seems, some switch that was 'repaired' in Antigua is now kaput. This means we must cut down on our use of electricity so as to conserve the batteries – which we can only charge when the engine is running. Meanwhile we're trying to keep engine use to a minimum.

There's a moaning halyard somewhere up forward that's flaying my nerves. It's been driving three of us crazy; Simon, who sleeps directly beneath it, hasn't noticed. Eventually, through a process of trial and error on a pitching foredeck, Charlotte and I locate and deal with the source of the noise. 'Cool!' says Simon, bopping away on the wheel, 'but it wasn't bothering me anyway.' Charlotte and I look at each other, look at Simon. Fortunately for him, sensitive soul that he is, he has his head down, has no idea how close he has come to being fish bait.

Today was sunny, a hard but not alien light, far less heat in the day. Tonight is beautiful; we're motoring with little wind, the barometer is high, there's a new moon, plenty of stars . . . It would be even better if there were wind: sailing the night is in many ways the best hit you can get on this boat.

Helming in a following sea, you look over your shoulder as often as you remember to, watching for the recurrent pair of bigger-than-usual waves — there is no really satisfactory explanation for where these pairs come from, they just do. You surf them if you can — it helps build up speed.

There is something very satisfying, beautiful even, in the way this hull slices into and through the water. She is wonderfully in her element.

Day 17

Saturday, 18 May
Pos. at midnight   N   36° 34′
                    W   41° 12′

Charlotte's log entry, going off watch before dawn, reads, 'Stars, stars, stars.' I'm in time for the last of the display. I find the North Star, tracing a shallow arc from the tip of the Plough. The conventional wisdom has it that the North Star is the brightest star in the hemisphere, but I can't see it. There are, oh, a half-dozen at least that seem to me as bright if not brighter – though at least two of these are planets. Is there something wrong with my eyes, or is it that so many genera-tions of sailors have built this up as an element in the lore: the North Star is the crucial star, so therefore it should be the brightest so therefore it is? Maybe. What else can I make out? There's the 'W' of Cassiopeia, the twins Castor and Pollux, one above the other, and there's Orion's Belt, like one of those mini-rosaries from my childhood – but that, I am half-ashamed to say, is it. I can find my way about Moscow with far more confidence than I can find my way in the night sky, and I feel deeply stupid that it should be so.

I remember a night on watch with Zaf and a man called John Gullery on the first trip through Biscay, the one that went well. Gullery had worked as a manager for the Dunlop Company – at the opposite end of the scale to my father, who'd worked most of his life in its Cork factory before it shut down more or less overnight, put 1,000 men and women out of work, and shagged off to somewhere where wages were lower. John is an amiable man, a kindly soul with a fund of stories and our favourite good-tempered breakfast cook of all time, so it's scarcely his fault that his tales of the good life in the upper echelons of Dunlop, when the company was riding high, exploiting the natives of Malaya and other outposts of the former or about-to-be-former Empire, chimed awkwardly with me. In those days Oliver still permitted cigarette smoking on his boat, and one night, when the Dunlop dichotomy was proving to be too much for me, Zaf and I had gone forward to have a smoke under the foremast. When Zaf went back to the cockpit, I lay on my back on the starboard deck, right forward; after a few minutes, with no warning (and with no sense of alarm or drama), I felt my self, my soul, being drawn up and into the heart of the starry heavens.

What I'd thought to do was no more than look at the stars, and I had got to the point where I was trying to persuade my mind to *feel* what it could assent to intellectually, that one might as well consider one was looking down at the stars as up at them, when, in a moment, all unexpectedly, I sensed/felt/experienced (I haven't the words for it) that the stars were pulling me up and in.

I couldn't say for how long this experience lasted, but it happened, like that, just so. I can't say the world had changed when I felt myself back again, climbing stiffly to my feet, trailing my harness line back along the deck to the cockpit; nor did I care to talk to the others about it, and I have not been inclined to talk about it since. Why should I? Such things happen all the time, are meant to be experienced in and of and as themselves, as phenomenal events or moments. I recall that moment now, listening to Charlie Piggott making magic on the box again, then I let it go.

'How are we doing?' Zaf is up, the wind is down, nothing to be done in the line of sail tweaking for the moment, nothing on the fishing line, the gearbox is cool – what to do?

'Have you ever made a pilotage plan?' he asks me.

'No,' I say, 'but I've seen it done. Sure, why don't I give it a try?'

In the nautical almanacs and pilot books which cover most of the world by now, if not indeed all of it, you will find sketch maps, sometimes photographs, and a wealth of painstakingly gathered information to assist the skipper in making a safe entry into, or a safe exit from, practically every harbour known to mariners. The prudent skipper, such as Oliver or Zaf, is never content simply to keep the relevant page of the book at his elbow when clearing in. Far better to write it all out for yourself, to keep those notes handy when guiding your vessel to or from anchorage or berth. There are many practical reasons for this. Books are unwieldy, and cockpits can be chaotic, unstable, exposed in a blow. A single sheet is more manageable, can be tucked in a pocket out of the weather, read under the lee of a jacket in the rain. There are other considerations: the pilot-book information is often in shorthand, and, while you will understand the shorthand in normal conditions, you'll understand your own version better when you're under pressure; the pilot book might offer more information than you'll need in your particular circumstances, or some of the information may be irrelevant – an alternative entry course suitable for a shallow-draught vessel won't be of much use to you if you're a deep-draught boat, and having to read your way through or past the irrelevant entry might just result in your missing the trawler that has suddenly appeared around the breakwater. Pilotage is a high-attention exercise. You want to have exactly the information you need, no more and no less.

I take down our trusty *Atlantic Pilot* from the saloon book-shelf, read through the entry and make the following notations in my notebook:

Pilotage for Horta

Lat./long.	38° 32′ N
	28° 37′ W
Faial	No serious outliers. Usual approach is to skirt S coast
	W end Vale Formosa light, range more like 5 miles than the claimed 13
	Airfield with control tower on W side island
	Coast may be closed to within 0.5 miles, Horta is near SE corner of island, facing Pico
	Pico is a volcanic island with a distinctive cone
	On rounding final headland coming from W, make straight for breakwater head
	Good depth close in
Buoyage	IALA
	Watch for Pico ferry when rounding in
	Fly Q
Radio	VHF 11 + 16
Pilot service	14 + 16
Marina monitors	11 + 16
Mid-Atlantic	
Yacht Services	77

Policia Maritima and Customs (Alfandega) on Reception Quay

Some of this ought to be explained. Outliers are submerged rocks or reefs that might endanger the unwary. There are no serious examples of this nuisance, which is good. 'Fly Q' means we hoist the yellow, or Q, flag from the starboard yard arm, or in our case spreader, signifying that we are arriving from outside Portuguese territory. The normal requirement is that you clear customs at the first port of entry when making landfall in a new country. I've put in the radio frequency for Mid-Atlantic Yacht Services because they are in the *Atlantic Pilot* as providing, among many other services, mechanics: the very worst time for the engine to pack in would be as we are entering harbour, so I'm making provision for the possibility that we will need assistance. Zaf can, of course, sail her on to a mooring, even sail her alongside a jetty, but not easily if there's a sudden gust, or if the harbour is full of boats going every which way at once.

I'm making a rudimentary breakfast, mulling over these notes, checking to see if I've left anything important out. Lured from his lair by the smell of toast, Simon has surfaced.

He comes to have a look. 'Looks good, but do you mind if I give you some advice?'

'Course not. What?'

'See the way you've drawn in the sketch map? It's much better if you draw it upside down, so that whoever's on the wheel can read the map the same way he's seeing the harbour open out in front of him. See the way you've drawn the harbour? When we're off the breakwater, coming in from the south, it's much handier if that's in the bottom of the map.' Smart boy, that Simon, always said so.

The wind all night was northerly, and had dropped by this morning when I came up. Now it's gone west, is picking up, and Zaf, ensconced at the wheel, wants us to try poling out the genoa and running out the cruising chute. Which we do, if not expertly, then with a certain dispatch. Was there a hint, the merest hint of swagger as Simon and I made our way back? There was, I'm afraid.

I make bread from packet mixes, and prepare lunch while it's baking; we eat in warm sun for the first time in a few days.

Last night's dreams have been niggling at me all morning. Now I make up my nest between the deck boxes, open my notebook, go in after the dead: Claire Barker, Bob Collins, Seán Dunne.

Claire was a friend from college days, a happy-go-lucky soul who fell in love with a man who treated her badly, would come round for comfort; a hill walker, a Christmas Day swimmer. Died at twenty-nine, cancer of the womb. I could never visit her in hospital, couldn't do that for her, reproached myself, tried often and unsuccessfully to understand why I couldn't. Bob Collins helped conceive, then directed, a TV books programme I presented. A Buddhist, a good, strong, gentle man, in love with a lovely woman, proud of his two talented daughters, a man of light. His last days in the hospice, I couldn't visit him. Not wouldn't. Couldn't. Out here, all this space around me, I call him up and see him laughing, laughing. He just looks at me and beams. Nothing to say, no blame, no messages – he just beams.

Seán Dunne surprises me; I had not thought to meet him here. We were friends in college, boy poets together. The day Saigon fell, we were there on the clock tower of the university, defending the red flag against engineers, commerce students, the shrill and spotty future luminaries of law and medicine. I carried him up Shandon Street one night on my skinny shoulders, barely able to feel his bones through his navy surplus great-coat; so thin, Seán, so driven, so brave. He became a reformed alcoholic, a man of letters, a denier of, and enemy to, certain of his friends. Including me. He made some fine poems, reconciled himself to the Christians, wrote sometimes good, sometimes ignorant journalism, won the hearts of many in his new manifestation, including some I admire and consider friends.

Sometimes, to make themselves new and safe, people are driven to deny the friends of their youth, even to do them actual harm. I am trying with an uncertain pen to work this out on the page, thinking it faintly absurd that I am out in the middle of the Atlantic Ocean, rising and falling in the salt air, under a hard sun, middle-aged, making myself new, beset in my dreams by dead companions of an earlier life, unable in this waking life to make sense of what they are telling me, what I need them to tell me. In the dream last night Seán was hale and hearty; we were at a bar with Tom McCarthy, a true friend still. I am reaching to offer Seán a cold, black pint of Guinness and am about to understand him, understand what happened to him, why he became so bitter towards me . . . and that's it, no more of the dream.

I have never dreamed of Claire, this long time dead, nor of Seán, nor of Bob so recently gone from us. It is to do with being at sea, this dreaming of the dead, but I do not grasp what is going on, I do not understand this.

No signal on the satphone. How long now since we spoke – days?

It occurs to me I should make a stocktaking note. Perhaps that compression of self will reach you, a signal down one of the lines that seem to be opening up around me?

The sun, astern of us, is getting ready to go down, we have about forty-five minutes of light. The ship is rolling gently. Simon's on the wheel; the others are below, probably sleeping. I'm between the coachroofs, facing aft. Blue fleece, that ancient grey shirt with the green woven cord through the buttonhole, grey baggy lightweight trousers, deck shoes. Lightly tanned. Your luck stone in my heart pocket, knife

on lanyard in right pocket, shades on a preventive strap, wide-brimmed
hat, notebook open, pen in my hand: me at forty-eight, thickset, still
fairly agile, getting stronger, still a believer, still very much in love.

Learning to be a sailor.

I am warm, borne up, being carried home on the bosom of the
indifferent, not hostile sea. Home, love. Home. So very fortunate.

Up pops the Lord of Misrule. There's a sail bearing 040°, been
there for hours. We're on 085° or so, closing the distance. Zaf
wants to hail them for smokes. I'm 50/50. If it were my choice
I'd let it go. If he gets some, I'll smoke one or two. We talk
about this for a minute or two, then Zaf shrugs; I shrug. We
don't hail them.

For no reason at all, the skipper decides we should all have
a whiskey. Then he's gone again – for a nap he says. Me, too,
says Simon. Charlotte appears bang on time for her watch; I
take my drink and my notebook below, sprawl out in my
cabin for a change, then I'm hearing this in my head, I am
writing it as I hear it:

'*Qu'est-ce que tu fais, Maman?*'
'*On fait l'amour, chérie.*'
'*Et moi, je peux participer?*'
'*Pas encore, ma chérie, pas encore.*'

Whatever happened to Victoria's dreams,
Of Paris and glamour and meaning?
Victoria lives on the rue Cherche Midi
In a *chambre de bonne* looking south.

Victoria works in a rue de Rennes shoe shop,
The shoes are up-market, the customers chic.
She smokes through the afternoon, back to the window,
She turns with a smile when she hears the door click.

Fille d'un boulanger, born in the Midi,
Never quite beautiful, never quite bright,
Whatever happened to Victoria's dreams,
Of Paris and glamour and meaning?

There's a tune with this, an indifferent tune – even I know that, and I'm tone deaf. I know I won't remember the tune.

Last entry in the log, 22.15, my hand: 'Main and motor. New moon.'

The official version.

Day 18

Sunday, 19 May
Pos. at midnight   N   36° 52'
                     W   38° 26'

Time does fall away; one day does blend into the next. The habit of constant attention becomes tiring. I know the instant I come on deck at dawn that this will be a day to be got through: it's chilly, we're motoring along, just the main up, keeping above six knots, maybe seventy-two hours from Horta – and that's about it, really, as far as I can see. Charlotte, going off watch, writes in the log, 'Nothing special.' By 10.30 we have the cruising chute and main up, the engine is off, Simon's log entry reads, 'Sailing nicely'; in my hand, 14.25, I find: 'Lumpy seas, 15 knots wind, getting there . . .'

We have been largely fortunate with the weather – no storms, and only a few days without wind. We would like about five knots more wind, and from south-west or north-west for preference – that would put some life into the sailing. Four is a small crew for a seventy-foot boat, but, if there are drawbacks, there are also, I see now, advantages as well – at least in our present condition. There isn't a great deal we can do about anything much, but there is always something to be done, and on a quiet day like today it's better to be dividing the tasks between four, rather than between six or eight. On the other hand, we could have a card school going, or a session – bound to be a few musicians in a larger crew.

Out of the blue I find myself wondering what's happened

in the general election at home. I say out of the blue because this is the first time I've thought about home, apart from speculating on our eventual arrival, and wondering how Paula is doing. I have a haunted sense there is something she hasn't been telling me in our brief conversations. My instinct is that someone has died; she's not telling me so as to spare me the grief of helpless knowing. If I do get through, I decide, I won't ask her – she'll know if it's something I would want to know.

Sometimes, on days like this at home, I open a notebook and just sit there. I mightn't even pick up the pen. I just sit there, vacant, perhaps ill at ease, perhaps not. I pick things up and put them down, stare out the window. Sometimes on a day like that, a day of not caring much about anything, I find myself writing. Or maybe I could say, I find I have written something. Late afternoon, sitting in the saloon to avoid having to talk when I've nothing much to say, I find I have been writing for nearly an hour, the mind (the moving hand) trying for a kind of order, a summoning which is also a summary, a latitude and longitude of sentiment, a log entry in the travels of the heart.

At 22.25, in my hand in the logbook: 'Kill the satphone.' I guess I must have been trying to phone home.

Day 19

Monday, 20 May
Pos. at midnight   N   37° 50′
                   W   36° 01′

Bach cellos this morning, nos. 4 to 6 with Paul Tortelier, after poor sleep and no memory of dreams. Wind all night was west–north–west, fifteen to twenty knots; we've been averaging six and a half to seven knots, motoring. It was chilly, says Charlotte at the handover, chilly but not cold. About 300 miles to Horta, the gunmetal wake behind us as the dawn comes up goes scrolling back 2,400 miles. I lash the wheel for a moment, go forward to have a quick check around. In the rising light, a ship ahead of us is crossing our bows, making west. Out of the Med, I suppose, heading, on that course, for Bermuda or the southern United States. I guess the distance at eight miles, go below, and flick on the radar to check. Yep, eight miles. Punch the rings out to sixteen, to thirty-two miles – nothing else inside the distance. Quick check of speed while I'm down here: seven knots, barometer still high. Very good, very good.

The skipper comes up all full of energy as usual, and the wind goes into the west, dead astern. There isn't, as far as I can judge, a causal link between these two facts, but it does mean we pole out the genoa and run up the cruising chute. The bustle and business pleases him and warms me up, so we're both pretty happy – the more so when we figure out we've added a half knot to our speed. We have big seas now lifting our stern, long swells rolling in from behind, a great impetus pushing us on towards Horta. Helming is tricky: with the wind directly behind you, the keel makes little or no contribution to keeping the boat on track. In these conditions it is all too easy to gybe the boat accidentally, the more so as you can't rig preventers to the genoa or the cruising chute, as you can with the foresail and the main. I prefer running downwind when the visibility is good: that way you have some chance of predicting a windshift, and taking precautionary action. Zaf is a wizard at this kind of work, able to keep up a full flow of conversation on several topics simultaneously, tend to his fishing line, give orders, drink tea and steer without ever seeming to be concentrating on any one of these activities. Put me on the wheel in these circumstances and I am watching the sails, watching the wind direction indicator and, just possibly, drinking tea – but that about exhausts the repertoire. I take a quick dive inside my head, rummage around inquisitively, and emerge with the conclusion that I have got better at this: not only do I know I should be watching the sails, but I find I am doing it automatically as well. I reward myself for this small step forward by eating a biscuit while drinking tea, watching the wind direction indicator and watching the sails.

I've been listening for a few minutes to Simon talking down below when it dawns on me that he's on the phone. Zaf sees my sudden agitation, takes the wheel without a word. Simon must be turning psychic because he suddenly pops up and says: 'Hey, Dorgan, I got a signal!'

I give Paula the coordinates without her asking, tell her we should make Horta in two days, then I shut up: all I want right now is the sound of her voice in my ear. Long after the signal goes down in the middle of a sentence I am still standing there, lost and glowing. I should feel embarrassed, at my age, but I don't.

It seems we are running low on diesel. From now on we'll sail as much as possible, conserve fuel. Zaf is still pretty exercised by something that happened last night. The radar gave him a target, bearing five miles, a single target which resolved itself into two fishing boats when he went back up to take a look. This far out, he reckons they must have been longliners. About a half mile off, one started flashing his white masthead light when he should have had a green over white to show he was fishing. It's hard to avoid a stab of anxiety at such anomalous behaviour. There's a fixed code for lights at sea, instructions for what to show depending on your size, nature, condition, the activity in which you are engaged. A sailing yacht under way at night, for instance, carries port and starboard running lights, red and green, respectively, plus a white overtaking light, usually mounted at the stern. The side lights should be visible from dead ahead and through an arc of 112.5 degrees when viewed broadside on. The configuration allows another ship's navigator to understand what kind of vessel you are, and therefore what kind of manoeuvres you may engage in, as well as permitting a reasonable understanding of what it is you are doing while under observation. It is particularly important to know what a trawler is doing – a drift netter, for instance, should show an all-round red light above a white at the masthead, as opposed to the green light above white of a trawler. Not all yachtsmen are as conscious as they should be that trawling is difficult work, that fishermen are out here under a different imperative and more often than not are far more constrained in their ability to avoid us than we are constrained in our ability to avoid them.

The salient fact about trawlers is that you never can be sure what the buggers are going to do next, so it's always best to give them a wide berth. Zaf points to last night as a graphic example of the wisdom of this: that pair were so close to each other at one point that they showed up as a single radar target, five miles off; by the time he passed them they had their lines out (or just possibly, he supposes, their trawls) and were no more than a half mile off, a near-miss in these circumstances. Simon, who's joined us in time to hear some of Zaf's tale, chimes in:

'Hey, Theo, do you remember the Dodger?'

Do I what? Biscay, last September, twelve hours before Finisterre, five or six trawlers on the radar, all inside a four-mile radius. Suddenly Simon the eagle-eyed spots a red, about a half mile off, closing us. It swings towards us; we can see red and green, which means it's heading straight for us, may be going behind us, then it's red again; he's turned away ahead of us again, then – nothing. I'm glued to the radar; Simon is yelling down, 'Nothing, I can't see anything. The fucker just disappeared.' I'm calling back up. 'Nothing here either. I've the radar right in, and he's not showing.' I come up – the visibility's lousy, but we can make out the lights of the other boats, all corresponding to their position on radar, but where's this guy gone? We puzzle it out for the rest of the watch and come to the conclusion, finally, that he must have thought we were a patrol boat, that he doused his lights and ran for the coast because he was over quota, or carrying illegal nets, or was on a drug run. The Dodger, we christened him, dodgy by name and dodgy by nature.

The skipper has decided we're going back on double watches tonight, as we're more than likely in a recognized fishing zone and can expect more trawlers when darkness falls.

I surface after a nap in the mid afternoon; the barometer's down three points since 11.00, sign of a freshening in the weather. If it keeps falling we'll get a blow, but it shouldn't, really. We're well into the Azores High, an almost-permanent zone of high pressure centred on the islands, extending hundreds of miles in every direction, and generally a guarantor of settled weather. Not that the sea gives guarantees. The swell is deepening, visibility is decreasing and we're rolling considerably in what look increasingly like Irish waters – iron grey, green streaked with white in the underlip of the crests as they curl over. Now the waves mounting up behind us are higher than the after rail; on the helm it feels as if we are keeping just barely ahead of them, though this is an illusion. We have about seventeen knots of wind; we're averaging seven knots boat speed, so in fact we are perfectly poised in the swell, lifted and driven on by it. It's tough on the shoulders and on the neck. From time to time a pair of higher-than-usual waves, one hustling in on the one ahead of it, will run at us from the port quarter – you need to keep an eye out for these. The regular waves, once your hands on the wheel and your feet on the cockpit floor have found the rhythm, these you can cope with after a while. It's as if the boat is communicating more clearly with you. You feel the flow between sea state, hull shape, set of the sails, the information feeding into your body – and you keep turning your head for the rogue pair that will knock you off course. You keep turning your head because, though the wind has gone north of west, you're still more or less on a run, and therefore vulnerable.

'What's it like?' Simon calls from the companionway, dying to have a go.

'It's a pain in the bloody neck!'

'Ah go 'way out of that. You're loving it!'

I am. Simon rustles up stew and spuds. Survival food. This close to land we're not as fussy as we used to be, and with the galley like a lottery drum we think a hot meal of any kind is a considerable achievement.

I take the first double watch with Zaf, 20.00 to 00.00.

Visibility is at best moderate. We have the radar on stand-by; from time to time we switch it on. Nothing. Every ten minutes one of us takes a good look all around: I've found it best to go clockwise from the port beam, a steady sweep first, then a slower, more methodical look, holding a thirty-degree section in view for about ten seconds, then moving on. It's good practice, too, I remember Oliver saying ages ago, to yaw the bow from side to side once or twice, to make sure there's nothing in the blind spot right on the bow. We're making 095° or so, on the port tack as we're just above our curving track into Faial and the wind is still west–north–west; we keep a sharp watch to leeward, our slightly blinder side. It's one of those nights when you're on watch with someone and reluctant to talk; we shift almost without speaking between time on the wheel and time off; every now and then one or other of us goes below to make tea, to check the instruments, to get a snack from the treat bag, but we're both caught up in a kind of spell.

The knowledge that we're approaching land has been a kind of undercurrent all day, flickering through in a word, a gesture or a look. Nobody's speaking of it; everyone feels it. And here in the cockpit the tension is ratcheting up; Zaf and I, the biggest chatterboxes on board, hardly say a word to each other tonight. The anticipation of landfall is part of it, but there's also the sailing itself – the swelling genoa in the running lights, the phosphorescent streaks running alongside, the soft moan as a bigger-than-usual wave lifts us just that little bit higher, then sets us down. Above all, there is the ghostly light all around us. Up there above the clouds the moon is rapidly filling. The clouds can't be very thick because a milky, diffused light is shining through. We get occasional skirts of trailing cloud, or it could be sea mist, and these are like swirls of the same light, only more intense. The reptile brain is prickling through the back of my neck, nothing that would appear in this light would surprise me: krakens, UFOs, a black-hulled privateer, a wrecked lifeboat, a submarine surfacing, a shining Buddha floating in midair.

As long as it isn't an unlit trawler . . .

Zaf is asleep five minutes after we're relieved, but I can't sleep. I read my book, potter about in stockinged feet, bring tea up to the watch, switch off my torch (no cabin lights – we're saving the batteries again, with the engine off). I lie there, too tired to think. I get up again and try to read. No good. I think I'm getting land fever.

Day 20

Tuesday, 21 May
Pos. at midnight   N   38° 25′
                   W   32° 51′

About 03.00 there's a sail change going on – I hear them moving about on deck. Want a hand? No, go back to sleep. I must have slept because Charlotte has to shake me awake, the first time I haven't lurched to my feet when called.

Back to single watches with the daylight, but 06.00 has now become 07.00 by order of the skipper, to bring us into line with Azores time. Too tired to work out if I've gained or lost an hour, I'm on solo until 09.00, but have the rest of the day off. I feel stupefied, seedy, unlovely and unshaved, until Simon brings me a coffee of what is surely near-lethal strength, and I suddenly feel I've been plugged into the mains.

We're barrelling along, maybe seven and a half knots under racing clouds, when the cruising chute rips from top to bottom. Ziiip! Now what have I done? I can't leave the wheel, and the sail has to come in immediately, before it falls away in the water and wraps itself around the propeller. I yell down below, and Zaf is up in a shot. I point forward; he sees what's happened, and with a huge grin of delight yells down: 'Simon, boy, come up here. Theo's gone and destroyed the cruising chute!'

I start spluttering, explaining I didn't do anything, one minute it was . . . then I see the two of them are cracking up, cackling dementedly at my indignation.

'Ah, sure, fuck it,' says Simon. 'Sure, that repair was never going to hold anyway. We'd better get it in.' And they do. But I still feel responsible, so I stand there, helming away, and try to figure out what happened.

Why did the sail rip? The simple answer is: a sudden increase in wind pressure. The wind is an absolute given out here; even on a baking day in the doldrums, when all your senses and instruments tell you the world is absolutely still, there is, however imperceptibly, some wind. Air in motion. When the wind is from behind the beam, the mid point of the boat, the sails act in much the same way as a parachute, the pressure acting overwhelmingly against one surface. This has, among other things, the effect of opening out the fabric minutely, putting the stitching under strain. If wind acted evenly as a force, going up or down in strength in gradual increments, this would not be a source of unbearable stress; the natural elasticity of the fibres would absorb the strain. But a sudden change in the strength or direction of the wind can snap even the strongest threads, and that's one of the things that happened here. Naturally, sails are designed and made (some sailmakers now say 'built') to cope with abrupt increases in strain. This cruising chute, made of lightweight fabric, was a strong sail, but time and wear had begun to take their toll. Plus, it had already blown on the outward leg to Antigua, and this made it more vulnerable. It's even possible that the repair was too strong for the original fabric – the new stitching may have simply pulled through the time-weakened cloth. We've had a steady twenty knots of wind for nine hours or so, Force 5 on the Beaufort scale, and it's been gusting, too. Add to this another consideration: sea state. We have a deep swell, fast running waves, considerable rise and fall in the hull's motion. If we fall off a wave, unavoidable in this kind of sea, the sudden motion can drop the sail fractionally out of the wind; if there's a gust as we come up, then the sail will have sagged in the trough, will belly out forcefully when the wind catches it and – well, that's just when a sail will blow. I retrieve the memory of the moments before the sail blew. I see it fold in for a second or two, begin to fill then suddenly snap out – there's a pause, memory on freeze frame, then I see the slow rip begin at the top, come ravelling down parallel to but, interestingly, not on the line of the repair.

So, is there anything I could have done? Nothing I can think of.

The days of long lunches sprawled *en famille* in the cockpit are long past. Now it's mugs of soup, crackers and cheese, packet-mix bread if anyone's made bread. Magellan is long-retired by now; we need someone on the wheel at all times, and the long-term fatigue is beginning to tell. People are snatching sleep whenever they can, retiring into themselves. Small courtesies are still observed – witness Charlotte appearing just now with mugs of soup – but we talk very little. There's a great deal of gazing thoughtfully at the horizon whenever any of us is on deck.

We're getting long, heavy Atlantic rollers now – there must be a big blow 500 to 600 miles north of us. The barometer is steady; the wind is still in the west; by mid afternoon we're only 100 miles from Faial. It appeals to us all that we're getting real sailing weather on the final approach.

I'm enjoying the long rollers – when I can get Simon off the wheel. I've taught myself a technique for surfing these waves: you cut across the face of the swell at a shallow angle, heading up into the wind, then, when she lifts and the deck comes up against the soles of your feet, you lean your full body weight on the wheel, fall off in the direction of the swell, keeping the feet planted; then let your body and the wheel fall back again to the vertical, the hands loose.

Get this right, and she surges forward on the chosen course, settling flat as on a cushion of air, the stern falling below and behind the centre of effort, the bow wave curling off evenly to each side. It feels like a kind of magic. I don't know if it's illusion or not, but there is a palpable sense that sailing like this you are picking up speed, too. The catch with this kind of fun is you have to keep a close eye on your average course. In the interests of keeping going, riding the wind as opposed to slavishly following the compass, we've been out as far as 127° magnetic early this morning; at this point we ideally need 095°, or 080° true, in order to fall in on the coast exactly where we want to be, a few miles north of Horta on Faial's west coast. If you stray off course for even five minutes, a big correction is needed to bring her back on line. You have to pick your moment for this, unless you want to get broadsided by a big wave which will roll the boat heavily over, cause chaos below and even, a hanging offence, tip the skipper out of his bunk. And, of course, you keep looking over your shoulder for the pair of rogues rushing up on you unexpectedly.

There are scraps and tatters of white cloud racing by now, out to the horizon. The waves are nearly all white-capped, the troughs look deeper than the waves look high, everything everywhere seems in motion, and the boat is a big, graceful and heavy thing, plunging on.

When Simon cajoles me off the wheel in the last of the daylight, I go below and potter. First, find the Q flag, yellow square. We need that for customs. Next, find the pilotage plan in my notebook, refresh the memory, double-check against *Atlantic Pilot*. Leave *Atlantic Pilot* at nav station for skipper, relevant page marked. Charlotte has been gathering up the used sheets, pillow cases, towels and tea towels. Black plastic bags are beginning to accumulate in the saloon. I bag my own washing; look out something reasonably smart for the morning. There's a deal of showering going on, now that the engine's back on. Zaf has been fingering his beard thoughtfully, obviously wondering whether to keep it or not. The door to Simon's cabin reveals something not unlike a pristine monastic cell, an apparition so unlikely we all keep glancing in every time we go into the galley. The galley itself is in mint condition – somebody's been polishing the stainless-steel worktops. The heads are gleaming, too; the saloon table has a rich sheen to it in the fading light of evening. Wet-weather gear has vanished from the heads and from the engine room; the empty water containers in the embryo bank have been separated from the full ones, ready to be dumped in a skip ashore with the rest of the rubbish. Now everyone's busy suddenly, as Charlotte begins preparations for dinner. The skipper lays the table, digs out a bottle of wine, polishes the glasses.

He's up and down to the cockpit, ensconced at the nav station, up on deck checking, checking, checking, unable to keep still. Now with the dark the restlessness is getting palpable; the air itself is beginning to prickle with unarticulated expectation. People's movements are quick but contained, as if muscles are tightening up as attention comes more and more alive. Seated at dinner, we are all of us constantly listening for shifts in the wind, glancing up and out through the portlights.

At 22.19 exactly the engine dies. Out of diesel. OK, says Zaf, tomorrow morning we'll rig up a feed from one of the jerry cans. We press on under sail, the main boomed well out, the genoa likewise poled out. The wind's gone around into the north, ideal for our purposes. We are holding a perfect course, and suddenly I get a rush when I think of this: fifty miles off Faial, nearly 2,700 miles behind us, and we're falling into port on a dead straight line. Hats off, I think, and puzzle the skipper when he appears beside me by actually raising my hat to him, pointing wordlessly at the chart. He peers over my shoulder at the latest position, looks at me over his glasses and gives a Robert De Niro shrug-and-headshake.

Off watch, nothing remaining to be done, the mate sleeps; we persuade Zaf to get some rest, and around midnight, to my surprise, I fall asleep myself.

Day 21

Wednesday, 22 May
Pos. at midnight   N   38° 28'
                    W   29° 18'

At 03.00 I am wide awake. I shake myself into a jacket and go up to join Simon on watch. There's a reef in the mainsail, the genoa is out full and we're powering along at about seven knots when, suddenly, the low hump of Faial appears on the skyline. There are a couple of trawlers off to starboard, a good way off. The night is so clear we can make out their hulls, never mind their lights, and Simon is absolutely sure it's Faial. I scramble below and flick on the radar, which takes an agonizing forty-five seconds to warm up; I punch the range out to thirty-two miles and there it is, dead ahead. Simon sticks his head down; I point to the screen. We grin at each other, him on the wheel, me back in the cockpit beside him; we nod one, two, three, and roar: 'LAND AHOY!' It feels so good we count to three, and yell it again.

'OK, OK,' from a drowsy skipper. 'Good. Excellent.'

'Land?' from the port cabin. 'Yeah,' says Simon, 'About twenty-five miles.'

'Right,' says the mate, falling back to sleep again with a faint grin on her face.

Simon beats me to the log: 'LAND AHOY! Bearing 101°, speed 6.7 knots, wind nor'-nor'-west, visibility good, 03.30 hrs. (Lights, even!)' We can't see the light itself, but we have the loom – like car headlights over the top of a hill before you can see the car – of Vale Formosa light at the west end of the island, dead ahead. Distance to harbour, thirty-five miles.

As dawn comes, so do Zaf and Charlotte. At 05.25 we have the Vale Formosa light in view, which puts us thirteen miles out according to the *Atlantic Pilot* – bang on, when we check it against the GPS waypoint. This convergence of reckoning and record is inexplicably pleasing. It's like that satisfying click inside your head that I remember from childhood when a geometry theorem proves itself out.

We are done with reckoning now; it's eyeball navigation from here on in. The past twenty days have been an exercise in instructed faith, a trust in instruments and chart, in the skipper's judgement, in our own capacity to be not deluded. We have been in a trackless place, making our own track to a place we believe is there, sustained by the record. I think for a fleeting moment of the thousands, the millions of observations, notations checked and cross-checked, distances measured, remeasured, measured again and noted down by generation after generation of seafarers, cartographers – all those who have literally gone before us. In Antigua, at the crew briefing, Zaf had spread the chart on the saloon table, traced out our likely course, his fingertip resting on the dot marked 'Faial'. Day after day we have marked our progress on this chart, each line pushing further and further out into the void, as sure as we could make ourselves be that the last short line would terminate on the flank of the island that we can see now, actually see, as the light grows in the grey sky and the black hump on the horizon turns slowly to red and brown and green.

But, we're not in yet. There's shipwork to be done. Up come the binoculars, both pairs. We pass them from hand to hand. We check the photographs in the *Atlantic Pilot*: that's Faial, no doubt about it; there's Pico to the east of it, the volcanic peak unmistakable, tip of it coming visible above the thick, banked cloud on its flank. There's grey cloud over Faial, right down into the treeline, but it's lifting. A white mark on the near face of the island resolves into the control tower for the airfield. We'll make in for that, says Zaf, sighting over the compass for a rough bearing, then turn to starboard, make our way down the coast. Simon heads for the galley; we harden in the main, take in a few rolls in the genoa. Zaf gets the jerry can of diesel from the cockpit locker, and we go below to the engine room. First we rig a siphon from the jerry can, a kind of header tank, then we bleed the engine into a shallow can. Zaf lashes the jerry can to some pipework, sends me up to start the engine. It fires first time; I throttle it back to 1,200 revs and, hey, we're motoring again.

I've just gone below to give Zaf the thumbs up when Charlotte above on the wheel calls, 'Dolphins!' We head up, Simon scrambling on our heels. Two pairs, on our starboard bow, rising and plunging, a welcoming committee. Charlotte begins to tack along the west coast of this Irish-looking island; we can't take our eyes off it, the greenness of it, the sight of an early car on the road to Horta. We want some kind of acknowledgement, I suppose, some sign that someone ashore is aware of our coming, but we are just the first yacht of the day. We run up the Q flag and a small Portuguese courtesy flag on a light halyard to the starboard main spreader. We bring up a kedge anchor and lay it on deck right forward, just in case the engine fails with the sails down and we have to anchor. We flake out chain on deck, in case we need to let go in a hurry. Now Charlotte calls, 'Ready about,' and we are past the south tip of the island; she gybes us and now we are making our ghostly way along the south coast, the spires of Horta and the cranes of the inner harbour just visible over the low neck of rock before the swell of headland that marks the turn east. Coffee in one hand, glasses in the other, I make out a small tanker coming in from Pico, her topworks just catching the early sun. Zaf has his eye on her, reckons that at this rate we'll make the harbour mouth before she does, throttles back to let her get in ahead. Now we can see the harbour wall ahead of us; now it's beside us, maybe a hundred metres off. Charlotte and Zaf in the cockpit are reading off the pilotage from my notes; Simon's on watch in the pulpit. I have a signal on my mobile, but I won't phone home, not yet. Zaf calls me back: time to call the harbourmaster.

Channel 11. I take the fist-mike in my hand, hesitate, shy for some reason, then press the button.

'Horta Marina, Horta Marina, this is sailing yacht *Spirit of Oysterhaven*, *Spirit of Oysterhaven*. *Bom dia*. We request a berth, please. Over.'

A pause, then:

'*Spirit of Oysterhaven*, this is Horta Marina. Good morning. What length are you, please? Over.'

We're seventy feet – what's that in metres? Charlotte, who's heard this before, says, 'Tell him twenty-two metres.' I tell him twenty-two metres. He asks what draught; I tell him three metres. Simon and Zaf have dropped the main, are flaking it on the boom. The genoa's already rolled in.

'*Spirit of Oysterhaven*, Horta Marina. Please go to the reception quay near the marina office. Over.'

'Horta Marina, *Spirit of Oysterhaven*, will do. *Muito obrigado*. Out.'

The tanker makes in ahead of us, low in the water. We've turned the wall now; it's wide in here, another wall to our right, a forest of masts sticking up over it, the inner marina. Ahead of us, big, white warehouses; a large container ship to port, unloading; the town climbing up in white and red and green terraces to the right. Zaf has taken over on the wheel:

'We'll come in starboard-to,' he says; we put out the fenders, tying them to the guardrail for now. There's the marina office; there's the reception quay. Men in white shirts are waiting to take the lines; the bow goes in, Zaf guns the throttle, puts the wheel over, a burst of reverse and we're settling to the dock, a soft hiss from the fenders as we touch. Simon throws the bow line, I throw the after line, and everything stops. The guys on the dock make us fast, give us a friendly nod and walk away. We just stand where we are for a second or two, looking at each other, then one by one we walk back to the cockpit, shake hands with Zaf; then we are hugging each other, nobody saying much, then everyone chattering at once. Zaf looks at us all, grins one of those face-splitting grins, pushes his cap back on his head and says: 'Well, looks like we made it, eh? Well done everyone. We made it, eh? Bloody hell, eh? Congratulations.'

I jump down on the dock, walk away a few metres, turn and look back. She looks beautiful, at rest. Some guy going by stops and looks at her. 'Nice boat,' he says. 'Where are you in from?' Antigua, I say, and hope it sounds casual. He looks me in the eye; he understands. Smiles. 'Good passage?' 'Fine, fine. Twenty-one days.' He has a cigarette in his hand; he sees me look at it, fishes the pack out of his pocket. I don't even hesitate, I take one, stick it in my mouth, bend over the match, inhale. I thank him, walk away, a bit stiff and dizzy now, sit down with my feet dangling over the dock, take the phone out of my pocket, tap in the number. She answers second ring, and for five or six seconds I can't speak.

In the log, in Charlotte's emphatic hand, it says: '10.30, arrival Horta! With champagne.'

PART THREE

Horta

Wednesday

After three weeks with nothing but the sea and the sky and the boat and each other to look at, it takes a while for the eyes to adjust to the closeness of things – the high-banked town, the regular lines of the buildings, the other boats, the variety of colour, texture, tone in the physical world: everything seems as if it is crowding in on you. We spend the first hour or so getting on and off the boat, looking up at the town, turning and looking out to sea again. Getting our bearings.

Yes, we walk funny for a bit, with the rolling gait of the cartoon sailor; yes, in the approved tradition, we all want a drink. First, though, and very much to our credit, we clean down the boat. The garbage is offloaded into nearby skips; lines are coiled and stowed; the sail covers go on; we get a freshwater hose from the dockside and wash an extraordinary amount of salt off coachroofs and deck, out of the cockpit and off the brightwork. This is practical, of course, but it is also a matter of pride: we want *Spirit* to look her best, and we want to give a good account of ourselves as businesslike sailors. There are dozens of boats in the marina, more arriving as we busy ourselves, others leaving; Horta is one of the crossroads of the ocean, and everyone is scrutinized, particularly new-comers. Already we are attracting visitors, sailors of all nation-alities who stroll up in ones and twos, with friendly questions and friendly advice. They study *Spirit* from stem to stern, eyes darting this way and that; we feel ourselves included in their approval. What I notice with particular pleasure is that we all get on with the work while talking, seeing what needs to be done and doing it, with no need of orders from the skipper.

Zaf gets the grab bag from the cockpit locker, the small yellow barrel we would have taken with us if we'd been forced to abandon ship, and brings it down to the saloon. Solemnly he hands us back our wallets, gathers up the papers and passports, and hands them to Charlotte. Nobody says anything, but we are all thinking the same thing: anything could have happened out there, but it didn't.

Charlotte and I go to visit the marina office, then the Policia Maritima and finally the Alfandega, the customs, in prefabs around the corner from where we are berthed. The officials are low-key and courteous in the Portuguese manner. When we are done, we step out into the bright sunlight and look across at *Spirit*. She sits to the wall, low and gleaming – I have no idea what Charlotte is thinking, but I have a strong and sober sense that this boat is a living thing, that it is she who has crossed the ocean, carrying us with her, and now she has gone to sleep, now she can rest.

'A beer?' I ask Charlotte.

'Certainly,' she says.

Zaf and Simon have changed into fresh clothes, and suddenly they have a thirsty look about them. I think I must have changed, washed and shaved all at the same time because I have the impression I'm back on the dock before Zaf has finished the sentence he was beginning when I flew below. We don't have to discuss where we are going.

Among yachtsmen, Peter's Café Sport may be the most famous pub in the world. Painted blue and grey among the white buildings of the waterfront, it stands over the harbour on a curving hill that runs from the marina entrance along a high bank and on down to the corner of the harbour where the local fishing boats are moored or drawn up out of the water. From Peter's, anything heading into or out of Horta can be seen. On the low wall across the road from the bar, looking down on the inner quay, out across the pontoons and across to Pico, there is a permanent parliament in session whenever the bar is open.

It's near noon when we get there, a three-minute walk from our berth, but already the wall is full of sailors, and the brown interior is throbbing when we push through the door under the carved whale and find ourselves a table near the bar. The barman with his hand on the tap raises an eyebrow, and Zaf shows him four fingers. The beers are long, amber and cool. We just sit there looking at them, then lift our glasses in a silent toast. As mine vanishes in one long swallow, I catch the barman's eye, or rather his eyebrow. He starts filling the next four right away. Menus appear, we order something to eat. The bar is a Babel of voices and accents – Swedish and Dutch, German and English, sibilant high-speed French and boisterous Danish. Red faces, sun-faded shirts, shorts and jackets, animated tables of six and more, occasional solitary figures staring bemusedly into space. Here and there, uncon-cerned with any of this, groups of local men and women, distinguishable by their business attire, their highly polished shoes. The walls are plastered with flags of every nationality, pennants from boats and cruising clubs, faded sepia photo-graphs of whaling and cable ships, carvings in whale bone, scrimshaw, testimonials from crews that have long since sailed out of harbour and turned their faces again towards the ocean. Plates of shrimp, fried potatoes, pan-fried fish, soup and God knows what else fly through the air, balanced on the hands of weaving acrobats in white shirts. Through the open door, framing a brilliant picture, we can see over the sea wall on the far side. We watch the yachts, the ferry from Pico and the occasional cargo boat come and go, and slowly, slowly, it is borne in on us that we are in, but we are not yet home. Zaf calls another round, we raise four fresh glasses and Simon, bursting out of his skin, sweeps the whole room in a look, turns back to us and says, 'Jaysus, lads, this is a great place, isn't it?' We're here for a while it seems.

There's a figure sitting on deck; we see her as we come down the ramp into the marina. Anne Boyd is joining us for the next leg, a racing sailor out of Kinsale who wants to get some deep-water experience. She appeared not long after we tied up, had been expecting us in the afternoon and took a bus tour of the island to pass the time; now she's back. We've been wondering what it will be like, having a new person join the trip. Disparate group that we are, we have forged a bond, naturally, in the three weeks we've been at sea, and there is a certain hesitation at the thought of accommodating a new personality. There's something else, too: will it somehow diminish the experience, making the last leg of the journey with an augmented crew? We set out from Antigua heading for Kinsale, having it in our minds that we would be touching down briefly in the Azores. Now we'll be setting out from here as a new crew, as if we have completed one journey, are embarking on a second. This makes Horta a destination, not a stopover, so that in welcoming Anne we are complicating our sense of where we are, what we are doing here. Anne comes with news from home – and we have been keeping home thoughts at bay, caught up in the spell of the journey.

Anne, unsurprisingly, is as shy of us as we are of her. Charlotte excepted, we are a ruffianly looking lot, and God knows what Oliver may have told her to expect. The universal solvent of awkwardness is a pot of tea, and two pots later we are all at our ease. The problem of where to put Anne is solved by my moving out of my cabin and permanently into the saloon. I disperse my effects between the hanging locker, the upper of the two pilot berths and a drawer under one of the seats. We are all at something of a loss now, the day drawing on and no changes of watch, no rumble of engine, no sound of water flowing past. We are so used to movement that this stillness makes us in some way uneasy, unsettled. Zaf is in need of sleep, Charlotte heads up the town to find herself a hotel room, Simon goes off in search of non-geriatric company and I wander up the dockside to phone home again. There is something I need to know.

'Tell me what it is,' I say. 'There's something you've been trying not to tell me.'

There's a long silence, so I know before she speaks that it's very bad. 'Joanne,' she says. 'Joanne hanged herself.'

I stop, everything stops, I have to sit down. This can't be right (but I know it's right). This can't be true (but I know it's true), not Joanne (but, yes, Joanne). I can hear Paula still speaking, then she stops. It must have been like this for her when she heard; she stops and waits while I wait, too, for everything to stop falling uncontrollably. Then I say, 'I'm here. Oh, love, Malcolm. Is Malcolm all right?'

'Ah, Malcolm,' she says – a long silence, our hearts are breaking for him – 'ah, Malcolm has been amazing.'

Joanne, bright eyes, that level look, her long luxuriant hair, such intelligent eyes. Such a gifted artist. This can't be right. That night in Vienna when they came down through the crowded tables and told us they had just agreed to get married – November, Jesus, only last November – the photograph on my desk at home, our four smiles, the light in their faces. Joanne – but, but how, why, in the name of God . . .

'Oh, I couldn't tell you out there. Oh, love, I'm so sorry.

It's so sad. I wanted to tell you, but . . . she'd been very depressed, much more depressed than anyone knew. Malcolm was back in Scotland, her mother had gone into town, she went out to the barn and . . . she hanged herself there. Her mother found her.' When? 'The day you left Antigua.' Another long silence, both of us struggling. Horta feels very far from home right now.

'What's Horta like?' Paula asks, and for a second I'm confused as to whose thought this is. It's a shrewd question, a gentle reminder that shock will absorb itself in time, that there's nothing we can say or do right now that will make anything come right. I describe what I can see of the town, clumsily; the boats around me, the boat nosing in beside me where I'm standing between the outer harbour and the inner basin. 'Dig where you stand' is a phrase we often use, and I hear it float by in the background now with its comforting echoes of home, mundane conversation, the blessed ordinary. I'll be home soon, I say, and she says, 'I know, love, I know. Look after yourself. Give me a call tonight.' She's going to, but doesn't, say 'I love you' because just as I'm going to say it, just as she's going to say it, it strikes us both that never again will Joanne say it, nor Malcolm to her, and it is all suddenly too much for the heart to bear. I have to phone Malcolm now, but I have to sit down somewhere safe first, collect myself, absorb this, find the words. Zaf sees the stricken look in my face when I climb back aboard; he takes my arm and asks what's wrong, what's happened. I tell him and he looks me in the eye, his grip for a second tightening, and he knows and I know there is nothing at all to say. Awkward, we half-embrace, as people do; I go below and curl up in the darkening saloon. I phone Malcolm when I wake, a long call; then I go for a walk through the empty tea-time streets.

It's dusk when I walk back out the long pontoon to the

reception quay. Directly in front of me, just ahead of *Spirit*, a Bavaria 44 has just tied up. Simon is talking to the crew, and I recognize the tall, commanding figure of John Pearce – Taff, the Welshman we met in the restaurant that last night in Antigua. There's Gordon, the jolly Scot, and Rab, the English lad. John sticks out his hand and I ask him what happened to the Irishman, have they eaten him or what, did he draw the short straw or were they just too quick for him? It turns out he never made the trip, got taken sick the morning of departure, day after we left, and had to fly home. 'Listen,' says Taff, 'we're off to Peter's. I promised Gordon's mother I wouldn't let him die of dehydration.' Gordon is sixty if he's a day; he must have a very devoted mother. 'Take Simon with you,' I say, 'I promised his mother the same.' I see the shadow cross Simon's eyes: 'You OK?' he asks, and I nod; I tell him we'll see each other later.

What can you do? It all goes on, and we go on. I find some work to do on deck, and gradually, hesitantly, everything settles. Every hatch and port is open, to air out the boat. Anne comes up the forward companionway with a mug of tea and says, 'I heard about your friend. It's terrible.' I am grateful for her simple directness; it is, it is a terrible thing. And there, as I turn, is the last of the day's light on the white-capped top of Pico, and beyond and all around us the empty sea.

Thursday

Waking, I hear voices, engines, water lapping against the sides of the boat, and I know immediately we are tied up in Horta. How does the mind work so fast? Up in the cockpit, Zaf is making lists, talking to Anne. Tell me about it, I say to him, and he looks at me over the top of his goldrimmed glasses. 'OK then, provisioning we can leave to tomorrow or the next day. We have to find someone to look at the gearbox, and the generator. Mid-Atlantic Yacht Services might be worth a try?' Sure, I say, give me a few minutes and I'm with you. The shore pattern has taken over already – neither Zaf nor I even glance at the nav station as we go by. It's a curious experience to shave in a stable head, and I nick myself.

A cloudless morning, a hot day in the offing. I feel more disoriented today than I did yesterday, less sure of my footing as I stroll off with Zaf along the quay past the marina offices. There's a large catamaran berthed behind us, dancing on the slight swell, droves of French youngsters coming and going. They have that raffish, mixed-up look that second- or third-generation French hippies have, a mix of rasta, hip-hop and old-fashioned down-at-heel. We stop to talk to them, discover they have been in the Azores for some time, island-hopping as the mood takes them. They are thinking of heading in the general direction of Africa, perhaps this week, perhaps not.

The boat is a curious mix of efficient gear and home-made embellishments – the cockpit amidships is half-playpen, the running rigging an eclectic mix of new sheets and old. It's the kind of boat that might set out for Dover and end up, months later, in Guadeloupe or Madagascar. Further in towards the town the boats are monohulls, newer, more purposeful – they lack the gaiety of this cat, the air of casual insouciance. Too many yachties use the term 'sea gypsy' as a slightly derogatory term: in the full and cheerful sense, these are sea gypsies, and one of the happiest crews in Horta.

There are paintings everywhere underfoot as we go. It has long been a tradition that every boat making landfall in Horta leaves behind a painting of the boat, or at the very least the boat's name and a crew list. Some believe that not to do so invites bad luck, and there are those who will list for you the names of boats and sailors whose skippers ignored the custom and subsequently perished. The far wall of this inner basin is where the custom started, and that is long since full. Now the quaysides are almost full, and as we go we are keeping an eye open for a spot that would suit us. There are a few beauties among the paintings, evidence that some crews came well prepared. Our Simon has been working out a design with me for over a week now.

For the moment, though, the priority is finding an engineer. In Mid-Atlantic Yacht Services there is an air of both bustle and exhaustion. A large portion of the Caribbean exodus is in port or has already passed through, and the staff has been working flat out. Engine oil, gearbox oil, some mechanical spares, filters – all these can be supplied, will be delivered tomorrow. A fitter or mechanic, though, may be a problem. They will see what they can do, but behind her butterfly spectacles the woman's eyes, it seems to us both, are not lit with the light of confidence. We browse in the T-shirt and souvenir shop next door, are pondering the omnipresence of the whale motif when suddenly the air is rent with the sound of sirens, long ululating sirens of the kind we associate with World War II movies, Luftwaffe raids on the docks of London. Whales, says the teenage shop assistant. Yes, we say, gesturing at the merchandise, whales. No, she says, and gestures out the door, they have seen whales on the north side of the island, where they usually come, and they are telling the boats. But, surely they don't hunt whales out of Horta any more? No, no, for the tourists only.

Ah. But it's all too easy to imagine stern fishermen racing for the boats, the American consul looking up from his papers, perhaps stepping outside to watch the galvanized fleet, hundreds of them flying the Stars and Stripes, jockeying and bulling their way out towards the killing grounds.

I wander along the seafront, climb up where the road at the top of the bank to my left splits in two. I choose the fork that heads inland at a slight angle and gradually lose myself in one of life's greatest pleasures, an aimless progress in a strange place. Horta is low-key, architecturally undistinguished, undramatic. Small shops that wouldn't be out of place in a provincial Irish town; people coming and going on small domestic errands. They are so used to boat people that we have become invisible. Walk into a shop and buy batteries: the courtesy cannot be faulted, but the owner keeps up his conversation with his old friend as if you are no more than a brief and unreal interruption. I like this a great deal, this sense that the relative importance of the permanent and the transient has long since been weighed up in the minds of the people, and the permanent has come out decisively on top. In too many places now you sense a predatory interest in the visitor which, while perfectly understandable in one sense, often becomes the established attitude in the shops, bars and restaurants, so that it is the local inhabitants who come to feel displaced. A great number of Mediterranean towns suffer to one degree or another from this malaise – Palma in Mallorca is only now beginning to recover, for instance, while Corfu is still running a high temperature. Horta will never become a mass-tourism destination, but I am also pleased that the innate gentleness of the people is appreciated by the many hundreds of sailors who bring a breath of the outside world, as well as a healthy dose of reliable money, to this island fastness. There is an air of tolerable melancholy to the closed houses, the short, sharp lanes that jink up from the long main street, the somewhat dowdy dress sense of the people. They are lively enough when stirred, but rarely if ever vivacious; they walk slowly, with purpose; a man may turn to look from sedate curiosity at a particularly exotic visitor, but he gives out no sense of insular disapproval: he is taking a moment out of a long tack towards butcher or bread shop to look at an interesting fish swimming by, that's all.

Mark Twain passed through Faial, in 1870; he was less than impressed, finding Horta populated by people low, importunate and unclean. We have no record of what these courteous people made of the bumptious Mr Twain, but I do wish he had been a better prophet:

Here and there in the doorways we saw women, with fashionable Portuguese hoods on. This hood is of thick blue cloth, attached to a cloak of the same stuff, and is a marvel of ugliness. It stands up high, and spreads far abroad, and is unfathomably deep. It fits like a circus tent, and a woman's head is hidden away in it like the man's who prompts the singers from his tin shed in the stage of an opera . . . a woman can't go within eight points of the wind with one of them on; she has to go before the wind or not at all. The general style of the capote is the same in all the islands, and will remain so for the next ten thousand years . . .

I should like to have seen one of those hoods, but they have, alas, vanished.

There's a jabber of voices from below decks when eventually I climb back aboard *Spirit*. Zaf has made a fine capture, a wandering mechanic of the French nation. A casting director would have Jean-Yves in wardrobe in minutes, the very model of a middle-aged buccaneer. More than six feet tall, large-handed as Depardieu, eyes scrunched up against cigarette smoke, long-haired and leather-skinned, he has the restless energy of the born hustler, is in and out of the engine room, up on deck and down again with a bemused Zaf trailing after him, drinking coffee, smoking, talking on his mobile and scribbling notes from what Zaf is telling him, eyeing me up and down, waiting to be told where I fit in the scheme of things. When Zaf introduces me, in a momentary lull, and I congratulate him on his strong southern accent, my favourite accent in France, he draws himself up to his full height and I get a very sober interrogative look. Excellent, I can practically hear him think: I speak English to the skipper, French to this fellow and in the gap between the two versions I increase my profit margin. It's so funny, watching the calculation flicker across his face, that I laugh out loud; he stops in mid sentence, looks at me, startled, then gives me a slow grin. And then he laughs, the fun of it all momentarily squeezing out the commercial rapacity. Laugh away, I think, as we circle each other mentally like knife-fighters, laugh away – you haven't met Charlotte yet. Charlotte pays the bills with Dutch suspicion, is notoriously and professionally resistant to being charmed out of Oliver's money.

Anyway, Jean-Yves has arranged with his colleague, Bertrand (the one who does the work, I think darkly), to call by in the afternoon for a preliminary inspection. Much handshaking, a clap on the back for Zaf, a knowing look for me, a touch of the old man-to-man stuff, and he's gone, striding off imperiously towards a big, blue-hulled motor yacht just settling alongside the jetty. 'Monsieur Fixer,' I name him, but I like rogues anyway, people who live by their wits. 'What d'you think?' Zaf asks. 'Let Charlotte sort out the money,' I say, 'and you keep an eye on him.' Zaf gives his special wolfish grin: 'Fucking hell, boy, he's something else, isn't he? Don't you worry, I have him spotted.' He has, too. Simon is wandering by, slugging from a can of Coke. 'Who's your man?' 'Him? Oh, just someone for Zaf to play with.'

Charlotte doesn't like Jean-Yves. That's immediately obvious when he arrives back that afternoon, and he walks around her with the nervous disdain of a large cat. Bertrand the colleague can do nothing with the gearbox clutch; he thinks, though, he knows what's wrong with the generator. Reserved, overworked, direct in his manner, he takes a coffee gratefully, like a man who needs it; his partner, on the other hand, drinks coffee for sport, to stay up there on the high wire. To nobody's great surprise, a part is needed. To Bertrand, getting this part means a fair chance of fixing the generator. To Jean-Yves, hands busier than Ariadne's, it's an opportunity to weave a bewildering tale of local parts suppliers, daily flights from Lisbon, complicated schedules, other jobs to be fitted in – the cash register is going into overdrive. Charlotte is unimpressed: he can try for the part locally; get back to her or Zaf if it can't be sourced. He is not – glacial emphasis here – he is *not* to order a part from Lisbon without first checking with her. I get the 'Women, what can you do with them?' look, am tartly pleased to see our happy rogue's confusion when I say Charlotte's right, of course, she's the boss here. He goes off, darkly disappointed that *l'Irlandais sympa'* isn't quite so *sympa'* after all. Stolid Bertrand, almost expressionless, gives me a quick look as he follows his partner off the boat. Is that a faint flicker of amusement? I believe it is.

We seem to have fallen into a kind of spell. There are brief flurries of activity, then long periods of mooching about the dock, short, aimless forays into the town. I'm rambling along the reception quay with Simon when we see the top of a tall mast go by the far wall. 'That's *Velsheda*,' says Simon, and dashes back for his camera.

The J-class yachts are the thoroughbreds of the ocean. Sleek, fast, tall-rigged and snooty, their low hulls and acres of canvas are irresistible when under full sail. They sweep you out into a child's dream of the sea and racing; to watch them go by is to feel your heart, literally, lift.

The entire marina grinds to a halt, to watch her come in. *Velsheda*, like her sister ships *Shamrock* and *Endeavour*, has been meticulously refitted at hideous expense. Millions of dollars have been poured into restoring these classics from the 1930s, and it seems to me that the awe they induce is as much to do with the fabulous expense as with the intrinsic beauty of the boats. Her brightwork is brilliant enough to shave in; her gleaming winches and deck gear flash and sparkle right across the harbour; her mirror-deep blue hull makes everyone sigh and, for a moment, think of the gelcoat scratches, the faint rust streaks, the scuffed timbers of our own humbler boats. It isn't the boat alone which is under scrutiny: her skipper and crew are under the microscope, and, if there's a murmur of appreciation ruffling along the dock as she sweeps around to and settles in her berth, there is here and there, perhaps, some faint regret that just this once there wasn't a fender in the wrong place, that the helmsman didn't lose concentration at the last second. Just one little sign that they, too, are mortal like us . . .

The saltier among us are derisive of the white-polo-necks-and-pleated-shorts brigade. The rich run their classic boats, and crews, almost entirely for display – or so the sceptics feel. Most people here in the marina have come in from the Caribbean, many have been at Antigua Classics Week, and we've seen the swaggering displays of wealth, the subtle and poisonous jockeying for position on the totem pole. We think the boats are beautiful, we admire in a distant way the superb professional skills of their skippers and crews, real sailors without a doubt, but something sours it. Deep down we have a profound unease about pride on the sea: we think it's dangerous to give yourself airs out there, that arrogance is a conductor for the lightning strikes of ill fortune. 'She'd be a witch on the water,' someone says, wistfully, and that breaks up the murmuring parliament that has gathered, sends us wandering off in twos and threes, looking back occasionally over our shoulders, shaking our heads.

We have lunch in the cockpit, five of us now, chatting away to the endless stream of people who come to see the boat. In her home waters, *Spirit* is almost invariably the biggest boat in the harbour; out here she's not, but something about her is definitely magnetic. Zaf is choosy about who he invites on board; they tend to be the more faded sailors, the weather-worn humorous ones, the ones who ask questions about sea-keeping, passage times, the rig. 'She'd be a good boat in a blow' is a common observation, as are 'good room below', 'a good boat to handle' and 'nice lines'. We warm to these people because this is precisely what we like about her, but what interests me most is the unspoken sense we all share that *Spirit* is a boat fit for the job. There are other longkeelers about, other steel boats, other boats that are both sturdy and elegant, but somehow this boat has a little of everything, perhaps a great deal of everything that experienced ocean sailors appreciate in a boat. Knowing this, we cheerfully list her faults, dwell on the minor problems that have cropped up, but we know and the people we're talking to know that none of these things matters. We mention them only to be matter-of-fact – and to deflect unlucky envy.

Anne and I wrestle the heavy mainsail over the side, stretch it out to its full length on the dockside, fold it carefully so that the torn patch is uppermost. This is a rip near the headboard, about a foot long; fortunately it's on a piece of the sail where the material is doubled, and all around it is heavily stitched. We spotted the rip the day we blew out the cruising chute, and studied it carefully through binoculars before deciding it wasn't going to go any further. Zaf wants to have it fixed here, before we get into the stronger winds of the northward passage, and Charlotte has pulled off the minor miracle of getting the local sailmaker to agree to do the repair. He arrives in a van, a genial, bearded giant of a fellow, Viking to the last strand of DNA, examines the problem and says, 'OK, sure, I have it for you tomorrow, OK?' Zaf is pleased. 'You must be very busy?' 'Oh, ho, yes, many torn sails, too much work, but what can you do? What are you doing out there with these sails, eh!' As if we were ripping them on purpose. 'Will this be expensive?' Zaf asks. We're quoted what seems to me a very fair price, much less than I would have expected anyway, and off he goes in his little red van, whistling a happy tune.

Simon, storm-faced after his labours trying to unblock the forward head, is not whistling any kind of tune. 'Come on,' I say, 'I'll buy you a beer.' He's halfway up the dock before I've got my shoes on.

The carved wooden American eagle in Peter's used to hang outside the door. It came from the stern of a whaling ship, wrecked after running aground during a storm. The blue-and-grey colour scheme on the outside of the bar has its origins in a gift of paint from Dutch tugboat sailors to the original owner of the Café Sport, Henrique Azevedo. These Dutchmen, stationed here from the 1920s, made a considerable living from going to the aid of distressed sailors in the brutal Atlantic winter, and they also, one fancies, made a considerable contribution to the building of the Azevedo family business, as they struggled to keep dehydration at bay through the long, dark evenings. The British companies engaged in the laying of transatlantic cables did their bit, also, as we are doing this early evening.

Henrique Azevedo was clearly an enterprising lad. He inherited the Azorean House, a combined crafts shop and drinking emporium, from his father, Ernesto, and moved the business into its present home in 1918, calling it the Café Sport. It was the arrival of a war-damaged British Royal Navy vessel that brought the establishment its present name. The eerily named *Lusitania II* put into Horta at the beginning of World War II, her stern blown off by a depth charge that exploded prematurely. A petty officer on the ship took a shine to Henrique's son, José, and nicknamed him 'Peter' because he reminded the officer of his own young son.

'Hold on a minute,' says Simon, as we digest this flood of lore from newspaper cuttings, leaflets, snippets gained from our fellow-topers. 'Why did you say the name *Lusitania II* makes you shiver?' I tell him it is because the original *Lusitania*, a Cunarder, went down off the Old Head of Kinsale, torpedoed by a German submarine on 7 May 1915 – the same submarine that, nearly a year later, would land Roger Casement on Banna Strand. He's a bit stricken by this, superstitious as all sailors are, so I go on with gloomy relish to remind him of the many times he has sailed all unknowing over her grave, as we'll be doing on the last leg of our journey to Kinsale.

The destruction of the *Lusitania* is part of the folklore of Cork Harbour. The bodies, such as were recovered, and the survivors were brought ashore at Queenstown, now Cobh, and there is a dark turbulence in the collective memory when that infamous afternoon is drawn up in conversation. That the *Lusitania II* should have been disabled by an anti-submarine weapon seems fitting, and reminds me of how susceptible sailors are to names, dates and other phenomena to which ominous weight may attach. For reasons I have not been able to discover, no one likes to put to sea on a Friday, for instance, which may be one aspect of the more general European suspicion of Friday as a day of ill omen (surely related to the traditional belief that Christ was crucified on a Friday); nobody likes to rename a boat either – guaranteed to bring bad luck, the old lads will tell you; it is considered unlucky to whistle on board ship, as it brings up the wind; flowers carried on board a ship evoke funeral wreaths, and are thought to put life at risk; the old windjammer men believed that, if a shark appeared alongside, it was because it knew that someone was destined to fall overboard. And so on.

Simon, God bless him, is suddenly hungry. On one of my forays into town today, or it might have been yesterday, I noticed that the hotel above the marina, once a fort which guarded the harbour, offers buffet lunches and dinners for a very reasonable rate. Simon has no difficulty translating 'buffet' into 'all you can eat', an idea that strikes him, child of the Irish boom that he is, as foolhardy on the part of the proprietors. Mentally multiplying his appetite by the number of sailors in port, then halving the result to allow for more normal appe-tites, I can see his point. We collect Anne, Charlotte and our trencherman of a skipper and go to try our luck. We are at first the only people in the dining room, with its polished silverware, small flock of waiting staff, linen tablecloths and substantial quantities of food. We feel somewhat under-dressed in these formal surroundings, but our shyness soon vanishes as the eager young staff encourage us to put their training to the test. Satisfied that there is no financial catch to the arrangements, five honest sailors proceed to put a dent in the Portuguese food mountain, and we are substantially better ballasted as we eventually hoist anchor and make our stately way past two or three other tables of furtively gorging salty types, out into the balmy air of evening.

Anne is for the bunk, Charlotte for climbing the hill to her hotel, and Simon and Zaf for Peter's; I want to call Paula again, have a leisurely ramble through the small detail of our different days. It's a pleasant thing, on a starry night in port, to sit with your bare feet dangling over the side of the boat, your back to a brightlit town, to chat of inconsequential things – who called to the house, what came in the post, how the garden is doing, how the writing is going, how the garden is doing, what she had for dinner, how the garden is doing – the small change of a rich and lucky life. It isn't like calling on the satphone, even apart from the fact that the signal doesn't go down after thirty seconds; without ever saying so we both realize I am three-quarters of the way home, and it will be a short, fast run when we get going.

Now, why does this nightwalking policeman have an American accent? Not American, he tells me as we shake hands, Canadian. He was born in Canada of Azorean parents. João, as I will call him, is a relaxed, friendly kind of fellow. He won't have a drink, thanks, not on duty. He likes the marina beat because generally the people are interesting. He has some good conversations with all the different kinds of people, you know? 'We get some Irish boats in, not many. Ah, you Irish like your beer, eh? But never any trouble.' 'João,' I tell him, 'you amaze me. Never?' He's laughing, but he really means it, never any trouble the Irish. It must be the salt air, I tell him.

It's a bit unnatural for me to be sitting here chatting away with a policeman. Something about my face makes officialdom in all its guises uneasy, especially cops. I have canvassed my friends intensively on this subject, and they are unanimous, almost, that I don't have a criminal aspect, so that's not it. We're having a quiet laugh about this and that, João and I, so I let him in on this little internal monologue. He stands back and looks at me, clearly giving the matter some thought. 'Tell you what,' he says, 'how long have we been talking? About five minutes, right? I bet you know more about me than I know about you. I'd say that's it. You ask people questions, and cops don't like that. It's unnatural. Makes them uneasy, see? I don't mind. I'm just having a chat, same as you.' Well, that makes sense. 'João,' I tell him, 'you're a smart cop.' He gives me a mock bow. 'Glad to be of service,' he says.

Simon and Zaf, arriving back from Peter's, want to know what's the story with the cop. I was trying to score some acid off him, I say. Simon's eyes go out on stalks, then he gives a snort – 'You're weird. Did I ever tell you, you're weird?' Zaf is impressed with how peaceful everything is around here; he likes the low-key way the place is policed. 'That's the Canadian fellow, isn't it?' 'Jesus,' I say, 'you don't miss much, do you?' 'Ah, I met him earlier,' says Mr Cool.

Something coming in. There's a masthead tricolour over the wall; it goes down as far as the turn in. We hear voices, the low hum of a diesel. She's maybe forty-five feet, new-looking boat, five men on deck, a windblown look to them. We keep a torch handy near the companionway. Zaf flashes them; they hail us; we call them in alongside. The dock is full, so they raft up beside us, Simon taking the sternline, me taking the bowline. We carry their lines forward and aft of us, make them fast ashore; they fix some short springs to cleats on our deck, and there's a deal of handshaking, shaky English, quickfire Spanish and French. Zaf ducks down for a bottle of Jameson and a fistful of glasses; we pour them a drink. François in the blond dreadlocks, chief communicator, is relieved that one of us speaks French. Zaf hands a large whiskey to their skipper, a smiling Spaniard with a sweeping blond moustache and big laughing eyes. *Salud!* He pours a mouthful into the water, and so do we three, then so do his crew. Quique, their skipper, dives down below, comes up with a bottle of Cuban rum and a box of Havanas. They're in from Cuba, a fast passage, delivery trip after a hectic cruise around the island. João is back with the marina night officer; he won't have a rum either, but he welcomes this new crew. Quique climbs over us to shake hands with him, chat with the marina man. Ah, tomorrow will do for the paperwork, no? They all insist on coming aboard for a good look around, are full of admiration for the boat. We swap passage notes, tales of our voyages; the talk is of winds and their absence, their vagaries, directions and strengths, of the longueurs of ocean passagemaking, the quirks and foibles of crews and skippers. It might be the night, the drink or the lateness of the hour, it might be anything, but round about 02.00 I catch a stray thought flashing past: I don't feel like an outsider any more. Somewhere along the way I have crossed the line between useful passenger and sailor. Steady, I tell myself, steady: you're only a very *beginning* sailor. I head for the bunk as contented, I think, as it is possible for me to be.

Friday

They're building new marina offices. The jackhammer would have woken me if the headache hadn't, and the thirst. I'm about to shave when Charlotte and Jean-Yves appear, their fates now intertwined until the money comes between them, as it must. I have no wish to be referee or interpreter, so I vanish into the forward head and discover in the mirror that what I took to be a headache may have a more interesting origin. There's a lump the size of a golf ball over my left eye, not painful to the touch, but throbbing. I lean in to examine it closely, can find no speck in the middle that would confirm my first guess, an insect bite. Here, Charlotte, what do you think this is? She examines it, Jean-Yves crowding in behind her. Neither can offer an opinion. There's someone on deck: the man from the Rosa Laundry, come to collect the bags. He suggests the outpatient clinic at the hospital. He even offers to drive me, but I take a taxi.

The hospital is small, clean, modern and efficient. I show the lump to the receptionist; she decides I'm not going to die on the spot and gives me a number and the duplicate of a short form she's filled out. I wait about an hour, then a young doctor examines me. 'Hmmm,' he says, or, in Portuguese: 'Hu-uumm.' Always pay the closest attention to medical para-verbals. This one means, 'I think it's probably something I

194

recognize, but . . .' – he pops out the door, returns with a younger, woman colleague in tow, hands her the magnifying glass and turns my face to the light. I regard her huge eye while she gravely examines my big lump. *Picada de inseto* is what I want to hear, insect bite: I looked it up in the waiting room, in my pocket phrase book. They confer; they peer through the looking glass again. 'OK, we are agreed,' he says finally, and she nods. 'It is a bite of insect.' '*Picada de inseto*, you are sure?' Now he smiles, wags a finger: 'Ah, you antici-pate; yes, look, it is very small, but here, see, this tiny black mark?' Handshakes all round; I leave much relieved. Still marching stiffly up and down is a man in sailing clothes whom I vaguely recognize, as he vaguely recognizes me. We nod, the relieved greeting the still anxious, and I'm off with my prescription. The hospital is on the west side of the island, and out there halfway to the horizon is a fairly sizeable yacht, making in on much the same track as we followed ourselves. Can it be only forty-eight hours ago? I walk into town, downhill, taking it all in – the clay-sand red soil; the fields as green as in Ireland, but with cane-brake fences; the Toyotas, Renaults, Fiats and Seats you'd find on the roads at home; the mix of bungalows and indigenous housing; the familiar brand names on goods in the shop windows and the curlicue flourishes on the church façades of the Portuguese baroque – I feel at home and far away, and the mixture is both reassuring and unsettling. Like the pharmacist who fills my prescription: she purses her lips when she sees my lump, shakes her head gravely, then hands me the tablets and says, 'Should be gone tomorrow. It is nothing serious. Probably.' And smiles.

Zaf is ensconced with Jean-Yves in the saloon: Bertrand has been and gone, there is nothing he can do, sorry, shrug, he tried. So, here is his bill. 'Oh no, no,' says Zaf. 'You have to fix up with Charlotte when she gets back. I have to see the diesel man now.' Jean-Yves is agitated, turns to me: cannot I make these arrangements, he is a very busy man, it is very inconvenient. I give him my best Gallic shrug – the palms coming up together then out flat, the head sinking into the shoulders, the corners of the mouth turning down at the same time as the eyebrows rise to meet the descending hair-line. Then I add, for good measure, a Portuguese medical '*hu-uumm*' and a sceptical Cork sideways look. Understandably confused by all this, he sweeps off like a minor demon, muttering.

Zaf's head pops out of the engine-room doorway. Is he gone? Yep. 'Jesus,' says my fearless skipper, 'where is Charlotte when you need her? And, hey, have you seen Simon?'

There's a big tug at the end of the dock, converted to a private motor yacht by a German who's big into ecological issues. One of his crewmen is a surfer, a callow young American who addresses everyone as 'dude'. Simon and he were planning to go surfing today, at a beach on the north of the island recommended by Peter of Peter's Café. We walk down to the tug to see if young Simon's there. He isn't, but *Velsheda*'s tender, a big motor yacht, *Bystander*, is tied up alongside, the big J lying outside her. The waterfront lore has it that *Bystander* was bought for the wife of *Velsheda*'s owner because she thought the yacht was too small to sleep in. We stand there, watching the crew wash *Bystander* down with high-pressure hoses. We wouldn't mind if they were giving her a quick wash to get rid of salt, but they are using hundreds of gallons of precious water, with summer coming on, to wash the dust off, to satisfy an owner's vanity, and we are disgusted. Somebody passing by stops, says she's a beautiful boat, isn't she? Zaf, with magnificent casualness, deliberately misunderstands him: 'Yes,' he says, and – gesturing to *Velsheda* – 'I like her dinghy.' I manage to keep a straight face, but only just. The man backs away from us, shaking his head, as if lunacy were contagious.

We find Simon where the marina entrance walkway meets the reception dock. He's taping a large rectangle of ground with green insulating tape, prior to laying down an undercoat. This is where we will put our painting. He has a can of white and a large brush in one hand, his sketchbook in the other. The plan is a rectangle inside a rectangle, the inner space to represent Irish skies and tropical seas with *Spirit* under full sail slantwise across sea and sky. Along the left and right margins I want to paint, in Irish, *'mairnéalacht'* (sailing) and *'filíocht'* (poetry), with *'Spirit of Oysterhaven'* along the bottom and five flags along the top, each crew member's name under their chosen flag – Turkey, Holland, Scotland, Mayo and Cork. To the casual passer-by we might look like idlers on a holiday, but of course this is really an on-site design approval consultation, an engineering and planning evaluation, a high-level decision-making forum involving all the principals – chief executive, contractors, designers and implementation personnel. The sandals, shorts and cans of beer are mere incidentals. On the chief executive's recommendation we adjourn the meeting to a suitable indoor location, where the ambience is more suitable to the decision-making process. From the front door of Peter's, as he points out, we can take a long-term perspective on the proposals before the meeting.

About an hour later we take a broad perspective on the arrival of Charlotte and Anne's provisioning expedition. By the time we get down to lend a hand the dockside is strewn with boxes, cases, bags and packages, enough to water and feed us all the way back to Antigua again – except for the meat, which will be bought at the last minute. The all-important cases of wine – one for each of us to take home – go into the pilot bunk alongside the new supply of water, and it is touching to see the seamanlike care with which we all ensure they are well and securely stowed.

While the loading is going on, Charlotte gets a shock at the bank. They won't advance her cash on her credit card (Charlotte pays ship's bills on her own credit card and is reimbursed by Oliver at regular intervals). There's 800 euros worth of diesel to be paid for in cash: we have a problem. The mate reckons that if we all draw the maximum daily amount from the machine at the bank we should have enough by Monday. As a solution, this appeals to no one: the diesel man and the newly arrived Jean-Yves want theirs now, and the rest of us want to be off to sea; we're all of a sudden landsick and aching to feel the lift under the keel, the wind in our faces. Now we are faced with leaving two days later than planned. And what if the cash machine breaks down? We fob off Jean-Yves and Diesel Man for the moment, while I try to persuade Charlotte to try Western Union. Finally she agrees, and I call Oliver back at home. By now he has forty-five minutes before the Cork office closes, and a thirty-mile drive to get there. I head off to the post office, only to be told they can't receive money before tomorrow. Back to the boat. Jean-Yves has an idea: we head off to his bank to see if the money can be wired via his account. No. Try the post office again: a cool shrug, nothing to be done. 'Come on,' says Jean-Yves, 'we'll have a quick drink.' We walk in the front door of a bar, down a brandy each; I put my hand in my pocket to pay, and he shakes his head. 'No, follow me.' We go down the stairs at the back of the bar, me thinking there's another bar downstairs, and before I grasp what's happening we are out on the street, his hand in the small of my back – 'Come on, *vite*, come on.' Christ, I think, we've just done a runner. No skin off my nose, but he has to live here, is the man mad? Mad or not, he's getting no change out of the brisk Charlotte, who tells him he can wait until tomorrow and anyway she's not happy with his bill; she will have to study it. Diesel Man, a gentle soul, stands there observing the ensuing comedy, volatile France meets imperturbable Holland, and, without a word being said, draws the correct conclusion: no money today.

There is money, fortunately, for our cheerful sailmaker, but then he's not looking for the price of a first-class air ticket out. The repair is excellent. We all tell him so, and get a big, happy grin for our troubles. 'Ah well, you see,' he says, 'it is just as easy to do a job well, isn't it?' Jesus, pal, I don't tell him, with that attitude in Ireland you'd be either a millionaire or a pauper.

Whatever about that, he's set me up for a very pleasant afternoon. There are plastic fittings, sliders, fitted at two-foot intervals to the luff of the sail; these sliders, T-shaped in section, fit through a gate into a narrow slot in the after edge of the mast and slide up the slot as the sail is hoisted. These are what hold the sail close to the mast – the top is secured by the mainsail halyard, the bottom by the tack, a reinforced hoop at the bottom corner of the sail fitted to the inboard end of the boom. Anyway, these sliders require work: many need tightening, some have to be replaced, and that's my job for the next while. Zaf helps me stretch the sail out along the dock; I get a pair of pliers and screwdriver, a bag of bits and pieces, a crate and a cushion. So, like an old-fashioned tailor, I drape the sail across my lap and start to work along the luff, tightening or replacing sliders as I go. I sit there at my ease in the warm sun, engaged in pleasant and useful work, chatting to occasional passers-by, pausing every now and then to watch someone come in, someone go out, and fall to thinking what it would be if this were my own boat, how it would be to have come in here off the sea with Paula and old friends for company – a reverie that presently takes hold, begins to put out shoots and roots, probing for the trigger of ambition. I've been content, over the past four or five years, to take any chance that came along to go to sea. So far, on this boat, I have nearly 6,000 miles under me, enough to have acquired a few skills and learned what my limitations are. I know what it takes to own a boat – money, for a start. I know what I want and what I don't want: I'm not about to start racing; I'd like a longkeeler for stability, a steel boat for strength, a roomy boat for living aboard when we're out, but also a handy boat for sailing singlehanded or shorthanded, perhaps two up. I want above all a boat of character, something that has, in the indefinable but definite way that *Spirit* has, a life of her own. I don't need what the old boys call a plastic fantastic: power showers, colour television, Kevlar sails, carbon masts, a stereo system. What I do need is a strong rig, sufficient instruments, good sails, windvane self-steering gear and a decent cooker.

Zaf breaks into my reverie: 'What were you thinking about? You're in a world of your own there.' So I tell him, feeling as I do that, far away as the dream might be, it starts to take shape when you put it to yourself, and moves into the domain of the just-possible when you speak of it to others.

'Tell you what I'd like in a boat,' says Simon, stepping on to the dock.

'No,' says Zaf, 'I'll tell you what *I'd* like first.'

Anne yells from the galley. 'Does anyone want tea?' We yell back: 'Barry's?' Anne is still mortified she didn't bring Barry's out from Cork, and we slag her every chance we get. Now, getting used to us, she calls up, 'Do you want tea or do you want nothing?'

'Tea would be nice,' says Zaf, 'thank you very much.'

And now here's Charlotte. No luck with Western Union, but the post office is open tomorrow. I think the unexpected business with the bank has unsettled us all; we'd had the notion we'd be three days here, now it's looking more like a week, and we're losing something, a sense of common purpose. Since we've come ashore, and since Anne has joined us, we've drifted apart. Anne is exploring the island and the town; Charlotte is in her hotel or in the Internet café when she's not doing boat work; Zaf is socializing among the yacht crews; I'm doing a bit of work, a bit of socializing, spending a great deal of time just sitting near the water, scribbling and thinking; while Simon, to his great relief, has found company of his own age among the crews about the place. We might as well all be on different boats.

It doesn't, however, look like that to someone on the outside. Hours later, on the wall outside Peter's, Taff is telling Simon and me how he admires the team spirit on our boat. 'You look out for each other,' he says. 'You see all kinds of crews at this game; you'd be amazed how often it happens that as soon as a boat docks everybody steps off and walks away from the others, as if someone had thrown a bomb down below.'

Taff mentions casually he was once SAS, so I ask him, equally offhand, if he really enjoyed those dark, wet nights on the Brecon Beacons, how he likes Herefordshire pubs, if he ever met David Stirling, how does a sailor cope with Oman, say, or Brunei . . . he wants to ask how come I'm so familiar with the history of the regiment, perhaps isn't sure he wants to know, so we bounce references back and forth until he says, looking me in the eye, that he never served in Ireland, and I, relenting, tell him about the Companion Book Club, which flourished in Britain and Ireland in the 1950s. My father must have had a subscription for a while, as most of the books in our house came from that source, and I read them all. One of the books was by someone called Virginia Coles: *The Phantom Major* is the story of how David Stirling set up the Special Air Service in the Western Desert during World War II, and it made as much of an impression on me as did Stevenson's *Treasure Island*, which I read at about the same time. Stirling's second-in-command was a Newtownards man, Blair Mayne, a tempestuous character who played rugby for Ireland at international level, won a slew of decorations and was inordinately proud that so many Irish men, from North and South, served in the regiment in the war. Somebody in Newcastle, County Down, told me a horrifying story of how Mayne died (in 1955, in a car crash), and I tell the story to Taff, who hasn't heard it before. I fall to wondering at the vagaries of life at sea. Under a starry sky in mid-Atlantic, a Welsh ex-special forces soldier and a freelance Irish republican, small 'r' important here, yarning the night away in happy equanimity; an ocean behind us, an ocean passage ahead of us both.

A passage by sea is a kind of stripping away, a scouring of attitude and habit that brings up the bone of who you most likely are. The process is far from an inevitable one – it's perfectly possible to come home as unknown to yourself as you were when you set out. And it's possible that the kind of confrontation with self that the sea may promote can leave you even more, not less, of a mystery to yourself. Well, who can say? We're enjoying the speculation anyway, taking turns to cross over to the bar, breaking off to engage in brief conversations with people who come and go. Gordon and Zaf are laughing their heads off with Quique and the boys off the Spanish boat, Simon is buzzing back and forth between us and knots of his contemporaries, when Taff says, out of the blue: 'I've been thinking about what we're talking about, and it seems to me that it's as simple as this: I'd be happy to sail anywhere with you lot.' Simon, fetching up alongside just then, impulsive as ever, says, 'And we feel the same. Actually, it would be the crack to go sailing with you.' In that artless and effortless 'we', Simon makes us a crew again.

I walk back to the boat, falling into step with João and his comrade-policeman the Smiler. 'Ah, Irish,' says João, 'the happy ship!' Neither of them will take a drink. Humming away to myself on the foredeck, I press redial on the phone, and I fancy I see the signal pulse arc up through the starry sky, an arrow speeding for home.

Saturday

Everyone got money from the hole-in-the-wall last night, and everybody gets the daily maximum again early this morning. Zaf and I are off on a tour of inspection, checking out the wall paintings, when we see Jean-Yves and Charlotte disputing back at the boat. 'Damn,' I say to the skipper, watching from a distance as the tall Frenchman storms away, 'I wanted to be there when that happened.' Zaf says nothing, but when I turn to look at him the penny drops.

Later, I ask Charlotte how it went. 'Oh,' she flaps her hand palm down, 'he had some ridiculous bill, but I paid him what was right.' 'Good, good,' says a solemn-faced Zaf. 'Oh, and the diesel man,' says the Iron Mate, 'him I have told I will pay him tomorrow.' A born fool, I ask: 'And he's OK with that?' 'Yes, of course. Why not? Now, we have to put these stores away.' I understand why the trains run on time in Holland, why the sea doesn't dare breach the sea walls. I rein in the impulse to give Charlotte a big hug.

We climb up on deck to watch *Velsheda* curving out into the harbour, her solemn crew at their stations. Most of the people around have stopped what they're doing. We are silent as she reaches the harbour mouth and the great mainsail bellies out. There's a flash as the helmsman puts the big wheel hard over, then the wind takes her and she gathers way at a surprising speed.

Beside *Bystander*, still with us, still dust-free, *Velsheda*'s crew has painted a large, grey diamond, bisected by a short, horizontal black line. Above the line is an imperious 'J'; below the line, in the same black paint, 'K 7'. Simon explains that that's what all the Js do; they have a big stencil on board, they all just put the J and the K, then whatever the boat series number is. *Velsheda* is the seventh J. 'What's with the "K"?' I ask him. 'Dunno.' I know by the way he's saying this that something about it gets up his nose, just as it's getting up mine. Give me that notebook, I say, and I sketch in a diamond with a crossbar, write 'SO' above the line, '1' below it.

'SO?' says Zaf, leaning in.

'*Spirit of Oysterhaven*,' I say. 'Or, shag off.'

'I love it, I love it.' Simon is nearly dancing with glee. 'Look, we'll put it here, yeah?' And he opens the notebook to his finished design.

'Maybe we should put in a pint of Murphy's?' – I wish Zaf hadn't said that. Earlier we had stood in reverent silence, bareheaded in the sun, gazing upon the painting left by an Irish boat, *Saoirse*: a meticulously painted, giant pint of Guinness, the boat's name where the Guinness lettering should be, even the fine lace frost that you get on a perfect pint lovingly detailed. We'd managed to shake ourselves out of that reverie, now this bloody Turkish Corkman is conjuring up visions of a cold, slow-poured pint of Murphy's incomparable stout . . . 'Get thee behind me, Satan,' I tell him, to the poor man's mystification. 'C'mon,' says the Mayo Leonardo, 'we should start painting.'

Everyone coming on or off the reception desk has to pass us at work, and most of them stop to watch the painting taking shape. Some have completed theirs, and now they're anxious to see how this will compare. Others have yet to start theirs, and a few are actually making furtive sketches as Simon's masterpiece begins to appear. He has made many pen studies of the boat on the way over, so now he sketches the lines of her at speed, a perspective drawing, the boat slanting across the two-tone blue panel with a considerable sense of energy. I'm the subordinate painter, charged with the lettering. For '*mairnéalacht*' and '*filíocht*' I use the old Irish script – a good decorative touch, we agree, but I just want this alphabet out in the bright air, by the sea, in the middle of the Atlantic, for the child I was who read his first poems in Irish in this script, before the Roman alphabet superseded it. The painting takes a couple of hours – with breaks every now and then to chat to passers-by, to eat the fresh rolls and Brie with salad that Charlotte and Anne bring, to drink a glass or two of wine with the shifting knot of art connoisseurs who tend to become suddenly numerous every time somebody pops a cork. We are perfectly happy to sit here by our masterpiece for hours on end, fielding compliments with, we hope, a certain modest grace. Word about *Shag Off 1* has got around.

We're scrubbing paint off our fingers, mid afternoon, when a big, shiny eighty-footer comes in, British flag. I can't be sure the Brigade of Guards accent was the genuine thing, but the skipper, a lad in his thirties, was giving it his best shot. As he was longer than us, would we mind awfully letting him in alongside the wall, then we could tie up outside him? If we didn't mind awfully? I still think that if his mate had asked, we might have considered it; the mate was everywhere at once, instructing his bowman and sternwoman, checking their throwing lines, rigging springs amidships, doing all the work. Hooray Henry was keeping his superior vision aloft by means of his upturned nose, and we took one look at the set-up and realized this guy was a dead loss. Even at that we might have made the effort, but then he took to shouting ill-temperedly at his crew, to no obvious point, embarrassing them and us, so we all looked at Zaf and Zaf just said, 'No. Can't be done.' A Swedish boat ahead of us on the wall would have had to move, and probably the boat ahead of them, too; we just might have all moved if there had been a hurricane imminent, but there wasn't, so we didn't.

Henry-boy would maybe have made it alongside us first go if he hadn't been in such a fine temper; he was lucky to get in the second time, with considerable unobtrusive help from the mate – unacknowledged, of course. Now this was a very handsome boat – all mod cons, a good seagoing design, handsomely kept – but nobody in the crowd that stood watching her berth would have sailed in her; I was impressed to see how quickly the look flashed around among us all, on *Spirit* and on the dock, the look that said *unhappy ship*. I admired the young mate, a fellow in his late twenties, for the skill with which he handled this delicate situation, saving his skipper from making a complete fool of himself, yet doing his best not to undermine his authority in any way. Watching him marshal the crew and reset his shorelines, I was thinking that lad's private journal would be a good read when Simon said, 'I'd like to have a look at *his* journal. Boy!' Then: 'What? What are you looking at me like that for? What?'

Sunday

At breakfast, it dawns on us that, with the exception of Anne, who was here before we arrived and who has worked at getting to know the island, we have none of us been out of the port. I want to see the *caldeira*, the volcano crater at the top of the island. Simon and Anne decide to come, too, so we three hire a taxi and set off. It's an overcast day and the light is flat, so that the green fields and the tall trees that line the hilly road are intense in colour and shape. I love this light, the way it emphasizes the *thereness* of things, just as in different mood I love the harsh, glittering Mediterranean light of high summer, when things seem made of light – fleeting. The vetches, foxgloves, grasses and herbs in rich profusion along the ditches are the same as, or related to, what you'd find in Ireland. There are pines in profusion, oaks but not our familiar *Quercus alba*, thorns, ferns, bracken; there are also large stands of eucalyptus, flowering shrubs I don't recognize and, marking the boundaries between fields, tall swaying hedges of cane. The *caldeira* is a great deep, green bowl with red scars of landslide here and there, and a poisonous-looking acid-green pool down in the heart of it, but it lacks drama, somehow. There's a broad panoramic view of much of Faial, nothing higher on the island than the ridge to our west with its forest of antennae in the now-encroaching mist, but I'm not so much taken with the land we see as I am by the odd scratch mark on the sea far below that signifies the passing of a ship.

We get the taxi driver to take a different route back, one that passes by the old windmill that looks down on the harbour. Just past this, one of the few tourist landmarks on the island, there is a large statue of the Virgin Mary gazing west over the island approaches, her gaze encompassing the harbour away beneath us. There's a walkway around the statue's base, a parapet then, and a steep green fall to the coast road. The walkway and parapet are covered with wax, to the extent that it's necessary to watch your footing, and in front of the statue is a three-legged cauldron, filled with sand, the remains of many candles stuck there at odd angles in the sand. I think of the three-legged cauldron of Ulysses; I see for a moment the view from the windswept site of his presumed home on Ithaki, the deep anchorage below, and I think of the three-legged cauldron in the cave of the Delphic oracle. I am a child again, in Blackpool church; there's a sharp reek from a guttering candle somewhere, the softer, more comforting odours of incense, and everyone's singing a hymn. I loved those opening words: 'Hail Queen of Heaven, the ocean star / Guide of the Wanderer, here below.' As a child they would make the hairs stand up on the back of my neck. I have for a moment that dizzy sense we all sometimes get when we feel uncertain if our lives are fore-ordained or not. Sometimes I think we are possessed of a faculty we use, but do not know how to talk about, an overarching consciousness to which everything that we experience as serial in our lives, one thing following another from birth to death, is somehow present as an eternal now. At the foot of this statue to the eternal triple goddess I have a profound sense of my life as a whole, a foretaste, perhaps, of that promised moment before death when all that we are and have been, all we have seen, tasted, touched and been touched by, is present at one and the same time. For just a moment I cannot tell if I am still that child, dreaming some Wanderer under Heaven's Star, or myself nearing fifty, a sailor of sorts, standing high above the sea, getting ready to go out on it again.

'You're very quiet,' Anne says, when we get back in the car. 'I'm not always,' I say, and Simon snorts. But I am very quiet somewhere deep inside that has not been quiet since I was a child. I realize suddenly that I desperately want a dawn watch: I want to stand at the wheel again, the dark fading, the light coming up, with everyone else asleep; I want the silence again that allows me to hear myself think; I want to feel the miles rolling away beneath us, the wind carrying me home with stories from out here in the world.

When we're down again at sea level I say I feel like walking the rest of the way back, but what I really want is to let this sudden feeling pass through me, to stop by the water and let myself feel that after all these years, after all the storms and banalities of an ordinary, yearning life, I have somewhere to go to, a place I can call, in absolute simplicity, home.

Well, home for the time being is this boat, as I realize when I get back. Zaf and Charlotte are hard at work, squaring away the last of the stores, tidying the saloon. I get to work on the galley, Simon and Anne on the heads, cabins and general areas, getting her ready for sea tomorrow. Charlotte has done a great job in keeping this berth; the reception quay is not a place you're meant to linger, but she's persuaded the marina staff we're constrained by draught and unable to move to an inside berth. Now she goes to tell them we're heading out tomorrow.

It's checking time again. Check the systems, the tanks, the supplies, the gas, the dinghy; check the sails are running free in their tracks; check the safety gear, the charts, the weather. Ah, yes, the weather. Paula has given me the Web addresses of the various sites she's found, Charlotte and Simon have been pulling down weather forecasts in the Internet café, and putting it all together we feel we have a reasonable chance of a trouble-free, fast passage to Kinsale. There's a big low off the coast of Newfoundland which shows signs that it may begin tracking east before too long; shouldn't be a problem, though, unless it dips south towards us in its progress. Depending on where it is when we get close to the Irish coast, it may even give us a strong lift for the last day or two. For all that, it would be good to have a source of weather information aboard – we've not been having much luck with the single sideband radio – and I promise myself that, if the lottery does the right thing for me while I'm out here, *Spirit* is getting a top-of-the-range Navtex as a present when I get home.

My list-making itch needs scratching. It occurs to me I should make a list of what I've brought on board as personal gear – not just as an exercise in clearing my mind, but to see, when we get home, what I needed and what I didn't. And besides, it's nearly time to put away the warm-weather clothing, dig out the fleeces, jeans, rain gear. Making the list will sort out what I can stow until we get home.

Clothing

Oilskins – jacket and chest-high trousers
Trousers, one good pair for shore, one extra-light for protection against sun, two pair ¾-length cotton, reinforced in knee and seat
Working shorts, two pair
T-shirts, four
Underwear
Socks, four pair, thick and woolly

Fleeces, two

Fleece hat, wide-brimmed hat for tropics, baseball hat for wearing under hood in rain

Sailing gloves, reinforced palms for handling lines

Shirts, three, one extra-light, two heavy

Footwear: sandals, deck shoes, waterproof boots

Big blue bandanna, for sealing neck against draughts, also for keeping sun off neck

Light cotton jacket

Gear

Knife with shackle spike

Pocket binoculars

CD player with discs

Camera and film

Batteries, lots of

Notebook and half-dozen pens

Books

Dictaphone

Towels: wash cloth, hand towel, bath towel

Sleeping bag

Toiletries

Shaving gear

Baby wipes

Sunscreen, one for high protection, one for medium

Sunblock sticks, applied daily to lips, eyelids and cheekbones

Tea-tree oil, sovereign antiseptic

Dioralite sachets, good for dehydration and hangovers

Add in passport, wallet and mobile phone, and that's it. Sipping from the mug of tea Anne has just handed me, I can't think for the life of me what I could have left out. It sure looks like a lot of stuff.

Now I'm, if anything, more restless. I look out the next chart, Admiralty 4011, and have a look at the course; I get out the dividers and measure the distance again. I take down the *Atlantic Pilot* and check the table of prevailing winds: this time of year it should be mainly north-westerlies – that tallies with the forecasts off the Internet. OK, now what?

I hear Simon talking on deck, pop my head up in search of diversion. Taff has arrived with a present for Simon, a fleece he'd admired for its crest – a lighthouse motif and the legend 'Lighthouse Marina, Hope Town, Abaco, Bahamas'. Simon will be twenty-one in July; this is a birthday present, and he's well pleased.

We're idly watching a forty-six footer coming in when somebody hails us from the wheel. We hop down and walk along the dock to take the lines from *Scudamore*, just in from Antigua. We remember the skipper, James, a thoroughly nice fellow, and we're talking to him when one of the crew, an elderly Englishman, says: 'Hey, aren't you Sweeney? Your father's the lighthouse keeper in Blacksod?' Turns out he lives two miles across the bay from Simon's house. The young lad handing me a sternline has a Galway accent. He's Ronan Hughes from Clifden; his family owns the hotel on the Sky Road.

Taff is standing to one side of this palaver, considering our artwork. 'Jesus,' he says, turning, 'you Irish are taking over the place. I suppose I'd better buy everyone a drink, keep in with you all.'

James, English to the core, shakes hands with Zaf, our

Turkish skipper, says hello again to Dutch Charlotte, is introduced to Scottish Anne, shakes his head, and turns to Taff: 'If you're buying the Irish a drink,' he says, 'there's an awful lot of us.'

PART FOUR

To Kinsale

Day 22

Monday, 27 May
Pos. at midnight   N   38° 40′
                   W   28° 45′

Charlotte has made the clearing-out arrangements with customs. We stow the anchor below; it won't come up again
until we're off Kinsale. It's just like the morning we left
Antigua, except now we know before setting off that we
won't have the gearbox breaking down – provided the engine-
oil trick continues to work. We won't have the 240-volt
generator this time; can't get the parts we need, according to
Bertrand. This means we'll need the engine on any time we're
in waters where it's prudent to have the radar working – off
Cabo de Finisterre, for instance, and on the approach to the
Irish coast. What else is different? Well, we won't have the
windseeker or cruising chute, but as we're expecting heavier
winds than we had in the tropics, that's not too bad. We're
ready to go, more or less, but some strange, last-minute reluctance holds us back. Zaf calls the safety briefing in the
saloon, spreads out the chart on the table, makes sure everyone
is familiar with our intended course.

Afterwards, Charlotte and Simon head into town to fire off
some final e-mails; I call home, using the mobile while I can,
before we get into satphone hell again. Anne is probably the
most impatient to be off – she came here to sail, and all she's
had so far is a prolonged island holiday in the company of
absent-minded half-ruffians.

We buy some funnels in a hardware shop, to make it easier for ourselves when we're topping up the oil in the gearbox, and I buy Zaf a white builder's helmet to protect his head when he's ferreting around in the engine room. Every single time he goes in there some bad-minded piece of machinery bops him on the head, and though a knock a day is doing him no apparent harm we feel delicate around Anne; we want to spare her the crude language in case she gets the wrong idea about us.

We plan to leave at 13.00, but succumb to the lure of one last lunch in Peter's. The unfortunate skipper of the English boat beside us is in danger of apoplexy. What do we mean we're not heading out after all? It's damned awkward, don't we know? 'Yes, yes,' says the imperturbable Zaf, 'we won't be long now.' And off we go to the pub. It's surprising how many people we have come to know. Somehow the quick lunch we'd envisaged stretches into a long afternoon of leave-taking; the mate next door is beginning to wonder if he's going to need the cardiac ambulance for his skipper when, finally, we find ourselves at our stations. Taff is ready to slip our bowline; the Smiling Policeman is standing by; somebody from the marina staff is patiently stationed at our sternline.

Zaf sniffs the wind. 'You know,' he says, 'we could sail her off the wall.' We think about this for a minute, gauging the north-west breeze. Someone ahead of us has slipped their moorings, is footling about off the dock; the Pico ferry is coming up outside the wall, preparing to turn in; the big English boat has moved out into the centre of the harbour – it's getting very crowded out there. 'Tell you what,' says Zaf to our assembled crew, 'we'll motor out to the middle, then as I bring her head around we'll run up sail, OK?'

There's a tension in the air now, a tension we mask as best we can in a barrage of farewells, jokes and insults. We suddenly want to leave Horta in some style, and there are a lot of people around.

Let go aft. Let go for'ard. We're drifting away from the wall; we're moving ahead at low speed; the dock and its knot of waving figures is moving away from us. Charlotte musters us forward, then the bow is coming around; I haul on the main, putting everything into it, winch it desperately the last two metres and make fast. Simon has the staysail up, Charlotte and I get the foremain rattling to the top of the mast in no time, then we are heeling over, catching the wind, gathering speed. Along the wall to our left people are climbing up and cheering, waving, cheering again, a long line of people. We feel like mighty sea dogs altogether, doing our best to hide it, but delighted with ourselves, delighted with Zaf, delighted with this lovely, lovely boat. We must make a brave sight as we thunder away down the harbour, the only boat this week to make out under sail. 'OK, OK,' says Zaf, 'get the fenders in and stowed, lively now' – but Zaf is the best pleased of us all, one hand on the wheel, the other waving his cap at the fading cheers, the dwindling figures on the long wall.

Spirit puts her head down and comes up in a burst of spray, shaking off the torpor of land, coming alive again in her proper element. Me, too. All of us. We look at each other covertly, as we scurry about doing small bits of necessary work and we are asking: You, too? Do you feel it, too?

The mate takes the wheel, we open a bottle of wine and I pour a glass into the sea, Zaf doing likewise. Anne hasn't come across this tradition before, and I'm at a loss to know what to tell her when she asks where I learned about it. I don't know, I tell her, I must have read it somewhere – 'Oh, it's always done,' says Zaf – but in truth I have no memory of reading it. When I pour the wine over the side it's like something I just *know* to do, from inside the meaning of the action. A similar instinct has me spinning a silver coin into the water, greeting the new moon and first star ceremoniously, if privately. We down our glasses, then Zaf gives me the look. We lurch forward to the peak, sea legs still not found, light a cigarette each and turn to face Pico to starboard. Ah, well, I think, we'll try again – and over the side goes the packet. 'You sure now you haven't got any stashed below?' No, I tell Zaf, and for a second he looks disappointed. We turn to watch Faial slipping away on the port side, the green sunlit uplands near the *caldeira* running down in deep gorges to red and white fans of housing at the shore. There's a briskness in the air, a sharp contrast to the balmy evening airs when we left Antigua so long ago. Northern waters, I think, and feel the shadow pass over for a second. A gunmetal hue and sheen to the water, a small, brisk chop.

There's an orange moon on the starboard quarter; we're heading almost due north now.

Dead ahead is Isla São Jorge with her lighthouse ('Fl W 10s' is the legend on the map – flashing white, every ten seconds), the last we will see of the Azores. Simon is trolling a tuna lure when we catch a shearwater. The lad is distraught. We haul the line in as fast as we can, but it's too late: by the time we get the bird on board the poor creature has drowned. Everyone is depressed by this. We treat it as matter-of-factly as possible, commiserate with Simon who's wracked with guilt. All those miles from Antigua with the same lure out and we never caught a bird. This is a freak accident; he shouldn't be so upset. But he is, and I am – for the bird, sure, but also because this death touches a literary-superstitious bone in me. True, that beady-eyed Ancient Mariner shot an albatross, not a shearwater, and he did it deliberately, unlike Simon. But part of me cringes to see the dead bird, thinks a dead bird is unlucky per se, no matter how it got to be dead.

Anne isn't feeling too good, retires to her bunk. Charlotte is fighting off her usual start-of-voyage blues. Zaf wants us on double watches until we get used to things again, so I take the 20.00 to 24.00 watch with Charlotte. It's a very strange experience. I have a kind of engine inside that estimates what's needed from the body, usually supplies the necessary energy. For reasons I don't understand, I am perfectly capable of running on empty for long stretches at a time. Tonight, though, I have to fight, actually fight to stay awake for the four hours. Charlotte hardly talks at all when you're on watch with her, which is pleasant usually, as we both like the silence, but it's not a good idea, perhaps, if you're struggling to stay conscious. We're motorsailing under a clear sky, moderate seas, no shipping in sight. I have to keep inventing little tasks for myself, anything, no matter how trivial, to keep my eyes from shutting. It reminds me of dead-end jobs I've had, the kind of jobs where the foreman or supervisor disappears at the start of the day and doesn't appear again until clocking-out time. I remember the metallic taste of slow time in those jobs, and how long, by the end of the day, it would take you to formulate the simplest thought. It's not as if Horta exhausted me; we should be – we are – well rested, well fed, eager for the journey; it's a crisp night, the boat's going well, we're headed home, for God's sake, but nothing engages the gears, nothing sparks. All I can think of is my sleeping bag; all I want is to stretch out on that portside bunk, the edge propped up by cushions in the old familiar manner, and fall into the trough, the deep backward and abysm of sleep.

Day 23

Tuesday, 28 May
Pos. at midnight   N   39° 09′
                   W   28° 26′

Couldn't, absolutely couldn't wake at 06.00 for next watch. A well-slept Zaf decided to stay on for three extra hours, then we went back to two-hour solo watches so that I was eventually due back on at 12.00. I struggled out of the cocoon about 11.00, shaved very slowly, made coffee for all very slowly, brought the log into the saloon and sluggishly pieced together the story of the night.

We've been making good time, from a low of four and a half knots just before dawn to a high of seven and a half at around 10.00, soon after the engine came back on and just before the mist came. Anne stood her watch, and there is a new hand in the log. She's enjoying herself, evidently: the entry at 02.59 reads, 'Brilliant speed for such light airs.' There speaks a sailor. 'Brightness to the east,' she notes, at 04.54, 'visibility uncertain, sky overcast.' Strange how even these brief entries in the log give you a sense of the person who made them.

The mist is clearing, as is my head. There's a slightly more pronounced swell, grey-black water, the crests sliding over rather than peaking, a skin-grain on the surface, as if from a thin film of oil though there isn't oil – there's no iridescence when the light flashes off the surface. The barometer is rock steady, has been since we left. I should be able to figure out what's happening and where, but I'm a little too groggy still. Maybe a spell at the wheel will clear my head?

It doesn't, not much. When I come off watch I help Simon make lunch – then, not due on watch again until 20.00, I fall asleep again.

I wake in the early evening to near-silence. The engine's off; there's no moaning of wind, but I can tell we're making about five knots. No hum of conversation anywhere, a faint periodic rattle of cutlery from the trays in the galley. I'm tucked up snug against the side of the boat, the sky through the starboard ports is grey streaked with blue-grey. No voices, so either Simon or Zaf must be sleeping: in any case, neither of them is in the cockpit. Anne speaks so softly, Charlotte is usually quiet, so it could be either one or both of them up there. We're on a starboard tack, so the wind must be still in the north-east; from the motion I'd guess the wind speed at ten knots. No banging or rattling anywhere, no slamming of bow, no dip and rise to set a lamp swinging. And from the light, without looking at my watch, it's after 17.00, but not much after. Rig? Probably full main and either staysail or genoa rolled all the way out.

I slip into my shoes, pull on a fleece and head up. Anne is feeling much better, thank you, and, yes, a cup of tea would be lovely. The others are asleep.

Zaf comes awake, goes through to the galley to make himself tea, appears on deck with mug, Simon and chart. I've been marking our position at four-hourly intervals, but from now on he wants me to do it once a day only. We plot today's position, and straight away we can see we've made appreciable progress. At this rate, we calculate, we should make Kinsale in nine days, perhaps a little more. The current plan is to go north to pick up north-westerlies or south-westerlies from the low now moving towards Orkney, or from the leftover winds from a big blow farther north. It's a gamble, I suppose, but an informed one.

A container ship comes up from starboard and astern, heading east to west, out of the Med, probably US-bound. She passes us about four miles off. These ships seem entirely unaffected by swells that make us heave and toss, though this might be an illusion caused by disparities in scale. We wonder if we're in a shipping lane. Time was when the routes were more or less fixed; nowadays there are thoroughfares, certainly, usually rhumb-line courses between principal ports, but there's a lot of unpredictable shipping, too.

Simon gets a batch of potatoes out of the deck locker, and we start peeling on deck. It's a mark of calm conditions, to cook something that can be eaten only if you use a knife as well as a fork. Tonight we have pork chops, creamed sweet corn, new potatoes – partly because we can, partly because we always eat the pork first of the meats we bring on board, and also because bland fare makes it easier for some of us to eat.

There's a sense that the whole boat has been in a sleeping spell, that we're beginning to shake ourselves out of it. Anne, despite her indisposition, is really enjoying herself, helming a boat twice the size of her own. Charlotte seems to be suffering less than when we left Antigua. We're not quite fizzing, but we're all in quiet and emphatic good humour. And Magellan is back from his hibernation in the cockpit locker, doing a good job, too, of steering while we dine.

Towards sunset, while we're finishing the washing up, there's a call from above: 'Basking sharks!' Zaf on the helm, we close in for a look. The indolent, insolent power of them. They laze on the surface, hence the name. No teeth, according to Simon. These ones are about twenty-five feet long. Not particularly fazed, one way or another, by our presence. I associate sharks, like the blues I've seen off the south coast of

Ireland, like all the sharks you see in movies, with controlled, purposeful intent. These boys are just lollygagging around; they can't even keep their dorsal fins upright, for God's sake! Damn things just flap there as if they were made of cardboard. We circle a few times, then head on.

A little later, between 20.00 and 22.00, still light after a colourful sunset, we spot a fin whale, and I pilot us gently towards her in smaller and smaller circles. She's docile, if anything more powerful than the basking sharks, beautiful but not awesome.

I like the sea, the sense that it is a rich and complex hidden world. I like having *laissez passer*, a permit to cross over.

It's going to be cool on my watch, so I go below for a jacket. Then Simon yells from the cockpit; everyone rushes up. Away to port, skittering at speed across the water, up on its tail, blunt head up, a whale! After sailing from Antigua to the Azores across what might have been an empty ocean, now we have this ongoing circus display. Of course, it's only to be expected, this close to the Azores, always a rich whale ground. These waters, in season, would have been thickly forested with masts, hard hungry men out of Bedford and Newport, down from Scandinavia, out from Spain and Portugal, scavenging the sea. A bloody business it was, too. No harm that it's over. Or nearly over.

To top it all, as if some cosmic prankster is making a point here, we have the sudden arrival of a half-dozen bottlenose dolphins. The usual daredevil antics off the bow, lancing through the water, daring each other to cut closer and closer in under our babystay. Simon, glancing over the side, says, 'Oh, hi, guys, how's it goin'?' We may be getting a bit blasé about dolphins.

We're bowling along, not a care in the world. I catch myself just about to start whistling. Steady now!

Day 24

Wednesday, 29 May
Pos. at midnight   N   41° 13′
                    W   27° 48′

Dawn patrol again. I love these hours. Castaneda has Don Juan describe the twilight as 'the crack between the worlds'. That's what it feels like at dawn, as if the world of night and the world of day are separate domes, or half-domes. I grew up the eldest of a large family, a voracious reader, a chatterbox perfectly happy in the silence of his own company. I learned early on how to shift the clock, to be awake when others are asleep. At home, our usual bedtime is 2 a.m., as Paula's childhood taught her the same lesson, and the habit took. It means, obviously, that we wake when the streets are well aired, when much of the world has been about its business for three hours or more. You live like that for a long time and the primal fracture between night and day gets fuzzy, blurred. When it's dark, you sleep; when it's bright, you wake and work: I've little patience with the kind of mind that elevates this primitive given into a quasi-moral imperative, but I see a certain attraction in being awake when the shift comes. At the very least it sets a long, slow simple pulse under the business of things. Lock on to that and you can slow down inside; you begin to notice things you might otherwise have missed.

Well, mooning about thinking this and that gets tiresome sometimes, and I'm getting stiff and cold as we plough on towards the north, so I decide to tidy the lines in the cockpit.

The lazy sheet to the genoa is sticking, the one that isn't under strain. There's always a chance the wind will swing, and just in case it does I figure I'll go forward to free the lazy sheet where it's hooked up on the forestay. It's makework, really, so maybe I'm daydreaming a bit up there, and when I turn to face back I get a shock: there's a freighter broadside on, dead astern, maybe four miles off. Heading, as far as I can judge, east to west. Where the fuck did that come from? I've become so accustomed to taking a good look around every ten minutes or so that I feel more spooked than shocked, as if this is an apparition. I can't figure what she's doing. As the light sharpens she seems closer, but her aspect doesn't change. No sign of life or movement. A ship, a black freighter. If Lotte Lenya's voice came booming out over the water, Pirate Jenny's mordant and cold-blooded aria, I wouldn't be in the least surprised. I tell myself rationally we were never in any danger, but my head is buzzing with questions: where did she come up out of? Why is she lying there, unmoving – engine trouble? Because if she's been lying there for some time, then we came up on her, passed her, left her astern, all without my noticing. In the end, because they are the only reasonable explanations I can think of, I come up with these: she may have been lying in a localized patch of sea mist that cleared away; she may have been coming up for a while astern on the quarter, and only stopped when I saw her; she was there all the time and I just didn't see her; or she's actually much farther away than I think, much bigger than she looks, and everything is otherwise normal.

She's a small dot on the horizon behind us when Simon comes up to relieve me. I point her out, and he just shrugs.

Five aboard is a great luxury: we have two hours on, eight hours off if Zaf stays in the watch system. He sometimes takes himself out of the rotation, on the grounds that he services the engine every day and supervises all sail changes. More than fair, by us. All the same, since we've changed the watch rota I miss that moment at the end of my watch when he comes up out of the companionway like a fox on speed, ready for anything.

Since yesterday evening we've been making a heading of about 040° true. This is a bit more north than we strictly need, but Zaf is still banking on westerlies up ahead.

There's an altogether more businesslike air about this leg of the journey. Partly this is because it's cooler, so we don't feel as if we're on holiday as much as we did in the tropics; partly it's because we stayed so long in Horta that we became impatient to be off; and partly it's because we are five now. We had a rhythm, on the long leg to the Azores, a rhythm based entirely on the watches; two hours on, six hours off, though in practice it became two hours formally on, two informally, four hours at a time for sleep. Now it's two on, eight off, and with more people to do the work there isn't the same need to be semi-available during your off-time. The unexpected effect of this, for these past few days at least, is that we all tend to sleep more when we're not actually on watch, which makes the time appear to go faster.

This is more like the coastal sailing I'm used to on *Spirit*, so there is a subconscious sense that we are day-sailing – or, to put it another way, less a sense of open-ended adventure. Setting out from Antigua, Danny the Rasta taxi driver's phrase was looming over us all: 'That's a vaaaast ocean!' It doesn't seem so vast now; it doesn't *feel* so vast – though it is still the ocean, and we are well out there in the middle.

On this passage Charlotte seems to be the one who's luckiest at getting a signal on the satphone. I talk briefly to Paula, and she has more sad news: Robbie McDonald's mother has died.

Sitting on deck this late afternoon I find myself, not for the first time on this trip, dealing with a growing sense of how much of my life is behind me. Thinking of Robbie takes me back to the late 1970s and the foundation of Cork's Triskel Arts Centre, driven by Robbie with the help of his cousin Anne. I had no idea, when I walked in the door to offer him some part-time help, that I was beginning a life as an arts administrator and manager, a life that would take me over for twenty years until I balked in 2000 and bailed out, seized by a terror that the books were never going to get written.

From Robbie I learned how to build an organization, how to deal with politicians, business sponsors, artists of all kinds, the press and broadcast media, budgets, planning, administration, management. From 'Wouldn't it be a good idea if . . .' to 'How do we make this happen?' is a monumental shift, and Robbie was my teacher. The best of it was, of course, that we were making it all up as we went along in those days, chancing our arms, half the time bringing a building, an exhibition, a festival into being mainly by willing everyone else to agree with us that it had already happened.

The French and German 68-ers came to a crossroads in the mid-1970s; they had to decide how to get beyond the streets, past the trap of direct action, the heroic but doomed gesture. The Germans coined the phrase 'the long march through the institutions', and that's what we were engaged in, though sometimes we had to create the institutions before we could march through them. I have a sudden vision of Robbie, and a handful like him, as privateer-explorers, charting and annexing new territories on voyages made without maps, and I am unaccountably moved. I think of *his* mentor, the late and much-loved Lar Cassidy, the man who more than any other believed in the Arts Council as a major force in the building of our civil Republic; I think of the light burning late into the night in his wind-tossed attic office in Merrion Square, his unquenchable enthusiasm, his battling spirit – and it comes to me that even out here in the heart of the ocean the dead are not dead. We leave no one behind us, ever.

I feel awkward, unsettled, almost embarrassed at what's going on in my head – as if standing here in the bows, an arm wrapped around the forestay for balance, I might be willing this journey to fill with revelation. It comes to me that it isn't the sea, the journey or any heightened sense of significance brought on by circumstance, it's just that out here, as nowhere else, I am learning to fall silent, to listen to the quiet music of my own life. More robustly, I realize that those two boys would love it out here just as much as I am loving it. God alone knows what arcane lore Lar would be coming out with, and Robbie, Robbie would be reeling in the fish, not a word out of him, grinning from ear to ear.

Back in the cockpit, Zaf and Charlotte are discussing the barometer. It's been steady from Horta until about noon today, but now it's falling, down five points in four hours, and it keeps on falling. The wind is still in the east, but there's been rain since 17.00 and a long swell from the north; probably, Zaf says, from a big storm way up there. He thinks the wind is going to shift, maybe south-east, maybe as far round as south. For the moment he orders a course change, and we head almost due north, keeping the speed over six knots. Anne, coming up to the wheel, is happy to have her sea legs now, happy to be at the helm in these interesting conditions. I think she finds it a pleasant change that we tend to hold our sails for long periods at a time, that you can settle into the helm, find the groove and just crack on. Like the rest of us, she enjoys the long, meditative silences, when there's just yourself, the boat, the wind and the sea. Also like the rest of us, she finds the helm heavy. In theory we shouldn't have so much weight on the helm: on a longkeeler like this, it ought to be possible to set the sails so that with a consistent wind, from no matter what direction, she can sail herself. This is an old debate on *Spirit*, but that doesn't stop the three wise men joining Anne in a rambling discussion while Charlotte is cooking up a storm in the galley. As usual with this topic, we can come to no conclusion. The favoured remedy is a deeper rudder: there's a kind of consensus that with her buoyant stern and steep cutaway over the rudder she tends to lift out of the water due to increased wind pressure on the main in a rising wind, especially in a quartering sea, but really we're all just guessing and, as both ways of finding out – fitting a new rudder or testing a model in a tank – are in the realms of fantasy, we don't really expect a resolution. Naturally this doesn't stop anyone from having a good chew on an old bone, and it's one of the pleasures of sailing, after all, this kind of aimless circular chat about the boat.

When I take the wheel at 22.00 we have 300 miles under us since Horta and seven knots on the clock. The wind has indeed gone into the south-east, twelve to fifteen knots, gusting a bit, and visibility is poor enough even when we aren't in mist. The bar is down another point. We've eaten well, I feel rested, perhaps a little flattened by this afternoon's thoughts, but I enjoy this trick on the wheel; when there's a swell running like this, coming in on the port bow while the wind's on the starboard quarter, there is a lively sense of having to keep the boat balanced. You are constantly talking to yourself – watch that one coming three crests back, a bit higher than usual, wind's dying back a little, point her into the swell a bit more, lovely, now here comes the wind again, point her up into it, yes, that's it, now ease her back again, watch the course, five points either side of 040°, lovely – and if you keep getting it right there's a sense of satisfaction that grows by increments until at midnight, when you hand over the wheel, there's a reluctance to give over. You want to stay on a little bit longer – the boat is talking to you, and you're talking to the boat.

It's sometimes wise to go straight down after a watch like this. You've taken some time to get into the rhythm of it all, and naturally the next person on will also take some time to get into the rhythm, and there's a danger, if you don't watch it, that you'll be hanging about giving unwanted, irritating advice. So I give Simon the course and go down to make us both some tea before turning in. Lying in my sleeping bag, rolled comfortably in against the side, I listen to the water sloshing along the hull, still second-guessing the swell against the wind, and fall asleep with my hands curled around the rim of an imaginary wheel.

Day 25

Thursday, 30 May
Pos. at midnight   N   43° 05′
                    W   25° 52′

The wind, while I was sleeping, went east again, then south-south-east; now, at 06.00, it's in the south, nine knots, and there's fog. The entry in the log says, 'Shitty Irish weather, motorsailing at 1,200 rpm.' A quick look at the radar, nothing in sight. I go up to stand in the damp and put in two hours looking at not much of anything. The attendant shearwater loops in from time to time out of the pearly grey void, like a mute Japanese poet on Cold Mountain. I wouldn't be too surprised, I think grumpily, if he shat a haiku on the deck.

I hate fog. Where there are other ships about it sets your nerves on edge; no matter how often you check on the radar there's always the skin-crawling sensation that something could loom up out of anywhere at any second. And even if you manage to convince yourself that there's really nothing out there, you get cold and clammy and dispirited anyway. There's nothing to look at except what you can see of your own boat, and somehow, in this atmosphere, you get sick even of that. It doesn't help my mood, either, that Simon early this morning had eight and a half knots on the clock: I was enjoying myself so much last night on the wheel, but how much better it would have been with another knot and a half up!

It's starting off a doubtful class of a day. When in doubt,

cook. The trick is to get the bacon under the grill while the oven warms up. When the bacon's done, into the oven with it; then get the deepest pan you can find on to the stove top and start heating the oil while the toast goes under the grill. You need the plates laid out behind you, the knife in the butter and the kettle boiling so that you can give your full attention to the circus skill of frying eggs in a moving boat. The good thing is we're not rolling; it's enough that we're rising and falling by the bow, the human wrist can cope with that, but there's no way you can keep a pan horizontal when the walls and the floor are all moving in different directions relative to each other. It's one hand for the pan, one hand for the toast and whatever part of your anatomy is nearest to a solid object for bracing yourself. With the galley stripped out, a slow-motion film of the contortions I have to go through would be a fascinating dance piece against a single-colour background. There's something almost supernatural about the smell of fresh-cooked bacon, hot coffee and fresh toast, the way the braided smells go sleeking about the boat, slipping in under cabin doors, invading the deepest sleep: by the time everything is ready, I've a full house in the galley – with the wheel calling urgently down, demanding she be not forgotten.

The log entry at 09.55 says, 'Wind south, 15 knots, main well out on starboard tack, very good speed, 7.8 knots.' That .8 is good – amazing how precise and good-humoured a cooked breakfast can make you. We've the mainsail and genoa out full, a fair bit of heel on and the bow wave is flashing past, white and green solid water against the grey swell. A blue sky now, streaks of cirrus to the north, a sense that we're romping on home. The wind goes south-south-east a little later; the speed picks up a notch or two until by late afternoon there's 8.6 on the clock.

Speed in a boat is a curious thing. Forty knots is hardly

remarkable in a fast passenger ferry, sixteen to twenty knots would be a fair average in a lot of ocean racing, particularly in the high-tech Open 60s, but 8.6 in a boat like this feels like Formula One driving. In this wind *Velsheda* would go charging past us, with her slippery hull form, her vast acreage of canvas, but the sensation of speed we're enjoying now is measured against what we're used to, and is exhilarating.

There is a theoretical optimum speed for every boat, her hull speed. *Spirit*'s is 10.38 knots, arrived at by the formula: hull speed equals 1.34 times LWL to the power of 0.5, where LWL is length of the waterline, roughly sixty feet in our case. To know that a boat is sailing at or near to her optimum speed, no matter how low that speed might be in comparison with that of the average family car, for instance, is satisfying. Sailing is an active verb, too: we speak of a skipper or crew sailing a boat well, and of all the things you can experience on a boat this is the most addictive. 'Sailing her well' doesn't mean only sailing her fast, it should be said. It means having an intelligent grasp of all the forces in play, from the boat's grip on the water to the winds, tides and sea state, condition of her rig, condition of her crew, and making the best possible course and speed in the circumstances. To be hove-to in a strong gale might be sailing her well, for instance, as might sailing her under-canvassed to slow her motion, in order to arrive at a port under optimum tidal conditions.

We know that we're sailing *Spirit* well today. Nobody wants to be below. A kind of gentle anarchy has seeped into the watch system. Zaf is too good a skipper to let the system slide, but he's also a shrewd man. He knows very well that we all want a turn on the helm in these conditions, so as long as the official watchkeeper is present for her or his duty, it doesn't matter who's on the wheel at any particular time.

Zaf, incidentally, I have taken to calling '*Reis*'. Boats can be surprisingly formal: in certain conditions we might address the skipper as 'Skipper', but none of us particularly likes the term. It's a bit too self-conscious for our tastes. 'Captain' appeals to none of us, least of all to Zaf. '*Reis*' is a term I've wormed out of him by asking what terms might be used in Turkey. It has overtones of 'boss', undertones of something with a little edge to it. Think of the way in American gangster films of the 1930s both criminals and cops would call their boss 'Chief', and you get something of the flavour of '*Reis*'. Think of it, maybe, like this: about five days after we turned east below Bermuda we heard from a passing ship that some Americans had been airlifted off a seventy-foot yacht a few hundred miles to the north of us, and she had been left to drift when they abandoned her; Simon, Zaf and myself had passed a happy hour or two discussing the possibility of turning north to find her and claim salvage rights. It was a pleasant daydream to Simon and me, but to Zaf – so I realized in retrospect – it was a live possibility: if his crew had shown any half-serious interest in the prospect, our *Reis* would have turned for the north, the grin of some happy privateer of old gleaming through his newfound beard.

Right now he's perched on the weather coaming, one hand on the lifelines, stroking the beard. 'Hey, *Reis*, you going to keep that beard?'

'I dunno, what do you think?'

'I think it suits you,' I tell him. 'It looks very dashing,' says Anne, seated behind the wheel, arms going this way and that, eyes straight ahead.

'The only thing is,' Zaf says, 'my daughters are going to make me shave it off.' We think about this for another minute or two – it's that kind of conversation, that kind of afternoon.

Eventually Simon changes the subject: 'What about when we get to Kinsale? How are we going to do it?' I know immediately, the way you do sometimes, that he's been think-ing about how we sailed out of Horta, cutting a dash. Now he wants to cut a dash coming into Kinsale, and he's not the only one. The four of us wait while Zaf considers his response – he's playing, really. We all know he's going to say what any one of us would say. 'Well,' he says, after drawing it out for as long as he can, 'I think the best plan would be to arrive in the morning and sail her in, you know? All sails up, right into the marina, then drop and stow the sails at the last minute, just use the motor to bring her into her berth. What do you think, eh?' He gets four big grins for an answer, then we all drift off into ourselves, imagining the homecoming. Somewhere up there, imaginable now, over the curve of the horizon.

Charlotte disappears below, reappears with a pot of coffee, an array of biscuits and fruit. 'Hey, Mr Calculator,' Zaf calls, 'what's the story today?' Down to the nav station with the notebook, scribble, scribble, back up. 'OK, the first thing is the bar has dropped about eight points in the past twenty-four hours; the wind's been going around from north-east to south-south-east.'

'Right, we've probably moved out of one high-pressure cell into another, and they're both probably still components of the Azores High. Those winds are pressure gradient winds, I'd say. What else?'

Scribble, scribble, calculate: at our present rate there is a danger we will arrive in Kinsale very late Monday night. 'Oh, that's not too good,' says Zaf. 'Better to arrive in daylight. We either should sail faster at about eight knots, a small bit more, or slower, so's to arrive Monday afternoon or Tuesday afternoon. What would that work out at?'

We would need to average 8.2 knots to arrive on Monday, 6.5 to arrive on Tuesday. The sage likes to err on the side of caution: 'Charlotte,' he says, 'if you get a signal, and you're talking to Oliver? You can tell him that at the minute we're thinking of probably Tuesday afternoon.' 'Jesus,' says Simon, 'that's, what? Just over four days?' Down he goes, like the White Rabbit. Back up again in minutes with a bucket and a bunch of socks. Anne, trapped at the wheel, can't shift to windward, so he's banished forward by common consent. I ask Charlotte to ask Oliver to pass on our ETA to Paula, lest the signal drops before I can talk to her myself.

Before the sun goes down, Zaf decides to put a reef in the main. Shortening sail is often a good idea before night comes on, and it's certainly a good idea this evening – it's been blowing twenty to twenty-five knots all afternoon. It's a straightforward job, and it turns into a masterclass moment. The usual procedure when putting in a reef is to go head to wind, pointing the boat into the no-sail zone dead ahead of us. This depowers the sails, makes them easier to handle. The drawback with this is the general banging about that ensues, the rattling of blocks, swinging of booms, rising and plunging of the deck, as the balance between sea and wind is upset, and the sea starts to knock her about.

Our lad goes off on a broad reach, the boom well out over the side, then we haul the sail down by the reefing line. When this is done we centre the boom and tie off the reefing pennants, the short lines that wrap the gathered foot of the sail into a neat sausage strapped to the boom. The final step is to put a safety leash through the reef cringle, the sewn-in metal ring at what is now the foot of the sail at the mast, and make that fast around the boom. This is a smart manoeuvre, and I write it in my notebook.

Full of dinner, Simon's famous spuds and beans, at about 21.00 I spot a large tanker ahead, on a reciprocal course. Zaf comes up for a look – it's a darkish night, no stars, visibility maybe five miles. He has a look at her on the radar, figures she's about four miles off. He comes back up, takes the wheel, tells me to call her up. 'Wait.' He squints at her over the binnacle. 'Tell him the bearing is 190°.' 'What?' I say. 'Just tell him,' says the *Reis*.

Channel 16, the listening channel. 'Big ship, big ship, this is sailing yacht, sailing yacht on your starboard bow, bearing 190°. Over.'

'Sailing yacht, sailing yacht, this is big ship. I see you.' This lad is talkative, obviously bored. 'Very nice boat, I like very much the look of it. Who are you? All professional sailors? Where do you go? Do you own the boat?' Stretching a point, I tell him, yes, we're all professional sailors, delivering this boat back to Ireland, and, no, we don't own the boat. 'I like very much sailing, too much work on this ship. I buy yacht maybe, near Piraeus.' A Greek lad, evidently. He names the marina where he thinks he might buy his dream boat; I think it's the one nearest Palaeo Faliro. When I say there is a good café, called Fatni, near that marina, he gets very excited. 'Oh, you know Greece! Very good, where else please do you know?' I choose anchorages and harbours, to keep the ball in the air: Aegina, Hydra, Spetses, Hóra Sfakíon, Réthimnon and Chania in Crete, Vathí on Itháki, Fiskardo in Cephalonia . . . Now he's becoming animated. 'Ah, very good, very good, excellent.' I am suddenly seized with a powerful desire to revisit all these places, not by ferry or hydrofoil, but in a boat of my own. There's something both touching and absurd in this conversation, the bored radio operator and the neophyte sailor in mid-Atlantic, each animated by a dream of Greece, of travelling for private reasons in those warm blue waters. For devilment I tell him our captain is a very good man, from Turkey. 'Ah! Also very good.' There's a cheer from Zaf at the wheel, leaning forward to catch this conversation. We sign off with warm regards for our respective voyages, then I am seized by contrition. I forgot to ask him for the weather. 'Ah, it's OK, it's OK,' says Zaf. 'I think we have a good grip of it anyway. Listen to me, boy, did you ever go into any of the harbours in Turkey? There's great sailing there, you know?'

Hold on, I say, hang on for just a sec, what was that with the binnacle? 'Ah, this is something you should remember, when you're calling a ship, have a look at him over the compass, then give him his course towards you, get it? That way he looks straight at you. Get it?' I do. 'Go on,' I say, 'tell me about sailing in Turkey, then.' And I should have got out my notebook and written it all down, but back on the wheel and more than happy just to listen to his reminiscences I let it go.

Day 26

Friday, 31 May

Pos. at midnight   N   44° 42'

                      W   22° 17'

The radar's on stand-by as I come up in the early hours for my next watch. Flick it on to warm up for forty-five seconds while I study the log and the instruments. The bar's down another two millibars, but that's not to worry about, as it's been a long, gradual decline. I'm cheered to see we've been hitting an average of eight and a half knots since 22.00 last night: everybody has been having fun then, and the engine's still off.

Way back, leaving Antigua, we were speculating about this last leg, figuring what the best winds would be to carry us in. South-easterlies were the consensus, and that's what we're getting now, for the past twenty-four hours. OK, let's have a look at the radar. Aha! Signal from astern, something substantial. I go up, and Charlotte says she's been watching the lights for a bit. It's about four miles off, so she goes down to the radio.

This lad is more laconic than last night's radio op.

'Big ship, big ship, this is sailing yacht on your port bow, bearing 210°. Over.'

'Ah, I see you, course 061°. I will pass you to your stern. Out.'

And he does, neatly, a large tanker making 080°, for the English Channel, I presume.

It's always nerve-wracking when a contact appears on radar at night. First you try to ascertain visually that it's really there, then you try to make out its lights, and hence its intentions. Anything other than a right angle to your own course takes a bit of working out.

A ship passing four miles away can seem as close as a bus on the other side of the street does, depending on its size and course. A ship seemingly coming towards you in daylight might actually be heading away from you – you just have to wait and see. (At night it's easier – you have the lights to go on.) Our rule is: if in doubt, call someone out; then, if you think it necessary, call the ship on VHF. It's kind of uncool, apparently, to call the ship.

I have yesterday's black freighter very much in mind and, left to my own devices, I spend a great deal of time, more than the usual amount, carefully checking all around, yawing the bow from side to side to make sure there's nothing in the blind spot dead ahead. Every time I look behind I half expect to see James and Co. on *Scudamore* coming up overtaking us. They were due to leave a day behind us, but they made a faster passage than we did from Antigua, and might make Kinsale ahead of us if things fall out right for them. I think we'd all like it if they appeared: with these winds and the ground we've been covering, we're keyed up enough to race them. Never thought I'd discover this competitive streak in my make-up, but, now that I haul it out into the half-light of the coming dawn, it doesn't have an altogether unfamiliar look to it.

Charlotte pops her head up to mention, with superb casual-ness, that she's just noted nine and a half knots in the log. I tell her what's in my mind, and her head goes up, she positively sniffs the air: 'Hey, you see a sail, call me, OK? We can give them a run for their money, yeah?'

The long swell from the north is still there, but there's a good fit between wind speed, boat speed and the periodicity of the crests. We're slicing through the water, rather than shouldering it aside. *Spirit* has clipper bows, concave on either side, so that the uprushing water, as her bow goes down, is thrown wide to either side in great flat sheets of spray. Like the famously fast Baltimore clippers of the early 1800s, she has a long, low hull, is deeper aft than she is forward, is cut away sharply forward and has long overhangs aft: the result is she's a fast boat for her length and tonnage, and also a very dry boat. A more vertical bow and flatter sections forward would mean a lot more water coming on deck, which of course would slow her down. This morning she's flinging out great sheets of green water tipped with white, a brave sight on a grey sea.

Towards the end of our stay in Horta, a Norwegian boat appeared at the far side of the marina, slipping in quietly one morning without any fuss. A trim forty-five-footer, dark navy hull, steel by the look of her, long overhangs, she was easily one of the prettiest boats we'd seen. There was something else, too, though I wouldn't have thought much of it at the time, a certain stillness about the crew that suggested not so much tiredness as thoughtfulness. Later that day, wandering the wall looking at the paintings, Zaf and I stopped to speak briefly to two young women hanging bedding out to dry on her booms. In from Providence, Rhode Island, they said, heading on for the North Sea. Had a good crossing? They looked at each other, shrugged. The older one said, 'Sure, it was fast, I guess.'

Later that evening, in Peter's, we came across them again, standing quietly in the corner by the counter where cigarettes and souvenirs are sold. Something about their absent air intrigued us. It turned out they'd been hammered by a Force 12 for two or three days off Bermuda, a tropical storm we'd been well to the south of at the same time. They still looked a little bit stunned by it all, the woman in her late twenties more so than the younger woman, a red-cheeked eighteen- or nineteen-year-old who giggled as she described the experience. It seemed ghoulish to dwell on the subject, intrigued as we were. All I could think of asking was, who did the praying? The older woman smiled wanly, gestured with her thumb: 'She did, Sophie.' Sophie went a bit redder, grinned even more broadly. 'Oh, yes, I was doing many prayers. But it was fine, you know!' Fine. Force 12 is a hurricane, winds of sixty-five to seventy knots, the sea completely white, the air full of spray and foam. You could be 200 metres from a large ship in such weather and not see it. 'How did she stand up to it?' Zaf asked gently, meaning the boat. 'Oh, fine, you know. We trailed everything we could from the bow – warps, sheets, buckets, anything at all you know that would float or drag. She's a lovely boat; she stood up to it well.' We felt a curious inhibition about questioning them further: I had a sense that they weren't out of it yet. We bought them a drink, and I found myself asking Sophie: 'What did you tell your mother?' They both laughed, such a normal question. 'My mother? Oh, my mother, I told her we had a bit of a blow, but that it's nice and sunny here in the Azores.' A bit of a blow? 'Yes, that's right, am I bad?'

I see Sophie still in my mind's eye, her long hair hanging straight down from under a pixie's woollen cap, her uncanny resemblance to the daughter of friends of ours, and I am no longer surprised at the sea voyages of the Vikings. I can see Leif Eriksson coming home to his mother, looking a bit sheepish. 'Where were you?' 'Me? Em, well, in America. You see we had a bit of a blow . . .'

Later, talking to Zaf about this, he says: 'You know what I can't figure out? When they trailed the warps and everything to break down the waves, to keep her up into the wind, why did they trail the stuff from the bow? You know you're supposed to trail warps from the stern, keep running before the wind?' Maybe she meant stern, I say, but he's not convinced, and he goes off puzzling this one out, shaking his head. One for the winter fireside.

We've had a good run on the wind, but it's dying back a bit now, so the engine comes on. We still reach down through that hole in the engine-room floor, but the trick with the engine oil is still working, and the gearbox is staying cool. Just in case, we keep the revs at 1,200, which also has the happy effect of keeping the noise down. All is quiet above decks and below; after yesterday's exhilaration, everyone has gone back to sleeping or reading when not actually required on deck.

Yesterday afternoon, Zaf asked Charlotte if she wanted to skipper a boat herself. 'No,' she replied, 'I think I would like to marry a rich man with a beautiful boat and spend my time sailing to nice places.' Charlotte is forty-one years of age, an intelligent and very capable woman. Zaf wants to know if I think she was being serious. He can't understand how anyone with the requisite skills wouldn't want to skipper her own boat. I'm a bit surprised myself, except I'm not sure she was being serious. With Charlotte you never can tell. Zaf and I are puzzled by different things here. He can't understand how any sailor wouldn't want to skipper her own boat, but has no problem with the idea of marrying a boat. On the other hand, that's the bit that intrigues me: I simply don't know anyone who would say such a thing. Or if I do, I haven't been paying attention. Among my friends there are none I know of who married, or has entered into long, stable relationships, for any reason other than love. Perhaps Charlotte's is a different kind of realism – or perhaps she was just winding Zaf up a bit, or testing one of the choices available to her by speaking it out loud? There was a time when I'd have got myself caught up in puzzling this out, as if it was somehow necessary to have a *position* on the matter; now, and much to my relief, I find myself thinking it's really Charlotte's business whether she means it literally or was saying it for fun, and there is no reason at all for me to give it head space. So I let it go, and feel neither better nor worse for having let it go. This is a state of mind I've been getting used to all through the trip, not so much detachment as non-attachment.

I'm still quite attached to calculation, though; some of my happiest moments on this boat have been spent at the nav station, poring over figures and readings, chart and *Atlantic Pilot*, scrolling through the various screens on the GPS, scribbling industriously with a soft pencil.

At 12.00 today we have made 194 miles in a 24-hour run, an average speed of eight knots. Since midnight last night we've been doing even better, averaging eight and a half knots.

What everyone will want to know is, when do we get in?

At six knots, ETA is 17.00 Tuesday.
At seven knots, ETA is 01.00 Tuesday.
At eight knots, ETA is 15.00 Monday.

I've been doing the calculations based on an estimate of 600 miles to Kinsale, but it's only when I go to mark up the chart that I realize what this means: we are now exactly halfway from Horta. I show the chart to Zaf, and he studies it for a while, then says: 'You know what our port of refuge is, don't you?' No, I say, where? 'Take a look at the chart again.' I do, and I realize it's Muros, in Galicia. We're standing in the cockpit, holding the flapping chart between us in the fresh breeze, when Anne comes up, asks what's going on. 'Zaf is just pointing out that Muros is our port of refuge right now.' 'Muros? Where's that?' Charlotte in her bunk opens her eyes, looks up at us, says: 'Muros? What about Muros?' There are five of us aboard, and three of us really, really do not want to think about running for Muros again. 'I don't think I want to go to Muros,' Charlotte says. Never mind, I say, you know where we are now? Exactly halfway between Horta and Kinsale. 'Halfway? That's good. Today we have a bottle of wine with the lunch. Wake me in one hour.'

We switch the engine off and forge on in comparative silence, just a steady drone in the rigging, the rhythmic slosh of water along our sides.

Soon after lunch and a nice bottle of Dao, with very little warning, the wind goes north-west; so we run in the genoa, gybe the main and run the genoa out again, this time on the starboard side, Zaf supervising, but scarcely a word uttered.

Late in the afternoon I talk to Paula on the phone, a surprisingly clear and relatively long-lasting signal. I don't mention Muros, but she says she knows where we are on the chart; there's a short reflective silence, then we move on. A proof copy of Ciaran Carson's *Inferno* has come in the post, she says. We've read parts in typescript. Has he changed it much? Not as far as she can see.

I have a small quote from Canto XXVI copied into my notebook, where the poet and Virgil meet Ulysses:

> So I set forth upon the open seas,
> with but one vessel and that little band
> of comrades who had not deserted me

I hear Paula scrabbling pages, then she comes back with:

> . . . in this last watch that still
>
> remains to you, I ask you not to shun
> experience, but boldly to explore
> the vast unpeopled world beyond the sun

'Well,' she says after a moment or two, 'perhaps not quite *that* far.' It's one of those conversations full of the right kinds of silence.

I'm still in good humour hours later when a halyard parts and the foresail comes down. I'd happily go up in the bosun's chair, except that Simon has done it a number of times before and this is no place to be making a maiden ascent of the mast. With Zaf on the wheel, Charlotte supervising, me grinding the winch, Anne tailing and watching the halyards to see the lad doesn't get in a tangle, we get him up there smartly and down smoothly. Even with no more than five knots of wind over the deck and moderate seas, it takes guts to go up. When I see on the television Ellen MacArthur, or anyone else, going aloft on one of those big Open 60s, singlehanding in a gale, I am awestruck at their courage. My respect is increased, not diminished, by the knowledge that they don't really have any other option, that seamanship demands it of them.

A black night, dark clouds, no stars: it's like driving on towards a solid wall, and I'm glad when my watch is over and I can turn in.

I make up my nest, settle myself, but I cannot sleep. I read for a bit, get up, make tea for the watch and myself; eventually I begin to understand this sudden insomnia. Muros, our port of refuge; Muros, where I stepped off this boat last October, not knowing for certain if I'd ever again climb aboard. Hunched up here now in the dark saloon, I am assailed by vivid images piled helter-skelter one on top of another, crowding in on me, lit by flashes.

Bay of Biscay, September 2001

There were blue-grey skies with racing clouds over Cabo de Finisterre astern when I came up for the early watch that Sunday morning. The seas had gone down, there was a fair chop and some foam about, but compared with what we'd faced in the preceding days it might as well have been a flat calm. The fields ashore looked rain-sodden. The steep headland astern was black and brown, with here and there glints of reflected light that might have been quartz seams or waterfalls. The dark coastline to port lay grim and unbroken, but none of this bothered me; still less did it bother the others. All five of us were up to savour the moment: Oliver, the owner, relieved that his boat had survived such a hammering; his fifteen-year-old son Al; Charlotte, the mate; young Simon and me.

I sat under the foremast collecting my thoughts, such as they were. The past four days or so we had been soaked, frozen, battered and anxious, but mostly we had been beaten into near-exhaustion. Now it looked as if we had broken through, beyond Biscay, out of trouble.

Wednesday, midnight, we'd come on watch, Simon and I, to a Force 7, gusting 8. Our wet gear hadn't dried out; the rain driving against our faces was nearly horizontal; visibility was shit. The boat felt bad-tempered, headstrong. Great blasts of black water came coursing back when she buried her nose more deeply than usual. We took it in turns to stand to the wheel, laboriously clipping and unclipping our lifelines as we moved about in the narrow cockpit.

Things were no better when we came back up for our first daylight watch. Al had seen forty knots of wind; Simon raised an eyebrow, and Charlotte just nodded to confirm it. We ploughed on through the day, on into the night, remorselessly tracking just east of our hoped-for course, into the bay. Nobody was surprised when, at midnight on Thursday, the BBC gave out a gale warning for this area. There were big, cold, heavy waves breaking into the cockpit by now, with only a second's warning. It was nagging at me that Paula would be checking the forecasts.

By midday on Friday we had chunky pyramid seas, ice-blue and grey, slashed with foam. The wind was still howling, we were still slamming and crashing, especially when we ran down the slope of a steep wave and banged off the next face in the bottom of the trough. We didn't go on deck unless we had to, but it was almost impossible not to go look when two sparrows, of all things, came frantically beating up alongside, then dipped and ducked aboard somewhere under the dinghy lashed to the forward coachroof. By late afternoon we had blue sky, a very pale blue admittedly, and a few racing cumulus clouds high up. For a while, tentative and unsure, we allowed ourselves to think we might have come through the worst of it.

Friday's night's watch was a doddle, we thought; the moon a delight, the stars brilliant and clear. At dawn on Saturday, watching the sun rise, glad we were still on a heading just west of south, I saw what looked like a squall in the distance. There was a tanker to the west of us, heading north, and I was distracted by this for a minute until I remembered the squall, mentioned it to Simon. Suddenly, two to three boat lengths ahead, a thick, high bank of fog appeared. I scrambled back to switch on the radar. Nothing showed – not even the tanker we'd just seen, and she couldn't have been more than four miles off.

Just before 18.00 the engine went. Not a good place to be without an engine – in a heavily trafficked shipping lane, with fog coming and going. Oliver was in the engine room, changing a clogged diesel filter, before bleeding the system. There were a few contacts on the radar – set to eight miles, with rings at two-mile intervals towards the centre. We hoisted the radar reflector from the starboard forward spreaders, Al showing nimble skills at rigging and hoisting. Oliver was calm, decisive, popping up and down between cockpit and engine room. He'd got the engine fixed and had decided to refit the first oil filter when Simon came running back to me, very pale and tense, to say hold your course, there's a ship dead ahead. Oliver came bounding up to take charge; how he heard this I don't know. There was a big, black trawler dead ahead; we could see her clearly in this fog, very close. She passed right to left, not showing on the radar. Oliver retuned the set, got three contacts on or near the inner two-mile ring. We could see two ships to the west, both going north, the tanker nearer to us, about one and a half miles, overhauling the container ship farther off. A small tanker crossed our bows, heading east. Al had been aloft, meanwhile, in the temporary ratlines at the forward mast, blowing his foghorn at intervals – until it broke.

Coming out of that fog into the clear skies and light winds of Saturday night, the easy going of this grey morning, seemed like a kind of deliverance. Agnostic that I am, I was still programmed, it seems, to think of Sunday as a day of rest.

Now that I had a signal on the mobile, I decided to call Paula. I knew she hadn't been sleeping, I knew she must have had a sense of what we'd been going through, so I waited as long as I could before calling her, to let her get some rest. We had a delighted conversation, then I did something foolish: I told her about the letter I'd left for her.

The night before leaving Dublin, I had a convincing premonition that this would be, at the very least, a rough and dangerous trip. I wrote her a letter, a very short letter, to be read in the event I should drown. I wanted her to have words that would say, if something bad should happen, how very much I had loved her. When I finished that letter I had a real sense of fear: I wondered if, by the very act of writing those words, I was initiating a chain of events that would cause them to be read as prophetic; I wondered, contrariwise, if it was already all decided, that I was writing those words because some disaster out there ahead of us in time was reaching its cold fingers back towards me, putting the pen in my hand? That was the fear I brought down with me into Biscay.

Of course, I should have kept my mouth shut about the letter, but I was so relieved to be out of that fucking bay that I wanted in some way to put it absolutely in the past; I wanted that to be over. And I wanted to stop being ashamed of my fear. It didn't even occur to me to stop to think what effect it would have on her to hear I had written such a letter. To me the worst was over, the letter a thing of the past; to her we had still three or four days to go, and it certainly was not all over.

Mid afternoon. I struggled awake hearing muffled noises overhead — then a metallic, slatting banging. There was a sharp chemical reek from somewhere. My watch said I'd had no more than half an hour's sleep. I swung my feet out of the bunk in the forward cabin, looked up through the hatch. The staysail was down, stowed on the boom. We were wallowing;

clearly the sea had come up. I struggled into my clothes, opened the door. A powerful smell of diesel, and something else, too, pungent and sharp. I made my way on rubbery legs to the cockpit. Everyone else was up, sitting there looking serious. The main boom was down, lashed to the starboard quarter. What had happened? Oliver and Charlotte were preoccupied, so Simon answered. The reefing blocks had sheared off. The inner cheekblock, holding down the second reef, just burst off the boom – and the force of the sail releasing had distorted and jammed the other cheekblock.

Absorbing as much as I could of the situation, I stood looking around. We were pitching and rolling in a lumpy sea. The sky was a clouded-over patchy grey, the wind keening through the bare rigging; it was cold again, and I had a sudden uneasiness in the pit of my stomach. I mentioned the smell in the saloon to Oliver, but he was focused on getting the mainsail up again. Then I smelled smoke, went back, saw it seeping out under the engine-room door. I called Oliver. He opened the door: so much smoke he couldn't see inside. 'Shut off the engine,' he roared; someone above killed the switch. Silence then. Oliver wrapped a towel around his face, stepped firmly into the engine room, came out coughing, trying to command his breathing. No flame, at least, nothing on fire. On deck, the rising south-westerly was blowing the fumes from the ventilators directly into our faces.

I persuaded Charlotte to come down into the saloon for a second: what was on my mind was that we'd just had, maybe, a small fire, and there seemed to be diesel slopping around somewhere in the saloon. We lifted the tops off a few seats: there was varnish spilled in the locker under the starboard seat forward, and the filler cap on the diesel tank for the generator, under the port seat forward, was half off. I used rags to soak up the varnish, while Charlotte screwed the top back on the tank. Oliver came down for a moment, wanting Charlotte on deck to help with the urgent work of getting the mainsail up. We told him, tersely, about the situation: he considered it intently for a few seconds, decided it posed no danger, headed back to the cockpit. I followed him up.

Oliver had figured out a way to reef the main, putting a reefing line over the sail from the outside. It was a tricky manoeuvre, first hoisting and then part-dropping the sail, then lashing it around the boom, putting a short, strong line through the cringle at the mast. I was a bit put out to be relegated to the subs bench, but it was a job for three, and of course Oliver wanted the vastly more experienced Charlotte and Simon. The boat was heaving by now, the heavy boom and sail lurching and swaying in the growing sea, the deck underfoot treacherous in the rain. I could feel the wind coming up, minute by minute. Al, imperturbable, sat there at the wheel, holding her steady to his father's commands. I sat on the lee side, watching everything, running the permutations through my mind, and for the next fifteen minutes I struggled silently with great fear.

We were maybe sixteen miles off what could rapidly become a lee shore, a notoriously pitiless lee shore. We had a south-westerly on the nose; even worse, it was veering slightly west, increasing the chances that we could be driven onto the rocks. We didn't know what was wrong with the engine, didn't know if we would be able to fix it, and Oliver's manoeuvre with the mainsail might not work. In a strange way, itemizing the elements of our predicament seemed to help. I became calm enough to name the fear behind the fear: we may die out here. Something nameless passed over us then, I felt its great wing brush me; my stomach turned to ice.

With the main up at last, they went forward to raise the staysail, too, then Simon and Charlotte fell back, exhausted, sprawled in the cockpit. Oliver went below immediately, rifling the *Atlantic Pilot*, watching the radar, waiting for the last of the smoke to disperse so that he could examine the engine.

I asked him to sit down for a second and talk to me. His principal concern, he said, was that it looked as if it was coming on to blow. We had two choices: stand out to sea as best we can and ride it out, or make for shelter. He reckoned it was better to get in now: if we went out and needed to come back in again later we might not be able to. I asked if we should be trying to organize a tow – from lifeboat, coastguard, fishing boat? I sensed he was offended, and didn't for a while understand why. What I didn't allow for was pride, not vanity, but right pride. He knew, and I didn't, that he had seamanly options; he knew, and I didn't, that he had the skills and the boat had the resources to get in out of this.

I felt ashamed to be another unstable element in the puzzle with which he was having to struggle. The ice-cold part of me sneered at this feeling of shame, another superfluous emotion, but the greater part of me felt I had been wrong to suspend my trust in Oliver. 'Right,' I said, 'just tell me what I can do.'

Oliver briefed the others on the situation as he saw it, opened the *Atlantic Pilot*, explained he'd decided to make for Muros, a fishing port near the head of a long *ria*, a deep fjord-like inlet maybe fourteen hours away. He broke off to call up the coastguard, explain our situation. They were pretty offhand: 'OK, call us later if you need us.'

Taking Simon with him, Oliver disappeared into the engine room. Charlotte sprawled at the starboard end of the cockpit, expressionless. 'What do you think, Charlotte?' 'Oh, this is sailing,' she said. Al, on the wheel, looked at her. Looked at me. Said nothing.

Now I was at a loss to know what to do. I sat there and watched the fog roll in, half-obscuring the coastline; I braced automatically to the odd bigger-than-usual wave, noted that the sea was still coming up, smoked a cigarette now and then, waited to see if the engine would come on again. And then it did. Oliver sometimes bears an uncanny resemblance to Tony Blair, something that comes and goes across his face, a fleeting expression, a trick of the grin. Sticking his head up just then he looked as if someone had told him that Gordon Brown was quitting politics. He wasn't, he said, quite sure what the problem had been. We would keep the engine running at low revs, and whoever was on the wheel should be ready to shut the engine down the instant they heard something out of the ordinary.

I went to cook dinner. I probably picked up more bruises in the galley in the following hour or so than I'd picked up in the previous six days, but the fact that it took me nearly an hour to rustle up a simple carbonara says as much about the state of my nerves as it does about the sea state.

When I brought the pot up on deck, the emergency tiller was laid out on the cockpit floor. What's up now? Al answered: the steering is sticking; there's only a small bit of movement to either side.

The worst carbonara I've ever cooked disappeared surprisingly fast.

We were making progress to shelter by now. The fog hadn't got any thicker; the wind and sea had calmed down a bit; we were inching along the coastline, looking for lighthouses, counting the flashes and the seconds between flashes, checking them off against the list of lights and their characteristics that Oliver had drawn up. I took a turn at the wheel; it felt sticky, lumpy. We crept down the coast as darkness fell. Oliver was like a big cat, pacing between the radar and the nav station, checking and rechecking the *Atlantic Pilot*, our course, our position, the pilotage into Muros, our position, the windspeed, our position . . . and us. He kept a close eye on his crew, everyone had a task, and round about 20.00 we settled into a kind of final configuration: Al on the wheel, Simon on radar, Charlotte on eyeball navigation, searching out lighthouses, assisted by me. Oliver has asked me to call him the depth at regular intervals, from the depthsounder gauge on the cockpit bulkhead. Somewhere along our plotted course, close in, there would be a sudden change in depth, where a big underwater rock comes near to the surface. We crept down the coast, coming very gradually into the lee of the southernmost peninsula at the *ria*'s mouth.

For the first time in six days that bloody south-westerly was doing something useful, pushing us up the *ria*. I perched on the coaming beside Oliver, a torch in one hand, the notepad with his hand-drawn pilotage plan in the other. Halfway up, the town lights dead ahead, low-riding concrete mussel rafts sliding by in the slack water to starboard, the red light on the disused mole just where it should be, Oliver suddenly broke the silence: 'Oh, fuck! Oh, fuck, fuck, fuck!' What? What? 'Nothing, it's OK, it's OK, nothing – some standing waves. There must be a sand bar. I thought for a second the whole anchorage would be like that. We're over them, it's OK.'

We rounded into the fishing harbour at last, the street lights a long crescent at the water's edge, the town asleep. The flickering disco light that Simon had been fixating on for the past fifteen minutes turned out to be a pharmacist's wonky green neon sign. There were clouds down to the rooftops of the stone-built town, but the wind had fallen away to almost nothing. We circled quietly under engine, all sails down and stowed, relief washing out of us in great gusts until finally Oliver was satisfied. He picked his spot, Simon and Charlotte let go the starboard anchor and the chain rattled out, the noise carrying over the sleeping rain-dark town, coming back to us in broken and muted echoes.

I went back to shake Oliver's hand. He was as awkward as I was, but he smiled, the first crack of exhaustion showing, and I hoped he could see in my eyes what I felt. Everyone was thumping everyone else on the back, embracing. Suddenly it was clear to us how tense, fearful and anxious we had all been. Simon broke out the beers, and in next to no time was breaking out some more. I heard myself singing, *sotto voce* at first, then louder: 'What will you bring me from beyond the sea? / Spanish boots of Spanish leather.' God bless Bob Dylan, a song for every occasion – but I never imagined I'd be planning a run ashore to buy boots under quite these conditions.

We stowed what needed stowing, in a half-trance, walking about on a flat deck for the first time since Kinsale, reliving the day in jolts and fragments. I dropped my jacket in the cockpit, kicked off my boots and socks, went forward as far as I could, bare feet on the wet wood deck, and when I thought I could speak without breaking down I punched in the number to call home.

Day 27

Saturday, 1 June
Pos. at midnight   N   46° 22'
                       W   18° 57'

Charlotte has to shake me awake this cold morning. It takes me a long time to drag myself out into consciousness of day, not quite sure where I am, here or there. Heavy in head and limb I go aft, make myself study the log before going up.

Around midnight last night, the wind went south-west then died away to nothing. The sturdy engine throbs on. We're 500 miles from Kinsale, it's cold, there's little by way of deckwork to be done, nothing at all I can do except be peaceful, stand to the wheel, go with the flow. Well, I think ruefully, there are far worse things than a flat sea, a mackerel sky and a bright sun at dawn.

Zaf appears with tea, toast, Charlotte and a sextant. Finally! I have little patience with those who sneer at GPS – to me it's a source of wonder, that a little plastic and metal box and a few cents worth of electricity links you to a net of man-made celestial bodies that can tell you to within metres where you are on the surface of the globe – but the sextant is older magic; maybe because it depends on the sun, the stars and the planets, it seems like a truer magic. Besides, celestial navigation, its practice and lore, inscribes us in a tradition that includes deep-sea explorers, merchants and traders, craftsmen, horologists, map-makers earthly and stellar, exporters, importers, fishermen, admirals, pirates and thieves.

Glance at the GPS and you know pretty much at once where you are; lift a sextant to your eye, bring the sun down to the horizon by means of mirrors, check the exact time, check the angle marked on the side of the instrument – you're engaged in work, skilled, satisfying work. It's a delicate skill, acquired over time by dint of considerable practice, and the literature of the sea abounds with stories of ships falling silent while the skipper pores over his tables and almanacs like a sorcerer or necromancer in communion with spirits and powers.

I've always wanted to try this. The sextant, Zaf explains, is a device for measuring the angular height of a celestial body over the horizon. I put the eyepiece to my eye, I can see two suns in the green glass. I'm not actually looking at the sun; I'm looking at its reflection brought down by angled mirrors. In fact, I'm looking at two suns, and the task is to bring them together by turning a knurled knob on the side of the instrument. Then, note the angle from the arc marked on the side of the instrument, calling the mark while somebody else notes the time. From this you can find a circle of position, a circle on the face of the globe; you are somewhere on that circle. If you wait a while and take a second observation, the point where the two circles cross is where you are – to within a few miles. (Of course, the circles cross each other in two places, but as they are on opposite sides of the globe, and you really should have some idea of which side of the world you're on, this doesn't matter.) You have to be able to tell the time to within seconds if you're to have any chance of extracting from the printed tables the magic formula which tells you where you are; that's why the search for an accurate chronometer was for so long the Holy Grail of navigation. Well, we take numerous sights, Zaf, Charlotte and I, we work meticulously, slowly, with as much precision as we can manage, but it's all to no avail because it turns out after a long and increasingly frantic search that we don't have the tables aboard.

It's a day for just plugging on, it seems. Flat, oily sea, high sky, trade-type clouds around horizon, some cirrus to the south. We steer with a short length of line tied to the wheel: Mac, son of Magellan. You can sit out on the coaming; a small pull on the line or a nudge with the foot is enough to bring her head back if she wanders off course. It's like being in a moving monastic cell. We are silent more often than not; we pass each other coming and going with a little nod, falling into a kind of spell. People find things to do – a little washing, a bit of tidying – but everything's low-key, matter-of-fact, the galley empty and shiny, the saloon polished and gleaming, the rich wood panelling calling to mind a kind of ideal library. For the first time in my life I'm not stealing time from work for reading; in fact, I have little inclination to read at all. What I'm doing, though I won't realize this until months after I've come ashore, is emptying myself out, letting the wind and the ocean and the work fashion a new kind of silence for me.

I open the hanging locker in the saloon to get a fleece. Down at the bottom, under towels and folded jeans and safety harnesses and sheets, I find a bag full of signal flags, hopelessly tangled. Now there, I think to myself, is a very pleasant way to pass an hour or two. I take the bag up on deck, drag it forward to where I can sit with my back to the coachroof, legs straight out in front of me, the sun gradually warming the back of my neck. Oh, good, I think, these are really in a terrible tangle. Excellent.

Simon appears with a mug of tea and a bar of chocolate. 'You must be mad. I'd hate to be doing that,' he says. 'We used those to dress ship back in Antigua. That's why they're all every which way.' And you didn't think of sorting them out then? A shrug: 'Well, I kinda knew you'd end up looking for something to do.'

For some reason I don't understand, there's been a football nestling among lengths of coiled line at the foot of the main-mast for weeks. Now Simon bounces it off my head. There isn't all that much room on deck for a game of football, but I think we manage very credibly for a while. Then I go back to the flags, and Simon goes below to cut the throat of a rabid sneaker or two.

Signal flags are a joy; a poet must have had a hand in their invention. As far back as 1653 the British navy was using a rudimentary set of signal flags, and the system went through a series of modifications, as did the systems of other nations, until the International Code of Signals was adopted in 1900, coming into worldwide use in 1902.

There are twenty-six alphabetical flags, bright-coloured, all square except for A and B, which have a triangular bite out of the right side; there's a red-and-white vertically striped cone-shaped one for 'code' and 'answer', three triangular substitutes, and ten numeral pennants, also cone-shaped, for numerals from zero through nine. As well as being used to form letters in sentences or short messages, each of the alphabetical flags (except R for Romeo, yellow cross on a red background) has a specific meaning attached. A ship flying V for Victor, for instance, red diagonal cross on a white background, is signalling 'I require assistance'; a ship flying G for Golf, three yellow vertical stripes alternating with three blue, is signalling 'I require a pilot' – though when made by fishing boats out on the fishing grounds it means 'I am hauling nets.' And so on. My favourite is J for Juliet – 'I am on fire and have dangerous cargo on board: keep well clear of me.' I am thinking of having a jacket made along the lines of this flag: two blue stripes horizontal, separated by a white stripe.

The flags are joined together by string which is so tangled and knotted I am disposed to believe that some malevolent intelligence must have been at work, down there in the dark on this long passage. It's a task conducive to meditation, daydreaming, the surprised retrieval of scraps of lore you didn't know you knew. Where and when did I first learn that the Blue Peter, P for Papa, small white square centred in a large blue square, means 'All crew should come aboard; the vessel is preparing to sail'? Perhaps it was on an afternoon like this, in the long doldrums of childhood, flicking through some encyclopedia, hesitating over a coloured page redolent of pungent inks.

I make up a hoist when everything's sorted into small bundles, neatly rolled, strings all tucked in: H for Hotel, one vertical white stripe, one red; O for Oscar, a red triangle over a yellow, red peak top of the right; M for Mike, white diagonal cross on a blue background; E for Echo, a blue stripe horizontal over a red.

'What's that?' says Zaf. 'HOME,' I say. 'I thought we'd hoist it on the portside spreader coming into Kinsale.' 'I like it,' Zaf says. 'Tell you what we should do, we should hoist the courtesy pennants of everywhere she's been since last September from the starboard spreaders.' Anne has joined us, says, 'I'll make that up. It'll look good, won't it.'

We allow our minds to wander ahead to the homecoming, familiar waters, the run in under the Old Head, staying west of the Bullman buoy, the harbour opening before us, the great bastions of Charles Fort that we will leave to starboard . . . Still 300 miles to go, we shy away by unspoken agreement from pursuing this line of talk.

We're waiting for north-westerlies or south-westerlies. Zaf is worried by the continuing high pressure; he thinks the last 150 miles may yet prove to be a beat into north-easterlies.

On watch after dark, someone spots two swallows, or the ghosts of swallows, bat-like, beating round and round the boat.

At 23.30, Simon clocks a ship dead ahead. Twelve miles off, according to the radar. It seems to be carrying red astern, white forward, on course towards us. Simon bears off thirty degrees to see what happens. Nothing much. Wait. Wait. Closer, the lights show as red over white over red, with deck lights or working lights aft. Either going away from us on our original course or stationary, hard to tell which. What is it, I ask?

Zaf: A longliner for tuna, or a trawler taking in nets.
Simon: A survey ship.

In 2,500 metres? Surveying what? It could be anything, I suppose – military or civilian, oil explorer, sonobuoy layer, submarine cable surveyor. Governments and business have long since woken up to the potential of the rich world under the waves: much of the extensive submarine military apparatus, for example, the sonar arrays for tracking submarines during the Cold War, all that sort of thing, uses technology first developed by the oil companies, who now in their turn are employing new technology filtering down from the military. Not that this is a particularly new thing: way back there off Bermuda, the Nares Abyssal Plain is named after a famous British rear admiral, Sir George Strong Nares, who led the *Challenger*'s deep-sea voyage of 1872–1875. This was a major hydrographic survey which did a great deal to explode the myth that the sea bed was a flat, uninterrupted plain of mud. It is only comparatively recently that we have come to realize that the highest mountains on the planet are under the sea, or poke their heads through the surface from roots far down where creatures use sulphur from volcanic vents as we and our kindred creatures use oxygen. Given the vast wealth still to be drawn from the ocean, I suppose it's a wonder we haven't seen far more survey ships than this possible one. It's probably also something of a mercy, given what humankind has done to the land in its care, that our exploitation of the sea and its riches is, like our collective moral sense when it comes to the planet's resources, still in its infancy.

It's a rolly night under engine and bare poles. I have difficulty sleeping.

Day 28

Jets overhead this dawn, converging probably on London, five of them. Such a high, clear blue sky. It's freezing cold down here, too.

The contrails make me think of missiles streaking in, the horror of all that. We lived with the fear of missiles for so long, for most of my life so far. Why are we so sure those days are past?

Those planes are out of Atlanta and New York, six hours, maybe less, to cross the Atlantic. We've made thirty-eight miles in the same time.

So?

So nothing. You are where you are. The wind overnight went west; it's blowing maybe ten knots; we're still making better than six knots boat speed. If the wind rises a little, as it gives every sign of doing, or if it goes north-west, which it probably will, we could be in Kinsale about this time Tuesday morning. I become aware of an underlying current of sadness as I come more and more awake. It's to do with the beauty and silence and solitude of the morning. This is when I feel the boat is a living thing, and myself in harmony with her; this is when I feel most alive inside myself; this is when solitude fills up, the internal chatter falls away, the voice of the turning world is most clearly heard. But soon I'll be ashore, and all this will be somewhere out there behind in the wake of days grown busier, noisier. I allow myself to feel this for a few minutes, then the watcher inside says, let it go, just let it go, don't sentimentalize this, just feel it, you won't forget it. And suddenly, a pang so intense I nearly double up, like I've been gripped from inside and twisted – I want more than anything else in the world to be waking up on a morning like this next to Paula in our cool white bedroom.

Up pops the demon Sweeney bang on cue, and says, 'Hey, Dorgan, I've got a signal. It's a good one, too.' It's a bit early, but she must have the phone by the bed, answers on the second ring. I tell her it's a glorious morning; I tell her Oliver wants to arrange a reception mid-morning Tuesday, we might even have to stooge around off the Old Head to kill time, it's almost certain now we'll be in on Tuesday, maybe she should come down to my sister Noreen's tomorrow night? 'Ah, here,' she says, 'I can't wait to see you. Curtis is on his way back from Listowel today. He'll hardly want to turn around to drive down to Cork, even though he's looking forward to it. I'll probably get the train and –' Naturally, the signal dies.

The poet Tony Curtis, our friend, has been planning for months to drive Paula down to Kinsale to meet me when I get back. The satphone indicator lights up again. I scramble below to find his mobile number, call him; he's already on the road home to Dublin, clear as a bell. 'Are you mad? D'you think I'll miss that? I'll drive Paula down to your sister's tomorrow night. You'd better get back to the wheel now. Ye might hit an iceberg, and I'll be blamed.'

There's something about the conversation niggling at the back of my mind, and it's only when I take the wheel back from Simon, fall into the rhythm again, that I realize what it is: he had the stereo on in the car, the tune in the background was Dylan singing 'Boots of Spanish Leather'. I wonder idly if Paula will be wearing hers in two days' time.

Zaf comes up, rubbing his hands, sweeping the horizon, sniffing the wind. He stands with his back to the sun for a while, turns to us and says, 'This'll hold – we should pole out the genoa. Be much better now if we had the cruising chute . . .' – this with a wink and a grin at Simon. 'Listen,' I snarl, 'you pole out the genoa. I'll see if I can pop that, too. OK?' I nearly catch him, but I'm in too good a humour to keep a straight face. He marches off forward, trailing Simon, cackling with glee, calling back loudly that I'm a bloody menace, I probably would shred it, too, given half a chance.

By midday we're all on deck; there's some cloud filling in, but nobody's bothered. Sweeney identifies a fulmar and a kittiwake, passing the bird book around for confirmation. One of them, I forget now which, shat on the genoa. We're all concerned, I hope not prematurely, about arriving in too early. Zaf, studying the chart, our course, my scribbled figures, says we'll make landfall at the Fastnet. We might, he says deadpan, consider the option of running in to Sherkin tomorrow night, leaving early on Tuesday to make Kinsale by midday? We all know what he means: the pub on Sherkin is famous for its excellent pints of Murphy's, and the landlord might well be persuaded, stickler for the licensing laws though he normally is, to make an emergency arrangement in favour of dehydrated sailors. Joke it may be, but at least three of us are giving this proposal serious thought.

I take a look at the chart myself, presently, get out the dividers, measure off the distance: Hey, Zaf, do you know that the nearest land to us now is Mizen Head? 'Is it? You know what that means?' What? 'It means that our port of refuge now is North Harbour, Cape Clear.'

'What do you mean, *now*?' Simon asks. 'What was it?' Zaf looks at me, back at Simon, answers, 'Muros. It was Muros.'

269

'Muros? Oh, fuck!'

I have a memory of Simon in the back of a taxi in Santiago de Compostela. We'd gone up in the bus, the five of us, to have a look at the fabled city. I was flying back to Dublin for work reasons, torn because it meant not completing the journey with the others, feeling that somehow I was letting them down. The driver had been asking us about ourselves, about where we'd come from. We told him and he turned to look at me, crossing himself: 'La Costa del Morte!' he said, and Simon went as pale as he is now, grabbed me by the shoulder, 'Tell him to stop saying that, will you!'

'I heard about that,' Anne says. 'Was it bad?' We look at each other, Charlotte and Simon and I, and Charlotte says, 'Well, you know, it was bad enough, but it was sailing, you know?' Anne says nothing, just looks at us for a second, looks at Zaf. I say, as simply as I can, 'I was frightened there for a while,' and Zaf says, 'I would have been.' Then there is really nothing else to say.

The day has slipped, grey overcast giving way to mist and fog, short, steep seas, fifteen knots of wind, but from the west so that all we can use is the genoa – which has been poled out since about 09.30. We take in a few rolls now to increase manageability as darkness falls. There's rain by the time we come to eat dinner; visibility is poor. We all get a little edgy, not liking this much now that land is getting closer. There's no particular reason we should be edgy, so I'm a bit puzzled for a while until I figure out what's happening. It's not just that we've had a good run from the Azores, we've had a good run for more than 3,500 miles, and some atavistic superstition is creeping around the boat, like a restless electric cat, some knowledge bred in the bone that says: at the end of every human endeavour, when you let your guard down, that's when it strikes. What 'it' might be everyone knows, but nobody can say. Nevertheless we're all, with never a word spoken, on our guard, watchful.

At around 22.00 the wind goes into the north-west, and it's in with the genoa, out with the yankee and main.

I like the yankee: high cut, strong, pulls her by the head. Like a genny, but more stable. And I'm particularly pleased to see the main up again; especially on the night watches, it's a big, broad, reassuring presence. The mist lifts; visibility goes out to maybe eight miles; all of a sudden it's an exhilarating starry night.

Landfall is out there, you can almost feel the pull of it.

Day 29

Monday, 3 June
Pos. at midnight   N   49° 45′
                      W   12° 45′

The wind at dawn from the north-west, a long swell running in with it, the boat unsettled, making better than six knots, but plunging a bit, pulling the wheel. It's cold up here, pale lemon sunrise, washed-out streaks of pink layered with high, thin cloud, cold blue sky. I stand, as much braced against the wheel as bracing it, stiff-boned, sore-eyed, watching a tanker coming up astern.

Finally satisfied that he's giving us a wide berth, that there's nothing else back there, I am turning around when I hear the words in my head –

Back erect, his head and shoulders bowed,
Diffident, courteous, reticent, certain, proud

– and I feel myself slowed, turning more slowly, heavier all the time, and then I am facing forward, and the poet Michael Hartnett is sitting there on the hatch above the companion-way, looking at me, unmoved and unmoving.

His black, black eyes.

He sits there like a tailor, his hands loosely joined between his knees, shoes brightly polished, a flat tweed cap on his head, wearing his brown tweed jacket and snow-white shirt. He sits there and looks at me, and he knows I know he's there. He somehow conveys this, but he says nothing, his face gives nothing away. There is no sense of anything uncanny; if he were to reach into his inside pocket now and produce a cigarette, I'd just toss him a lighter; if Simon were to come up now with tea, I'd expect him to go get Michael a cup as a normal courtesy; if Zaf came up he'd just offer a hand to Michael, introduce himself, ask simply, 'Where did you come from?'

This is absurd, of course. Nothing like that could happen because Michael isn't there. Except, he is. Michael is absolutely there and absolutely not there, both at the same time. Perhaps it's a kind of mercy that we are forced to choose at such times – how could we otherwise get on with making a life between us all, an agreed life with a common frame of reference? Singlehanding, perhaps I could have kept him longer. Stirrings below, rattle of a kettle, I know that he'll vanish with a revenant's impeccable tact as soon as another voice is heard, another person appears.

We address the dead directly, don't we? 'Michael,' I ask him, '*Cad tá uait a chroí, an bhfuilim faoi gheasa anseo?*' – What do you want, dear heart, am I under some kind of obligation here?

He looks at me, I look at him, correcting the wheel as it pulls now to port, now to starboard, the wind gusting and dying, then he's gone.

All this long journey there have been these encounters with the dead, coming in and out of dream and daydream, the shifting sea underneath us causing the mind itself to break free of its mooring, the play of thought to imitate the play of light on water. I know there will be a connection if only I can be still, quiet, attentive to what is playing back there in the never quite silent conversation with myself. Sometimes you taste what it is; sometimes you see it. Today I hear it, high and clear: my boy self in primary school, moved in a way I was far too young then to understand by the song we are singing, 'Rosc Catha na Mumhan'.

Rosc translates as war cry or rhapsodic chant, and the line that snagged my attention then was '*Torann na dtonn le sleasaibh na long, ag tarraingt go teann inár gceann fé sheoil*' – how hard it is to convey in English the assonantal thunder, the hiss of the water on the ship's side, the boundless power of a ship coming towards you under full sail. 'Thunder of wave on the skin of the ship, pulling powerfully towards us under full sail' gives some of the sense of it, but it can't make the water hiss by her hull the way '*sleasaibh*' (sides) does by the very sound of it, nor is it possible in any translation to give the sense of contained power in the rhyme of '*teann*' with '*gceann*'. I loved then the very sound of the word that describes the particular glory of the line, onomatopoeia, sound echoing sense. Singing that line, swept up in the broad swing and dip of it, gave me my first intimation of the uncanny powers of the sea and of poetry. 'The War Cry of Mumhan', Munster, my native province as it was Hartnett's – and there in the song was a first call to native identification. That's what drew Michael out this morning, the line and the song, going round and round in my head all unbeknownst to me until now.

Driving on Munster from the sea, from the south, our Munster of Gaelic and English, of plain and hill farm, mountain and sea, of snug towns and confident cities, I am gripped in a kind of vision, a disjointed and overheated scrambling of sense and sight and sound. What I have seen and what I have heard, what I have read and what has been sung. Hartnett's sweet province of plenty and heartbreak, of ruin and peasant, of famine and greed, of great houses and fallen lords, of hazel grove, pasture, moorland and bog. Munster where Spenser, that 'epic idiot' as Curtis brands him, fell on the oak woods like a storm, a province raped to build the warships of a nascent empire. Munster of swordsmen fleeing to exile, to die in the service of foreign kings. Munster of famine ships making west out of Queenstown, their holds crammed with destitute labourers, singers and servant girls, thieves, teachers, farmers and craftsmen, new-wrenched into exile from a land where soldiers rode escort to grain and cattle and hides bound eastward for Bristol and London. Munster where Spanish traders shipped wines and silk from the south, where Viking invaders found refuge and founded cities. Munster whose poor shipped out in the British Navy, died in red uniforms in desert and jungle and mountain far from home. Munster whose educated sons officered regiments and commanded districts in the ranks of Empire. Munster whose desperate sons and daughters would battle the Empire in their native hills. Munster whose Fusiliers fell in their thousands, like scythed grain in the harvest of the Somme.

Coming up on Cork from the sea, crossing the tracks of so many ships: the great grain traders from Australia; Barbary pirates from Algeria in 1642, led in by native pilots to Baltimore, which they would sack and leave in flames, carrying off, some say, more than 700 souls; coasters and traders with coal and grain and wine and cloths and beer and butter and timber and manufactures, heading east and west in a scurry of commerce; great transatlantic liners – *Titanic*, Queenstown her last port of call, *Lusitania* bound for her fiery rendezvous off the Old Head of Kinsale; the French fleet bearing Theobald Wolfe Tone to Bantry; the fast ships out of France and Spain carrying boys to the seminaries of the Catholic South, bearing priests north again, years later, to a forbidden native country; my own native city which in 1919 sold the first agricultural machinery into Soviet Russia, from the factories of Henry Ford, himself the great-grandson of a woman of the lanes;

Cork of the great harbour, Cork of the merchants and canny dockworkers, Cork of the troopships, Rebel Cork, Cork of the martyred Lord Mayor; stone quays from which tens of thousands sailed into loneliness and dispossession, quays known to sailors of every nationality under the sun; my waterborne city built on a marsh, her motto 'Statio Bene Fida Carinis' – A Harbour Good and Safe for Ships; Cork with her tower of Shandon topped by a golden salmon, Cork with her back to a sufficient province, her many faces turned always to the south and to the sea.

'Would you like some tea?' Simon is standing there blocking my view of Michael, but Michael isn't there. Nothing behind the lad but the canted deck, the full belly of the mainsail, the poled-out genoa beyond. Have I been raving out loud? 'Want me to take the wheel for a bit? You look pale.' I nod and go forward, I say I'll be all right, I'm fine, just thinking something out, and I go up to the foremast, stand in front of it and look north, as if I could see over the curve of the world, and after a while I sit down because now my knees are shaking, and I feel very lonely for Michael and for all the dead.

The morning wears on; the day warms up. By noon we're 150 miles from Kinsale. At 14.00 we switch the radio on and hear Irish voices – chat between fishermen, desultory talk of work and weather. The wind has gone west, the boat is as tidy as she will ever be at sea, all we can do now is sail her and be patient. Another tanker comes up on us from astern; for a while it's not clear which way she'll go, but it's bright afternoon, she can surely see us. We watch her all the same, ready to duck left or right if she closes, and are relieved when eventually she peels off to port, making for Limerick or Shannon, we suppose.

Everyone's picking out shore clothes now, making domestic forays up and down. Charlotte and Anne are planning an elaborate dinner. We're out of bread, but for the past few days have been making out OK with baking our own from packet mixes. Anne brings up fresh loaves and an array of snacks to the drinks reception the skipper is hosting at 17.00. It's cold in the cockpit; the sky has turned grey, and the sun has more light than heat in it. We stand, then sit, a little awkward with each other for the first time. Charlotte pours, and we raise our glasses, but nobody makes a toast; we are caught in a between-time, 130 miles from Kinsale now, maybe thirty from the Fastnet, almost home but reluctant to admit a sense of occasion. For myself I know I'm still a bit lost inside, still grappling with ghosts. Or maybe some enormity is making us silent, the scarcely graspable idea that tomorrow, at this hour, it will be over. Maybe it's just that we're all afraid we won't know what to do with ourselves.

Zaf is reaching to refill our glasses when there's a sudden stench of whale breath. Simon springs up, scans all around us, yells and points. It's a pod of pilot whales, ten or so, adults and young. There's an adult to starboard while the pod is ahead to port, as I lean on the wheel and *Spirit* starts to come around; I'm watching the adult to starboard as she begins to move purposefully towards us: proud, slow, powerful, she dives beneath us as our paths cross. Adults like this one will reach about thirteen feet, will commonly weigh about 1,800 pounds.

According to Zaf, pilot whales congregate in pods of about fifteen. They live out here on the 1,000-metre line to protect their young – sharks don't come out this far, usually. They socialize during the day, feed on squid by night. Some of the adults will dive and circle, creating a vortex in which the squid are sucked to the surface as food for the pod. Others will act as sentries, keeping watch for predators. They are undisturbed by our passing, and I am uncomfortably aware, for the first time in a long time, that we are guests out here.

Zaf is in the saloon when I go below, poring over the

well-used chart of Ireland's south coast. We've sailed these waters before, and *Spirit* is well known in Crookhaven, Schull, Baltimore, Glandore, the array of harbours that lies in a fan due north of us now. We look at the faint lines of passages past, erased but not totally effaced; we murmur bits of pilotage at each other, come out of small silences with scraps of memory; we are beginning to dream ourselves in, locking on to familiar lines. Charlotte and Simon, as they pass through the saloon, come to lean in over our shoulders. I have been in these waters before, with everyone except Anne, but this is different. I feel it bear in on me, the doubled mind I have been in for five weeks and more: at sea, moment by moment; in a boat, moving but to nowhere obvious, making imperceptible gains along an imaginary line from a starting point to a finishing point. Here is where body knowledge and geometry stand back.

Darkness falls and we come and go, singly and in small constellations. When we speak it's in fragments of sentences, half-thoughts left hanging in the air. Secretly we all want a big fuss, flags, rockets, cheering, champagne – and at the same time every one of us would like to slip in quietly, perhaps in fog, or maybe beat in against a headwind in a steep sea like salty characters who have fought their way over an ocean, tight-lipped and offhand.

Sailors are paid in accidents and delays at the ends of journeys. The *Reis* has his eye on us all, has a very good idea of what's going on with us. He's alert, watchful, constantly touring the boat, checking the set of the sails, testing the blocks, tidying the falls at the winches. Now he's down in the engine room, checking the temperature of the gearbox; now he's at the nav station; now at the radar.

Charlotte, near 23.00, is convinced she can smell land. Nobody else can, but we're watching the gulls now, coming by in the glare of the running lights; there are trawlers about, shooting their nets or hauling them, or heading out to some further station.

Simon the sharp-eyed stands up abruptly, stiffens, blinking his eyes rapidly. Then Zaf is up, and I'm up, staring straight ahead. It's almost too good to be true: on the stroke of midnight we raise the Fastnet, north-east of us, maybe twenty-five miles. There's a long, long silence, then the three of us yell at the top of our lungs, 'Land Ho! Land Ho!' Charlotte and Anne come scrambling up, and we're all cheering like mad things, by turns exultant, frustrated and relieved. 'Well,' says Zaf, judging the moment perfectly, 'I better get some sleep.' 'Me, too,' says Charlotte. 'Me, too,' says Anne. We have twelve hours before us; I need some sleep myself, but not just yet. I imagine some sailor, or perhaps that anonymous wet nurse who must have kept him alive on the long trip from the Horn, lifting my infant grandfather in the air on a night like this; a child brought home from the sea, seeing his home-land for the first time. I remember now that he worked as a young man in New York; he must have come this way then, too, going west. Had he, I wonder, any thought for his infant self? Did he feel, as I feel now, that prickle along the skin, that sense of fate at play on these open, indifferent waters?

Day 30

Tuesday, 4 June
Pos. at midnight   N   51° 07′
                       W   09° 59′

I should be sleeping, but it's like a circus out here, lights everywhere. I can't figure half of them out. It's Simon's watch, but I think it's better we have two up for a while. I count six, maybe seven vessels, a low, bright confusion of reds and greens. Trawlers, says Sweeney, the lighthouse-keeper's son. 'I have them sussed,' he says, 'don't worry.' The radar is set at eight miles, two–mile rings, and every now and then we bring it in to four miles, with half-mile rings. One red has us puzzled for a long time, we can't figure out what she's doing, then the penny drops: it isn't a boat, it's the mast on top of Mount Gabriel, behind Schull. There's something going away from us, ahead and to port, eventually she crosses our track, making east like us. 'Small coaster,' says Sweeney, calm and authoritative at the wheel. 'We're out of the worst of it. I have them all figured out, you should get some sleep. I'll stay on for a bit with Anne when she comes up.'

My bag is packed, standing upright in a corner of the saloon; my shore clothes are neatly laid out on a seat, the hoist of signal flags and Anne's roll of courtesy flags laid out beside them. I lie in the dark, sleeping bag pulled up to my chin, and think of Paula, asleep now in my sister's house.

When I open my eyes again, maybe four hours later, I can smell cow shit. I dress in a hurry; it's daylight outside, 06.00.

There's a traffic jam in the passageway by the pilot bunks – Charlotte coming back to wake me, Zaf emerging from the shower. I climb on deck, and there's Galley Head to the north and east a bit. Zaf takes a deep breath. 'Jesus, do you smell that?' I do, I tell him, I do. He's just had a look at the GPS: we're early. We'll make on, but we'll probably have to hang about off the Old Head. He goes below to make coffee. We're all a bit underslept, and nobody wants to screw up at the very last minute. A pair of trawlers out of Kinsale goes by, heading south-west; there are gulls and gannets in the air, sound of a car engine from the shore, then the growl of a tractor, white scrawl of a jet in the bright sky overhead. Now we're all up, someone's making toast, Charlotte's in the shower, Simon takes the wheel and I dive down for the signal hoists. Port spreaders, Hotel, Oscar, Mike, Echo. Starboard spreaders, the courtesy flags of the places that *Spirit* has been since she left home last year. We're making seven knots in a light north-westerly, romping along. Anne spots the markers for a salmon net dead ahead. Simon bears off. It's coastal sailing now: we're watching for pot markers close in, small boats are appearing in the early summer light, lobster boats, beam trawlers. Seven Heads, we're on 074°, parallel to the coast. At 08.00 Charlotte calls Oliver, then I call my sister's. Paula answers. They're all heading for Charles Fort; they'll be on the ramparts. I put a mug of coffee down in one swallow. At 10.00 we're hove-to off the Old Head.

Now we're all on deck. Simon is hunched in the forepeak, handing up the fenders. Zaf calls the marina.

'Welcome home, Zaf. Oliver said to expect you. Tell everyone welcome home. What time will you be in?'

'Ah, about twelve, I suppose. That OK?'

'That'll be grand. I'll see you then, so. Kinsale Marina out.'

My phone rings. It's Paula; she's in the Fort with Noreen,

Tony and my sister Margaret. Margaret? She came down from Dublin, too. Oliver has just arrived.

It's time to go in. We've made some leeway in this north-westerly; we've drifted from under the black-and-white banded tower of the Old Head lighthouse. We'll have to tack, says Zaf, and we do, leaving the Bullman buoy to starboard, then we come about and begin the long run in under main, foresail and genoa, as much sail as we need, more than enough to make a brave show, and we want to make a brave show, by God. We want to stomp in there as gallant as can be. Charles Fort ahead, the great stone bastions pale in the sun. Green everywhere to left and right, such rich and lustrous colours, such rich land. Such a strong fort. The year 1601, I think, the Spanish force under Don Juan del Aquila making in, O'Neill and O'Donnell camped to the north of the town – suddenly it's that classroom again, and time is thickening around me. I shake it off, punch redial on the phone, Paula is shouting, 'We see you! We see you!' and we whip out the binoculars. We see them, waving madly. A boat coming out gives us a cheer and we cheer back, then we are under the walls; they're cheering us from the walls and we're cheering back; I can see Paula, phone to her ear, and now she can see me; I go forward waving her blue scarf; we're nearly hoarse now on board, then we're past; they're scrambling to the cars; we're in the inner basin, we run the genoa in, we haul the sails down, stow them, tip the fenders over. Kinsale is humming, traffic noise, voices calling here and there, a coaster at the deepwater pier unloading grain, a trip boat going out, trawlers manoeuvring. Zaf throttles back, starts a long glide in to the dock. Everyone's down at the water's edge, Oliver brandishing champagne: we can see the gold foil on the bottleneck. I keep seeing Paula's eyes.

There's a moment, a moment only, when the crew is

tumbled together aft. We stand just there and look at each other, then Zaf says, 'Well done, everybody, well done. We did it, eh?'

Everything is fragile and solid all at once – we've been together for so long, and now at the end we are breaking apart. Without fuss or time for reflection, we have ceased to be a crew.

The starboard side touches, the merest kiss of the fenders. The lines go arcing through the air. Oliver, Tom O'Leary and the harbourmaster make us fast.

Simon has got the ladder down; now everyone scrambles aboard. Oliver pops the champagne, happier than I've ever seen him; Curtis has a grin on him that could give him lockjaw. My sister Martina pops up; we're mugging for photos with Charlotte's Rasta wig. People we half know are appearing on the dock, and I have Paula in my arms, speechless with happiness, when Simon calls through a momentary silence: 'Hey, Dorgan, what do you say? *Abair rud éigin*, say something.'

I look at him, trusty Sweeney, at Anne hand in hand with her husband, at Charlotte raucous with sunny happiness, at Zaf, my teacher, my friend. At Oliver, remembering Biscay. I feel 4,000 miles of water and light and weather inside me, the great weight and curve of the Atlantic, then I say the only possible thing to say, the bronzed faces of my fellow crew shining before me: 'Comrades, that is a vast ocean! Here's to the ship that brought us home!'

I hold Paula close. I look down at her feet then, and she puts her arms around my neck, she sings in my ear softly, 'Oh what will you bring me from beyond the sea . . .'